The Modern English Novel:
the reader, the writer and the work

The Modern English Novel: the reader, the writer and the work

Edited by Gabriel Josipovici

Open Books

London

First published in 1976 by Open Books Publishing Ltd,
87–89 Shaftesbury Avenue, LONDON W1V 7AD

© Open Books Publishing Ltd 1976

Hardback: ISBN 0 7291 0037 5
Paperback: ISBN 0 7291 0032 4

Photoset, printed and bound in Great Britain by
R. J. Acford Ltd, Industrial Estate, Chichester, Sussex

Contents

Introduction **Gabriel Josipovici**   1

1 Reading: who is doing what to whom? **George Craig**   15

2 Vitality of language in nineteenth-century fiction
Rachel Trickett   37

3 Towards a reading of *Dombey and Son* **Gabriel
Pearson**   54

4 Reading late James **Tony Inglis**   77

5 Taking a nail for a walk: on reading *Women in Love*
Gāmini Salgādo   95

6 His master's voice? The questioning of authority in
literature **Jeremy Lane**   113

7 Difficult language: the justification of Joyce's syntax in
Ulysses **Roger Moss**   130

8 Figures of desire: narration and fiction in *To the Lighthouse* **John Mepham**   149

9 The innocence of P.G. Wodehouse **Stephen Medcalf**   186

10 The fictional topography of Samuel Beckett **Robin Lee** 206

11 Muriel Spark and Jane Austen **Bernard Harrison**   225

12 'But time will not relent': modern literature and the
experience of time **Gabriel Josipovici**   252

Notes on contributors   273

Index   275

Introduction

Gabriel Josipovici

Once upon a time there was a merchant who had to go off on business but was afraid to leave his daughter alone because there was a king who had designs on her.

'My daughter,' he said, 'I must go away, but I want you to promise not to set foot outside the house or let anybody in till I return.'

That morning the girl had seen a beautiful parrot on a tree outside her window. It was a highly educated parrot and she had found its conversation very entertaining.

'Dearest father,' she said, 'it breaks my heart to be left alone at home. If only I had a parrot to keep me company!'

The merchant, who doted on his daughter, immediately went out to buy a parrot. He found an old man who sold him one for a few pence. So he gave the parrot to his daughter and, after repeating his instructions, he set off on his journey.

No sooner had the merchant left than the king decided to try to get in touch with the daughter. So he wrote her a letter and gave it to an old woman to deliver.

In the meantime the girl had started talking to the parrot: 'Tell me a story, parrot,' she said.

'All right,' said the parrot. 'Once upon a time there lived a king who had a daughter. She was an only child with no brothers or sisters and no one to play with. So they made her a doll, and this doll was exactly the same size as the girl, with the same face and dressed in the same clothes. She took her doll with her wherever she went and nobody could tell which was which.

'One day, as the king, his daughter and the doll were driving in the royal coach through a wood, the king's enemies set upon them and killed the king and carried off his daughter, leaving the doll alone in the coach. The girl cried so loud and long that

1

the king's enemies were fed up and let her go. So she wandered about in the wood till she came to a queen's court, where they took her in as a maid of all work.

'The girl was very sweet and well-mannered, and soon became a favourite of the queen's. All the other servants were jealous of her, and out of spite they said to her: "Though the queen loves you better than us and confides in you, there is one thing she hasn't told you which we all know, and that is that she had a son who died." The girl went to the queen and asked her: "Is it true, Your Highness, that you had a son who died?" When the queen heard these words she almost swooned, for it was an offence to so much as mention this fact to her and anyone who did so was immediately put to death. So the girl was condemned to death. But the queen relented a little and had her imprisoned in a dungeon instead. In the dungeon the poor child was quite desperate. She refused to eat and cried all the time. At midnight, as she sat there sobbing, she heard the sound of clanking chains and saw five men passing by. Four of them were magicians and the fifth was the queen's son, whom they kept prisoner. Every night at midnight they took him out for a few minutes' exercise.'

Here the parrot was interrupted by a servant who came to bring a letter to the merchant's daughter. It was a letter from the king. But the merchant's daughter wanted to hear the end of the story which was getting so exciting:

'I shall read no letters till my father comes back. Do not disturb me. Parrot, on with your story!'

The servant went away with the letter and the parrot continued:

'In the morning the jailers saw that their prisoner had not touched the food they had brought her and they told the queen. The queen sent for the girl, who told her that her son was alive and imprisoned by four magicians in the dungeon, but that at midnight he was taken out for a few minutes' exercise. The queen sent twelve soldiers armed with crowbars down into the dungeon at midnight, and they killed the magicians and the queen's son was set free. The queen gave him in marriage to the girl who had saved him.'

Here the servant knocked once again on the door to give the merchant's daughter the king's letter.

'Well, now that the story is finished I can read my letter.'

'Oh, but it isn't finished,' said the parrot. 'There's a lot more

I haven't told you. Listen. The girl refused to marry the queen's son. All she wanted was a purse full of gold and a suit of men's clothes, and she went off to another town. In this town the king's son was very ill and not one of the doctors who had seen him had been able to cure him . . .'[1]

This tale has many things to tell us. It tells us first of all that narratives, like all works of art, are willed into being, they do not grow like trees and flowers. The parrot could have ended his story there, but instead he *chose* to go on. When he does finally allow the king's daughter to marry a king's son, this is because his task is done: the merchant has come back and there is no longer any danger of his daughter being seduced. At this point the parrot can reveal that he himself is a king who has disguised himself as a parrot because he is in love with the merchant's daughter: 'I knew that another king wanted to kidnap her. I have entertained her innocently in my parrot's guise and I have thus saved her from the clutches of my wicked rival.' He is of course rewarded for his services by being given the merchant's daughter for a bride, 'and the other king was so angry that he died'. But the story could have gone on. The young husband might have turned out to be a parrot after all, disguised as a king . . .

Stories, then, are the products of certain choices, from the choice of initial plot, through individual incident and down to the words themselves out of which the story is made. These choices are determined by a number of different constraints, some public, some private, some conscious, some unconscious. There is first of all the language in which a writer is working, which imposes its own rules; there is the tradition in which he finds himself (a novelist would set out to do rather different things in 1750, 1850, 1950); there is the kind of narrative he wishes to produce (romance, novel of manners, *Bildungsroman* and so on); there are the unspoken assumptions of the society in which he lives and works; and, finally, there are his own unconscious desires. Because the novelist partly moulds his material and the material is partly moulded by constraints of which he is not even aware, the term 'choice' does not seem to be quite the right one, and

3

it might be better to speak of different mechanisms being at work. Neither term really explains the mysterious business of how narratives get made (for reasons I will touch on later), but they do at least serve to point us in the right direction. The novelist, we can say, is like any speaker of a language, and structuralist critics have been right to attempt to study narrative art as though it were indeed a language whose grammer we could try to understand. This has not only led to an awareness of the ideology of traditional fiction, its function as a feature of bourgeois society, it has also led to impressive analyses of individual works. It has done this because it has released for us the notion of *alternatives*.

Let me give an example from another field. So long as dreams were seen merely as distorted and embellished accounts of reality, all one could say about a dream was: 'How beautiful!', or: 'How prophetic!', or: 'How odd!' When Freud began to explore the nature of dreams his first thought was that since something in us *makes* dreams, what we need to do is to grasp the process of this making, which he called the dream-work. And to do so we need to look not at the entire 'story' of the dream, but at each separate element. If, for example, we have dreamt of a house with a flag on it and a child peering from an upstairs window, we must not look for a single meaning that will contain all these elements. Rather we must ask of each item in turn: 'Why is it there?', and: 'Why is it as it is?' After all, the house need not have had a flag; there need have been no one at the window; or there might have been a weathercock instead of a flag, an old man instead of the child. In similar fashion, once we grasp that all novels are made—made of words, incidents, plots—we can better begin to appreciate why just these combinations have been chosen and no others. Instead of being condemned to discuss novels only in terms of character and ethics—as though we were dealing with a particularly stable portion of the real world—we can start to ask ourselves why Dickens, for example, chooses certain kinds of characters and situations, uses certain areas of vocabulary and not others, and so on. Moreover, if the novel is recognised as being the product of multiple choices or mechanisms, it is clear that the critic will not be able to find refuge in a view of it that relates it back to the novelist's own life or to his society. For these too are not 'natural', are themselves to be questioned in the light of the works one is studying. As Gabriel Pearson points out in his essay, the man Dickens is no more 'real' than his books. The books, the writing of the novels, are part of the total project of the man, and in *Dombey and Son*, for example, we find him almost consciously asserting himself as The Novelist. In similar fashion, as John Mepham shows, *To the Lighthouse* must be read not as a story 'about' certain people and events, but as Virginia Woolf's way of coming to terms with failure and loss.

It is the extreme case that alerts us to the norm. Oliver Sacks, in his extraordinary book *Awakenings*, describes how the patients he was treating would either rush forward or stand rooted to the spot, but could not walk in a normal fashion; and when they spoke it was either in a gabble or with extreme difficulty, but never as we do. This makes us aware of how extraordinary is our own 'normal' rhythm of locomotion and speech. Although it seems perfectly natural to us, it is in fact made up of innumerable subtle adjustments, and it takes very little to throw the mechanism out of order. Again A.R. Luria, the great Russian psychologist, in his book *The Mind of a Mnemonist*,[2] and Borges, in his strangely analogous story, 'Funes the Memorious',[3] recount the story of a man with perfect memory, a man who can forget nothing: every leaf he has ever seen, every face, every poem he has ever memorised. But the very sharpness of his memory, the power of his visualising imagination make living an appalling problem. For here is a man who cannot abstract; he thus has the greatest difficulty, for example, in recognising people, since people never look quite the same on any two occasions. For us this is no problem: we select enough for our purpose and pay no attention to the rest. A case history like the one described in *The Mind of a Mnemonist*, a story like 'Funes the Memorious' wake us up to what is really extraordinary about those aspects of our lives we take completely for granted. And this is the way modern literature often functions: the excesses of a Beckett, a Robbe-Grillet, like the books of Sacks and Luria, make us look again at the world we live in and recognise it not merely as 'given' and 'out there', but as the product of innumerable choices, decisions and adjustments.

In this way modern fiction has helped us to look afresh at the novels of the past, just as modern painting has renewed our appreciation of the great realist masters. But it is also possible to use the insights thus provided in a more purely critical and 'demythologising' fashion. Thus Jean Ricardou, one of the finest living French critics, wittily castigates those who go on believing that the word 'knife' can cut anything at all, or that one can sleep in the word 'bed'. And he quotes with approval Valéry's famous remark: 'What a confusion of ideas lies hidden under such terms as "psychological novel", "the truth of this character", "analysis", etc.! – Why not speak of the nervous system of the Mona Lisa and the liver of the Venus de Milo?'[4] Other contributors to the journal *Tel Quel* have an even more obviously polemical intent: not just to castigate the banality of much nineteenth-century talk about art, and of much nineteenth-century art, but, by revealing the made and chosen quality of all artefacts, to uncover the ideology which brought them into being and makes for their continuing popularity, thus speeding on the revolution. And though we might feel that Mallarmé and Mao make slightly uneasy bedfellows, it is certain that the best work of two of the greatest critics of the century, Walter Benjamin and Roland Barthes, has sprung from just such a desire to unmask the bourgeois ideology behind the 'commonsense' and the 'taken for granted'.

And yet such a project, when it is incorporated in a theoretical framework, leaves one very uneasy. For if modern literature reveals the *how* of artistic creation, and thus blows wide open the Romantic myth of the artist as prophet, it also demonstrates, as Robin Lee shows in his essay on Beckett, that none of us can get outside and above language in such a way as to deal with its products in the authoritarian manner favoured by French critics. Indeed the belief that one can do that is itself a Romantic myth, as George Craig points out. 'I feel', says Wittgenstein in the *Investigations*, 'as though, if only I could fix my gaze absolutely sharply on this fact, get it in focus, I must grasp the essence of the matter.'[5] Who has not felt this? But is it possible? Is it even desirable?

Not, at any rate, where narrative is involved. For this is the second lesson to be learnt from the tale of the parrot: that while the story lasts we listen as though under a spell. 'Suspension of disbelief' is a misnomer, because it suggests effort. But the effort for us, as for the merchant's daughter, is to emerge from rather than fall under the spell of the parrot. And even when we have done so it takes only a few seconds, a couple of sentences, no more, to plunge us back inside the story. And that is why Valéry's remark about the Mona Lisa, though true, is profoundly misleading. Again, Wittgenstein's remarks on our relation to language are apposite: 'But the difficulty is to remove the prejudice which stands in the way . . . It is not a *stupid* prejudice.'[6] To talk about characters in novels as though they were real is not stupid. It springs from a real need. The fact that we enter the world of the story without any effort at all, that though we know it is not true – the parrot is making it up as he goes along – we nevertheless experience it as so real that it could be happening to ourselves – this is itself as important a *fact* about narrative as the fact that it is the product of multiple choices and made always and only with words.

The power of the story-teller, as Rachel Trickett shows in her essay on the Victorian novel, has always been strong in English writing. It emerges powerfully in writers as different as Dickens, John Buchan and P.G. Wodehouse. And there is nothing really surprising in this. We do not form part of a community such as the one in which the tale of the parrot, for instance, was elaborated. We do not come to that tale sitting round in a group that suddenly falls silent as the barber, perhaps, well-known for his story-telling skills, stands up and starts to speak: 'Once upon a time there was a merchant who had to go off on business but was afraid to leave his daughter alone because there was a king who had designs on her.' Instead we read these words off the printed page, in silence, by ourselves. But the old magic starts to work at once: we forget our immediate surroundings and enter the world of the story.

The activity of oral story-telling takes place in a special mode of public time, a mode which has more in common with rituals than with daydreaming. From the moment the voice starts until it finishes all those who listen are its willing captives. What is important is not that anyone should understand, but that the story should be completed, with nothing missed out. Anyone who has ever read to a child from a favourite book will know what I mean. What is vital for the child is not so much 'what happens next' as the meticulous repetition of every word. The story here functions rather like a *mantra*, a grid on which the voice can be spread out, and though the child may not appear to be listening, woe betide the weary or distracted parent who skips a page or even a line.

However, once the story-teller as a living presence disappears, the hold of the voice is naturally weakened. As soon as we start to read we are indeed constrained to enter the world of the book, but now it is possible for us to put the book down, to linger over a page, to turn back to the beginning. And this means that we inevitably start to ask questions of this book: What is it about? What is the author trying to say? And as soon as *this* occurs, as soon as we start looking for *meaning* in what was once taken for granted as an *activity*, we create insoluble problems for ourselves.

Let me give an example from a different but related area of social activity. At the time of the Reformation – just the time, incidentally, when oral narrative was giving way to written – it suddenly became vitally important for men to answer the question: Are the bread and wine of the Eucharist really the body and blood of Christ, or only symbolically so? (And in that case what does 'symbolically' mean?) But such questions do not admit of any satisfying answers, for the simple reason that to ask them at all is to have prejudged the issue. They are a symptom, not a cause, of crisis. What has in fact happened is that the mass has ceased to be conceived as an *action* and attention has instead become focused on the reality or otherwise of its constituent elements.[7]

In much the same way the transformation of oral tales into novels, and the emergence of a class with leisure enough to read these, led to the asking of questions whose answers were bound to mislead rather than enlighten.

'The attribution of sense is an essential aspect of symbolic development in *our* culture,' Dan Sperber has pointed out in his brilliant recent book, *Rethinking Symbolism*.[8] What he means is that a central source of error has come from the implicit assumption that *symbols mean*, or that there is a 'true reality' behind cultural phenomena, which, with enough thought, care and effort, we should be able to get at. But this is to begin by denying what we have seen to be a central fact about the experience of reading narrative fictions. What the sophisticated reader needs to recognise is what every naïve reader instinctively knows, that symbolic systems, including novels, are not repositories of meaning but invitations to take part in certain kinds of activity. (Each of us, of course, harbours both types of reader within himself.)

'Philosophical problems arise when language *goes on holiday*,' says Wittgenstein.[9] And literary problems too. The act of reading narrative is extremely simple, almost natural. Yet *what happens* when we read is far from simple. Our errors in dealing with novels rarely spring from a false response, only from a false interpretation of that response—it's when we 'try to put it into words' that the mistakes creep in. Again, though, this way of putting it suggests two distinct activities, which is clearly not true: just as anyone who uses language at all cannot help 'doing philosophy', so anyone who reads is bound at times to reflect on his reading. When this happens what we do is to reach for the nearest, ready-made sets of explanations and use those. But with narrative fiction as with philosophy, we are too often betrayed into false interpretations of our responses by the language that is available to us. So here too we must apply Wittgenstein's famous aphorism: 'Philosophy is a battle against the bewitchment of our intelligence by means of language.'[10]

Critics have in the past been anxious to write about the theory of the novel, the grammar of narrative, the meaning of *Ulysses*. But to remain true, at a conscious level, to our instinctual response is extremely difficult. Even one page of a novel may be more than we can easily deal with. Roger Moss, in his essay, hardly moves beyond the attempt to explain the way Joyce asks us to read a one-word sentence at the very start of *Ulysses*. John Mepham, trying to analyse the function of the brackets in one novel by Virginia Woolf, gives us here what is only a tiny fraction of an immensely rich and complex argument.

What unites the contributors to this volume, then, is less a set of beliefs about the novel than the common feeling that discourse about fiction is usually conducted in terms wholly inadequate to our experience of it. Their only principles are: (1) the recognition of the need to go slowly; and (2) the recognition that it is very difficult to put into words *what happens* when we read a novel. Thus the most valuable thing they do, it seems to me, is to give the reader confidence in his own puzzlement. It may, after all, be just such a sense of disorientation, of bafflement, that the modern novelist seeks to instil in his reader, though one instinctual response is to fight this by forcing meaning and clarity to emerge at whatever cost.

As a result of the application of these two principles (I hasten to add that none of the contributors has consciously formulated them as I have here), many critical terms, used unthinkingly by generations of critics and reviewers, are seen to be a hindrance to understanding, rather than a help. To begin with, once it is recognised that narrative is verbal and sequential before it is anything else, a whole spatial vocabulary can be got rid of: 'point of view', 'round' and 'flat' characters, even the 'house of fiction' itself, with its implications of windows giving on to 'reality' – these terms do not merely not *advance* understanding, they positively block it, as Rachel Trickett and Robin Lee, in their very different essays, demonstrate. Other terms too, like 'stream of consciousness' and 'intentional fallacy', which were useful enough in their day, helping readers to combat certain false ways of thinking about literature, and especially the fiction and poetry of their day, have long outlived their usefulness. Even the terms 'author' and 'book', as Jeremy Lane and

Gabriel Pearson show, are by no means to be taken for granted, for to do so is to adopt, from the start, a misleading model of the processes of reading and of writing.

It is particularly interesting to see how nearly all the contributors struggle with the definition of the term 'the traditional novel'. In including essays on Victorian fiction we felt we were escaping from the fruitless aridity of debates on the relative merits of 'traditional' and 'modern'. Yet nearly every contributor has felt the need – in forwarding his own argument – to define what 'the traditional novel' means for him or her. But the reader should not imagine that, having gone through all the essays, he will finally be in a position to grasp what 'the traditional novel' *really is*. For the novel, unlike more obviously 'made' modes like drama and poetry, is really as close to us as our own bodies, as our own language, and we can define it as little as we can (usefully) define time. That is why it seems to me to be of great interest to see how the different contributors struggle with the problem, and to be made to realise that there is no such thing as an 'answer'.

The very notion of a search for answers is itself suspect. That is why these essays do not try to explain what the novel is, what novels are, or even what the novels of James or Lawrence are, but focus instead on the process of reading. And this not because 'a criticism based on a theory of reading' will 'minimise boredom', as one recent critic has suggested, but because what is important is to understand the richness and complexity of the activity we call reading, whether it is reading *The Unnamable* or *What ho, Jeeves!*.

But phrases like 'the activity we call reading' do not sound quite right to me. My feeling about the essays that follow is that if they are worth anything at all they are worth it because they are written not from the standpoint of the educationalist or the scholar or the scientist, but from that of human beings whose lives have been affected by the works about which they are writing, and who wish to share that experience with the reader. It is difficult to speak about these things because they immediately sound pretentious and embarrassing, and academics in particular prefer to find refuge in theories about 'truth' and even 'value'. In a letter to Oskar Pollack, written when he was twenty, Kafka said:

It seems to me that one should only read books which bite and sting one. If the book we are reading does not wake us up with a blow on the head, what's the point of reading? To make us happy, as you write to me? Good God, we would be just as happy without books, and books which make us happy, we can at a pinch write them for ourselves. On the other hand we have need of books which act upon us like a misfortune from which we would suffer terribly, like the death of someone we are fonder of than of ourselves . . . a book must be the axe which smashes the frozen sea within us. That is what I think.[11]

In the essays by George Craig and Jeremy Lane, which, it seems to me, set the tone for the whole book, such sentiments are taken seriously. Neither would be writing, we feel, if he did not think as Kafka does, if books were for him no more than a diversion, or the object of his professional curiosity.

There is one final question to answer. The reader of a collection like this is bound to ask himself why certain writers have been 'dealt with' and not others. If Dickens, why not Hardy, if Lawrence, why not Conrad, if Wodehouse, why not Waugh, if Muriel Spark, why not William Golding? There are a number of answers to this. First of all, since one of the aims of the book is to rekindle the reader's interest in the complexity of writing and reading narrative fiction, the essays that follow need serve as no more than examples. Hardy and Waugh would have done as well; it just so happened that the contributors were at the time interested in Dickens and Wodehouse. But this raises a further problem: any book of this sort can easily be accused of failing to 'cover' the period. But what do we mean by 'cover'? As George Craig shows, Biggles and Borges (Captain W.E. Johns, he should have said, but there is a shrewd point about the way we instinctively latch on to books here, as well as a love of alliteration) – Biggles and Borges have more in common than either has with football or caving. Where, then, are we to draw the line? Why should we include Graham Greene and leave out Lionel Davidson? Why include Conrad and leave out the Biggles books? There is in fact no limit, and every textbook attempt at 'full coverage' sets up only one tradition and thereby effectively cuts out others. Art is not like an apple tart, finite and half an inch thick, waiting to be cut into neat segments and then eaten. One book, one little story, like James's 'The Middle Years', can sink so deep that it alters our lives, and we know, on first encountering it, that its reverberations will never cease to be felt until the day of our death.

Nevertheless, the characteristic tone of the book that follows is clearly different from what it would have been if we had taken the French or German or Russian novel as our field of concern. It is perhaps no coincidence that of the ten authors who are dealt with in any detail, five – Dickens, Joyce, Wodehouse, Beckett and Muriel Spark – are masters of the comic mode, and, moreover, of a comic mode that is dependent primarily on linguistic agility. I feel sure that French criticism would have developed along very different lines in the last twenty years – to the impoverishment of us all – if the French literary tradition had had Shakespeare and Dickens instead of Racine and Balzac at its centre, and Lear and Lewis Carroll in the place of Sade and Lautreamont on the periphery.

This, then, is neither a random collection of essays nor the manifesto of a group. The contributors have for the most part been known to one another for some time. We met twice in the course of a year and early drafts of many of the essays were read aloud and discussed by all of us. Later drafts were passed round and the comments of the other contributors often incorporated into the argument. Not all the contributors agreed with either the formulations or even the choice of subject-matter of the others. I too have my areas of disagreement with this or that essay. Some of the essays seem to contradict what is said in others. But how absurd it would be to try to get it all straight. It is an enticing myth, and one that must be resisted, to present criticism as if it were written from above, by perfect and immutable beings. The contributors to this volume have only tried to express what many readers must have felt, but which they have perhaps ignored because they were unable to bring it fully to consciousness. I hope that the essays that follow will help those who want to become better readers of the great novels of the past and, what is equally important, of the best novels of today and tomorrow.

One thing remains to do in this introduction. This is to record the tragic death of Robin Lee at the age of twenty-nine. He was one of the most promising poets of his generation and, as the essay on Beckett will make clear, a critic whose intelligence and human sympathy would have led to remarkable work.

Lewes
31 December 1975

1   This is a traditional Italian fable from Pisa and Monteferrato. The version I use is the the composite one made by Italo Calvino and published as no 15 of his *Fiabe Italiane* (Turin, 1956). It has kindly been translated for me by Sacha Rabinovitch

2   A.R. Luria, *The Mind of a Mnemonist* (Harmondsworth, 1975)

3   Jorge Luis Borges, 'Funes the Memorious', in *Labyrinths* (Harmondsworth, 1970), 87–95

4   See Jean Ricardou, *Problèmes du nouveau roman* (Paris, 1967), prologue and chapter 1

5   Ludwig Wittgenstein, *Philosophical Investigations* (Oxford, 1953), 113

6   ibid., §340

7   See Gregory Dix, *The Shape of the Liturgy* (London, 1945)

8   Dan Sperber, *Rethinking Symbolism* (Cambridge, 1975)

9   Wittgenstein, op. cit., §38

10 ibid., §109

11 Franz Kafka, *Briefe 1902–1924* (Frankfurt, 1958), 96

14

1 Reading: who is doing what to whom?

George Craig

Our attempts to account for the processes of fiction seem to involve us almost at once in spatial metaphor. Directions, roads, tangles, peaks, *romans-fleuve*, fissure, territory, mapping – whatever their value individually, the cumulative force of these and a hundred others must eventually draw our attention to the phenomenon itself. We may buy time by talk of meta-languages and the constraints which shape them, but a doubt remains: infectious habit or essential perspective? Comic inflation or serious search for a currency? Of the many pairs of contraries which suggest themselves in any attempt at resolution, none, perhaps, throws a longer shadow than 'simple' and 'complicated'.

Thus what we call our response to a literary work includes elements as different from one another as, say, the perceived design of a text and temporary changes in our psychosomatic condition. It may be easy to give some account of the first (which is, ostensibly at least, something out there), but peculiarly hard to talk well or convincingly about the second. Everyone has, one imagines, experienced the shock of surprise, fearful or joyful; it is indeed one of the most important and powerful signals we know. Yet our efforts to describe or catch it ('My heart missed a beat' or whatever) fall hopelessly short. Shifts of feeling, of energy, of absorption do not just accompany the act of reading: they are the form of that act for any given instance; and they are, unsurprisingly, at least as hard to describe as is surprise – since after all this last is merely one example of them.

However many other elements may be present in the act of reading, and even if all of them can be satisfactorily described, we are in the end left with a basic opposition:

15

that between relatively describable complexities (the formal realities of a literary work, processes of appraisal, ideological determinants and so on) and something relatively indescribable but unarguably elementary (the excitements caused by inflections of our attention – fear, hope, joy, the stasis of blankness, the chill of despair). Even before literary criticism had achieved academic respectability this was an embarrassment; since that time it has been still less acceptable. If, as I want to suggest, that embarrassment is misplaced, the commonest way of dealing with it is, or ought to be, genuinely embarrassing: the claim (implicit, for example, in the pejorative force attached to 'subjective') that the reader is an observer, a neutral witness more or less acute, more or less experienced. The more sophisticated version of this is that, with experience and guidance, the reader may attain the status of observer. But however the claim is elaborated, whatever concessions it may include (the reader as supremely sensitive receiving device, discriminator, active participant), its structure remains the same, dependent on an essentially romantic wish to be outside language in the moment of attending to it. For if we may indeed suspend disbelief, we may no more remove ourselves from the language-world than we can stop breathing; while our performance in the language-world is at all points uncertain. Whatever the reader may be a neutral witness of, it is not words. And the elimination of the false problem – the persistence of unwanted subjective elements in an objective process – allows sight of a real one: the continuity between extraordinarily complex and extraordinarily primitive elements within a single process. Psychologists inquiring into how people learn to read, critics writing about what they and others have read: both may enlighten us in innumerable ways, but will leave us with the question of that continuity. Since most writing is about the complex end, we might turn rather to the other end. At once the scale of the difficulty is revealed: if there is this continuity, and if already we fail in accounting for psychosomatic change by itself, can any discourse respect the continuity while not converting it into one more observable phenomenon?

A first clue comes from the earlier moments of reading

16

as a learned practice. Once the beginner accepts the notion that he may make a connection between a given printed symbol and a given, presumably familiar sound, the possibility of something like a game exists, the more excitingly in that he will not yet know how big a game it is: it is too early to look for answers to questions like, 'How many connections can I make?' or 'Does it always work the same way?' Success in a new venture of uncertain scope seems likely to associate, for some little time at least, deciphering with pleasure, particularly as acts of deciphering will be brief forays rather than extended scrutinies. There will be a point, however, at which the notion of a possible, even a necessary continuity (of deciphering and of what is to be deciphered) appears in the consciousness of the reader. From this point on the reader's situation is entirely different; he is faced with choices and decisions that are only marginally connected with deciphering. Brief forays, like muscle-flexings, sketch the possibility, even the imminence, of a new activity, but without committing the venturer to the venture; the base, in our chosen example, is still non-reading. What is now possible is prolonged absence from that base, indeed the coming into existence of what looks like an alternative base, from which a bit of reality is explored indirectly. Both elements are important: the absence because it involves a serious redirection of attention (and in particular a turning-away from what other people are doing); and the indirectness because it restarts and extends a crucial process previously lived through only in pre-conscious experience: the infant's discovery that a known figure who has disappeared from view can reappear with all the same characteristics. Some of these notions can of course be applied to games or to daydreaming, or for that matter to sleep; but there is a marked difference, a new factor. Over sleep the child has no control; daydreaming arises from inside, leaving no gap in which choice has to be made; games offer the lure of activity and the participation, real or imagined, of others. The decision to read is rather closer to any decision which puts the self at risk – a first dive, for example, or a musical solo – but, unlike these, it leads to no more direct involvement with the world, no externally sanctioned release. What is new, then, is that the apprentice reader has to decide to withdraw attention from the external world (including the book as object) *and* from his own internal world as a preliminary to an experience which is unpredictable and, in an important sense, unshareable. We can hardly be surprised that many gifted and sensitive children show reluctance to let reading get beyond the earliest stage. They are aware, even if in pre-verbal ways, that the recommended activity is one which involves a serious, because partial, lack of control, but brings no certainty of reward while offering no noticeable challenge (unlike, say, rock-climbing). The reader must agree to a surrender before fighting the battle. What is surprising is that, on the whole, these children do learn to read, sooner or later, for they have hit on a central and uncomfortable truth, one that we find again as part of the force of these words, from a rather more experienced word-user: 'Strictement j'envisage . . . la lecture comme une pratique désespérée.'[1]

The order of truth involved is uncomfortable in more than one way: the emphasis on struggle, risk, reluctance as readerly experiences tends to shut out the potential glories of reader–writer encounter; and the focus on decision, on boundaries (whether to 'go into' this partly alien territory or not), may have something of the effect produced by an unexpected intrusion of self-consciousness during physical action (to become conscious of one's way of walking can have strange results). Much teaching – and many assumptions underlying the more 'advanced' language of criticism – will for obvious reasons play it down, or at least suggest that it is a consequence of inexperience, a mere stage, perhaps even an accident of mood or disposition. But there is a third form of the discomfort, and one which makes dismissal rather more obviously suspect: the concentration in the present argument is neither on the time before any given decision about reading has to be made, nor on the later time when a given reading is actually taking place, but on the segment of time between. The relative security, or at least familiarity, of the first and third times, their long and memorable rhythms contrast sharply with the unknown and unpredictable urgencies of the second. It is this contrast and our general reluctance

18

to linger on it which act as warning signal: when we hurry away from any experience not already placed on some scale of social or moral unacceptablity, it is at least probable that more is going on than we are prepared to admit. Our language and our practice are, as ever, one; there is no familiar body of discourse concerned with this intermediate time; no equivalent of that branch of learning theory which bears on reading, or, on the other side, of literary criticism. There are of course plausible enough practical reasons why this should be so: the activity of reading and the activities of non-reading already generate and justify all the attention we can give them. But it is not just some preference for leaving nothing unexamined that makes these reasons seem, in the end, evasive. For, apart from the knowledge that it can be an enjoyable experience (to put it no higher), we are not yet clear what reading actually is; whether there really is an alternative base. To say that it can be enjoyable but also disappointing or even sickening is to make it sound a hit-and-miss affair which could not so easily be contrasted with earlier indecision or unease. If it is more than that, we still have to understand the unease; if less, the relative popularity of reading; and in either case, more of what goes on when we read. Most of all, unless our behaviour is merely random, there must be a connection between the time of unease and the time of reading. It is that connection which we must get clearer if we are ever to understand what the total process involves.

For as soon as we turn our face away from the problems of the beginner (when decipherment is no longer an issue) we realise that most, if not all, of the elements can be found too in the experience of practised readers. We need think only of the writer with whom we 'can't get on', yet who evokes no easily discernible hostile feelings in us. The confidence of experience allows us to find ways of disguising failure: 'The words stay on the page'; 'No matter how many times I read over the beginning I can't seem to get into it', and so on. But it is a failure to make the move from the first base to what for the moment we may still call the second; and if it were to happen several times in succession with different writers we might be, at the least, seriously

19

embarrassed. This embarrassment is interesting for the light it throws, not on us as variable individuals, but on the vague assumptions we appear to make about security. If defeat is a possibility, then the notion of the second base as a zone of ease is a hope, not a description; we are confusing our pleasure in successful reading with the activity as a whole. But if risk and challenge are involved as permanent factors whose distinctive force is neutralised *only* when our reading is successful, then the notion of a base must be revised; and the word 'activity' takes on an oddly ironic quality. In other areas, too, we confuse occasional pleasure, or the possibility of pleasure, with the framework of that pleasure, and rely on our successes, real or anticipated, to cancel out our failures. Games and acting, two of the most familiar, will serve our present purpose admirably, for both in their different ways show how much of ourselves we, literally, bring into play when we engage in them. The contrast with reading is immediate, and begins with the bodily: here movement is to be avoided as far as possible; excitement or self-control are tolerable only from within a reading already successfully begun; awareness of the presence of others must be minimal; and consciousness of any or all of these constraints is seriously or totally inhibiting. The activity must be played out, at a first and yet also a permanent level, in the narrow limits prescribed by the eyes' ability to identify with certainty black marks on a page. Such constraints would be bearable only if the results of respecting them went beyond success in deciphering; conversely, even those readings which may be for us supreme experiences must take place within the constraints.

We can now perhaps see our way to clarifying the notion of base, and in particular of 'alternative base'. Paradoxically, it is the emphasis on results (pain of failure, pleasure of success) which has obscured the issue by compounding the original error: that of the either/or. There is no question of denying that readings may be successful or unsuccessful; the point is to know what happens in reading such that words like 'successful' or 'unsuccessful' can be invoked at all. It must be clear that they cannot refer to an *event*, something that happens at a particular moment, but must bear retrospectively on a *process*. Either /or will serve very well for retrospective judgement; its relevance to the earlier process is not so clear, because the process itself is not clear.

The first 'base' is simply that of our hold on the world: the particular state of readiness, sensory and affective, in which at any given moment we engage either with what we perceive as not-us (people, objects, weather changes, noise, whatever) or with drives or impulses arising within us from below consciousness. Since all our responses and decisions, whether consciously formulated or not, must issue in performance here, it is not a state we can compare with anything else; this is what it is like to be alive and awake. It is of course by no means necessarily a comfortable state: our hold on the world may be or feel extremely tenuous. Among the forces constituting us are desires or fantasies that it should be other, and these are fed and fanned by that part of our experience which takes us beyond base: sleep and, more specifically, dreams. Longings for omnipotence, for freedom from responsibility, for effortless fulfilment steer us in their turn towards certain kinds of activity which, belonging in real time (the time of life at base), seem nevertheless to legitimise, by way of a new and different set of constraints (their internal rules), the switching of our attention away from the endless unpredictabilities of our world over on to a carefully delimited segment of it. In the best examples, permission ('You may safely redirect attention') is reinforced by necessity ('You must redirect attention or you'll miss the pleasure'). Even the thin gratifications of watching a television soap opera so as to re-experience its 'badness' are available only to those who attend. Examples involving a more thoroughgoing commitment (to games, to arts, to gambling, whatever) demand and deserve fuller and more differentiated scrutiny than is possible here. What we might do is distinguish those which allow *inter alia* direct expression of aggressive impulses and fantasies of omnipotence, or at least of potency and control (the *practice* of the arts, or of games, or of gambling) from those which entail a preliminary subordination of the self to the enterprise of another or others (listening to music, watching a play or a contest, looking at a picture).

Of the first we might say that they do not so much belong
with the hope or illusion of an 'alternative base' as extend –
and, it may well be, complicate – the primary base, since they
offer instances of our hold, however partial, on the world.
With the second we appear to be in rather different territory:
the handing-over, the deferring to another's venture have
more about them of the yielding to daydream which bespeaks a
loosening of that hold. But while they may foster this inclina-
tion to let go, they need not by any means do so. There is
another, and equally relevant, sense of 'deferring' here: that in
which, as a moment in a total experiencing which by definition
is part of our positive action in the world, we agree in the first
instance to wait for the performance of another. But whether
we are listening to a story or a quartet or watching a dance or
a match, there is an 'it' to engage with: the other's performance is offered in directly perceptible terms (however complex those terms may be). And that is where the difference
from reading shows. Just as, a moment ago, we noted that
the severe physical constraints of reading can never be re-
laxed, even where a given act of reading allows access to intense experience, so we can say now that the other's performance will never be directly perceptible: only the written or
printed symbols are immediately available. Neither of these
facts might seem to weigh very much against the possibilities
reading offers, but once again it would be a pity to confuse
process with effect. What in reality they draw attention to
is an extreme constriction occurring where two immeasurably
larger phenomena touch; where, for example, one imagination
approaches another. What starts by looking like a mere convention, a rule of the game ('Just follow the printed marks and
you'll . . .') reveals itself as a central structure, the physical
and perceptual constraints imaging a basic human situation in
which any contact we make with another person must pass
through language. And if, at either end, language is that which
expands to accommodate the whole play of desire and intention, it is, in the middle where one person's language-world is
pointed towards another's, dauntingly less open, since that
pointing is the reminder of the other's freedom within his
language-world. And all the time language goes on existing

independently as the summarising name of all those symbols and practices which either, or indeed anyone, may have recourse to.

There is an immediate and necessary parallel. To want to meet someone face to face is to carry towards the projected encounter an indeterminate mass of hopes and fears, efforts and flaggings of the will, musterings and dispersings of energy; indeed the stronger the wanting, the greater will be the felt force of this alternation. Success and failure lie some distance ahead, beyond a ground signposted with questions like: 'Will I be up to it?' But signposting, like any attempt at ordering, implies the other, less straightforward reality which is to be thus simplified. Wanting is so powerful an ordering that it will drive a path towards success and constitute that path as the dominant feature of the terrain. Such a venture will meet resistance, as will any move away from the already experienced; but where the goal, as here, involves a creature capable of independent choice, that resistance is much more intense, and may release very primitive feelings. The possibility that the hazarding of the self (explicable only in terms of desire) may be undertaken for nothing (meet no corresponding desire in the other) is a profoundly disturbing one, for in it desire is seen both as the only procurer of satisfaction and as that which may, once acted on, expose the self to humiliation and the denial of satisfaction. And with that we are back in the infant's world: wanting our wanting to be a necessary and sufficient condition. But, rare cases apart, we can't stay there. What one learns to do is to point a version of oneself towards the other, resolving the rest by focusing attention on his response so that tactical mistakes can be redeemed or surprising counters accommodated. Suddenly, in the present, two people are in conversation; anticipation is overtaken by experience; two mutually unknown worlds touch in an exchange of words, hallowed and governed by immemorial practice. Where there has been no wanting on the part of the other there has been its equivalent: the mustering of as many resources as seem necessary to sustain the encounter without hurt or strain. The soundings and explorations which follow are the constituents of a new reality, the unknowable scope of which commands a new attention. Yet even with the greatest possible goodwill from both parties, and however wide the verbal territory each has covered before arriving at the encounter, connection can be made only through the language of each to the other.

Here, surely, we have our first serious clue to the nature of reading, which does not so much *resemble* what we have been looking at as form one apparently eccentric mode of it. Such eccentricity as it may have is in the *form* of the encounter, not in the forces at work in it; and we shall see later that even that concession may be too great and, for this and other reasons, misleading.

' For the moment let us rather concentrate on the ways in which connection is made: how the small range of gestural and spoken language that makes up conversation, or the compressed offerings and decipherings which join writer to reader, can carry enough of the flow from each of two distinct personalities to allow even the hope of pleasure. We can see straight away that there can be no question of a direct exchange: although we talk of 'throwing ourselves into' this or that reading, we are unlikely, even in fantasy, to conceive the possibility of ourselves ending up inside the writer's reality; becoming one with him. We remain witnesses, and witnesses moreover to the product of that reality, not to the reality itself, however much the first may suggest about the second. And of course the product is available to us in one form only – written words. But if it is true that we do not in reading become the originator of the words, it is also true that they are not simply made over to us as some raw material which we might, gratefully receiving, transform into a private artefact. (We may and do play at this, but this mild cheating hardly affects the general argument. Nothing can annul the anteriority of the other's words; and, as we shall see, the metaphor of raw material is illegitimate.) If, to put it more simply still, we can neither offer nor absorb the words of another, the connection must be indirect. It remains for us to see just how indirect it is, and what form the indirection takes.

One feature perhaps deserves immediate attention: the way in which it is established in time. The other's words are, in both senses, there before us; we follow them. This situation can be described in several ways, but what is most interesting in it is that some of these ways not only may be but frequently are contradictory. In one version, for example, the writer has, by allowing this arrangement of words to reach us in his absence, given us, silent judges, all the evidence we need in order to formulate a verdict. From the writer as prisoner we pass to the writer as invader issuing an unbroken series of instructions for the direction of our attention; as procurer, knowledgeable in the illusory relations we crave; as isolate, arrogantly or humbly recording the inside of his head without reference to our concerns. And of course these and their like, with or without the caricatural edge, are not types of writer but kinds of relation between. So while the priority of the writer's words has, as we have seen, blocked any possibility of substitution and appropriation, it does not by itself determine the nature of the relation. What the examples make clear is that that relation has to do with *control*; with what might, at an appropriately primitive level, be pointed at in the question 'Who is doing what to whom?' (I ask or allow a clown to do his turn, and from my freedom laugh or don't laugh; I shiver and submit to the unexpected anger of an intimate; I behave erratically when faced with a behaviour I can't place; and so on.) Now this connotation of control, endlessly familiar from our direct dealings with others, is a little more puzzling in the indirect contact of reading. The priority in time of the other's words is given spatial expression as well: we hold in our hands the entire body of the words.

And of course it is not only in this sense that the connection is indirect: there is the question of address. We know one context where there is no mystery as to why connection can be such as to release the full play of dependent, dominating or submissive feelings: the reading of a letter from a valued other. It would be tempting to say that what really happens is that, wanting certain kinds of things to be said as tokens of a pre-existing relationship, we scrutinise the letter for their presence or absence, either of which, by setting off an echo in the continuing relationship, will belong to the mode of direct connection. But even in this instance, and however charged certain phrases may, by custom or desire, have become, there is no connection to be made except with the words, which here must take the strain of what, in face-to-face encounter, is carried by bodily presence: gesture and voice as well as word, experienced not only as immediate but as part of a history, a continuity.

So since we can notoriously be led into intense turmoil by reading the words of the letter, while recognising that these words have no predetermined value, we move to thinking that the unifying factor is our awareness of the other's characteristic linguistic performance: shifts in tone, surprising emphases, familiar patternings perceived in a context shaped by habit and the assumptions and predictions it generates. But, relevant though such developed awareness is, it cannot give us the whole answer. We may know or guess, for example, that venturing into writing is experienced by the other as hazardous or even frightening; written performance may then be so much at variance with spoken that it is to that fact (maddeningly, saddeningly, fondly, embarrassedly) that developed awareness draws our attention. Now we have layer on layer of indirectness: ultimately what we are seeing is not simply the achieved performance of the other but evidence of something more elusive – his relationship with his own words; the extent to which this other that we know is vested in verbal representations, and the manner of that investment. In this connection, the timorous letter-writer is not the least interesting example. The general wish, however strong, to 'be in touch' with someone else is only one of the factors at work, and is indeed unusual in being positive; but then it arises from non-particularised desires originating in a relationship between persons. It functions, in fact, as a simplifier, promoting the wish to be in some way directly available to the other, without reference to the mode in which availability can be realised. The other factors, however, bear on the mode as well, and it is these which bring hesitation, constraint, even occasionally contrary desire (where the risks seem to outweigh the pleasures conceived earlier; this is the letter that will not be written or will be postponed). And they turn on the writer's freedom in relation to words. He may, for example, have been earlier ravished by words from his other (may even, along the lines we are pursuing here, have grasped how such excitement can have arisen from reading them); but that offers no guarantees or even hints for his own subsequent performance. Indeed the other's words have introduced two new constraints: the felt need to do other than borrow or repeat them; the felt need to be all the same 'up to' them. These would be alarming enough if they were merely challenges to ingenuity or range or capacity for intensity, issued to someone who had all the same free access to words. But access is not free. Dictionaries may suggest that words can be arranged in such a way as to be, so to speak, equidistant from our central fears and desires, sitting like tools on shelves. We may like to contrast the disturbance produced in us by contingent verbal events with some ultimate possible equanimity about words, but we're unlikely to know many people who have ever found or even glimpsed this paradisal state. What starts for each of us with the unobserved chargings-up of certain words and phrases in early experience continues with the endless implications of our discovery that all others are other, and cannot speak even the same words as ourselves without being other. From this comes an unsought awareness of boundaries, of limits and limitations, and, with that, the notion of performance. Performing means risking: facing the double challenge of our private attitudes to words and of others' reception of those we utter. And while we may persuade ourselves that the exchanges of speech are so quickly over that risk is bearable, we are likely to see writing as giving hostages to fortune.

If there is little we can do about unconscious or pre-conscious revulsions or preferences, we are quick to learn a way of apparently answering the other part of the challenge: anticipating the judgement of others by imagining ourselves to be receiver as well as sender of the words. This familiar and, on the whole, painful and unsatisfactory practice is, like many of those we are considering, profoundly ambiguous. In one conception of it we are close to the assumption of omnipotence: I predict and make bold to determine your response by the manner of my saying. In another we are closer to self-abasement: unless I can make this good enough – and perhaps even then – you will destroy me. And of course we could add other versions. Any or all of these will repay attention, but none has such general interest as the practice itself, however particular needs may colour it. Because it inevitably emphasises the implied response of the other it tends to play down the extent to which the imaginary judge is attending to the self. For here is not only 'What will he think of me when he reads this?' but 'What sort of me do these words suggest?'; not only an awareness, welcome or unwelcome, of the other's freedom, but an intuition, clear or confused, of distance between intention and performance. Memory and desire may sustain the hesitant letter-writer for a while, the surge of unconstrained words momentarily drowning out hesitation, aligning permission with wish. But if the surge is over before the letter is finished and dispatched, the doubts return intensified.

The writer's clear, if by no means necessarily exhaustive awareness of intention reappears and is at once directed on to what has been produced during its brief abeyance. By a harsh symmetry, it is now the imagined permission which is withdrawn: the words written must stand alone to face the test of intention. Yet if desire cannot guarantee the desired result, intention, for all its implied awareness of self, of other and of the offering that purports to connect them, can do little more than make clear the size of the difficulty. The hesitant writer must either give up or move to a different conception of the enterprise. If he does finish the letter he will have made this move, even if he feels he has merely failed to satisfy the earlier conception. What he has done, however reluctantly, is to allow to go out a body of words which stands in a certain relation both to his own desires and to what he believes are the desires of the other, without being in a position to determine what that relation is. The body of words will be neither wholly justified by his desire nor wholly deprived of its informing strength; neither, since it is the body of *his* words, can it be wholly appropriated by the other. So it comes about that the writer of the letter, whatever his attitude to the relationship with the person to whom it is addressed, can work only on the words of his letter; and then only in hope, not in knowledge, of success. And with that, for all the weight of special circumstance (awareness of a particular other, shared experience, immediate desires and fears), he reaches the position of the writer *tout court*. By his work on and in the words, his provisional and simultaneous resolution of private attitudes to them, designs for them, reliance on them, all accompanied by his recognition of necessarily partial hold on them (they are his words but they are also drawn from the common stock) – by this work he is establishing in words the constituents of a possible 'I'. It is as yet no more than a possible 'I'; there remains the perceiving of these constituents and the synthesising of them; that is, the other work we call reading.

Of these two central notions, 'work' and 'I', let us look first at work. When we have reminded ourselves that even in letters to intimates, and despite the desire for immediate presence which impels the writing of them, there is no possibility of operating directly on the other, we reach a crossroads. The energy which accompanies and sustains the writing does not function in a void: if some part of it goes to feed the fantasy of direct connection, it must be part only. The scrutiny of our own words which we are drawn to is already evidence that something else is going on. The severity of our judgement will vary with temperament and circumstance, but these cannot account for the judging itself. Energy flows because in the moment in which we set about writing we re-enact in transposed form the irreducible human experience: a self confronting another self or other selves in the world. Just as the self cannot, outside madness, wholly determine its own reality, so it cannot, in the transposed encounter which is writing, exhaustively prescribe the terms in which the words are to be received. But this means, among other things, that writing is the ground of yet another encounter, located this time within the self: that between desire and experience. Whatever the form, intensity or direction of the desire, writing is inconceivable without it; while, at the same time, what we discover to be the impossibility of controlling the enacted form of that desire (the words written) entails its partial frustration. The blank page and the other's absence offer the writer an apparently total freedom; but whatever the nature of his relation with the other, the only way in which he can exercise that freedom is through the signs by which the other's freedom can alone be expressed. Nor do attempts to break the pattern of indirectness ('Please believe me; I really mean this') have privileged force. To write at all is to settle for the desire over the fears of frustration. The 'work' is what goes into the resolution of a conflict in which not only these two elements but also residual longing for direct connection take part. Thus, against the odds, what starts out from a spontaneous wish to connect in the most personal way moves inevitably towards an exercise in composition; and the effort to reach the other, towards an argument with the self.

One extreme form of this argument (that in which the self, writing, tries to short-circuit response by assuming the judicial position of the other, reading) is so familiar in its barrenness that it has tended to obscure what in the central process is neither wasteful nor even avoidable. For the fact that our words belong to the common stock is relevant in more than one way. It is not possible for us to identify the moment at which, on the way to writing, pre-verbal sensation issues in words. But, for as long as the prompting lasts, the emergent words are experienced as continuous with the sensation. It is when, the prompting over, the words have taken their place on the page that the continuity is broken. The separation, symbolic and actual, allows renewed awareness of the words as having an existence independent of us; as being part of the common stock and so the property of none, as registering the absence of the previously sustaining continuity, as precariously viable, and so on. This moment is a node; through it pass in lines the several ways we apprehend it: the line that runs between intention and realisation, the line connecting private-and-continuous with public-and-disjoined, the line from manic (the confident surge of creativity) to depressive (the verdict of the internal 'hanging judge').

But, as the metaphor suggests, the moment contains elements of all these oppositions: we are looking at both/and, not at either/or. And, because of that, the moment is dynamic, not static. The energy generated to deal with the tension between and across these oppositions, must, if it is strong enough to overcome the paralysis or renunciation which is the only other resolution of that tension, catch up all the elements (temperamental, experiential, intellectual) in a single complex act. The territory of that act is, however, and can only be, words; resolution, therefore, however provisional, is accomplished in a stylisation which promotes one of the elements to the central position: the opposition between language as private and continuous and language as common and disjoined. The 'work' is the effort to resolve, at each point of the writing and in the whole of it, that particular opposition. And because this is a 'both/and' (we arrive at verbalisation in strictly private ways but are at the same time always aware of language as functioning outside us: as something we react to, have views on), the writing we do is not our considered 'answer' to a stated 'problem'; it is the form of our response to a situation we cannot control but find ourselves, through desire, involved in.

But if the writer's 'work', made necessary by the encounter of desire with the later oppositions, yields for the reader the form of the writer's response, it has by the same token achieved something else as well: the establishing, by way of words, of the writer's 'I'. For, whatever apparent permissions the intimate letter offers its writer for display of the *word* 'I' (or of course for coyness about such display), the controlling, intentional aspect is merely a component of the perceived 'I'. My words, the form of my response to desire and its oppositions as instanced in my struggle with language, in fact allow the reader of my letter to see the 'I' who is engaged in that struggle – whatever I am saying. But then my reader is not outside the struggle either: no matter what the force or direction of his desires or memories, they cannot play direct on 'I', any more than on me, while the reading is going forward. For that which enables him to perceive the 'I' of the letter is only partly memory and expectation (forms of attention which make of the letter a mere token or trigger); the other part is his awareness of how the form of my language-struggle is related to the experience of his own. Locked for ever in the attempt to resolve our own language-conflict, we watch, with the fascination of familiarity, the attempt of another. Thus, even in the most safely circumscribed of verbal relations – no doubt as to who is being addressed and who is making the address; shared experience; the justification of temporary absence and nameable desire – the relation between writer and reader is shaped by processes that have only indirectly to do with the person-to-person connection.

In turning, then, to the more open territory of fiction we are not so much moving to a separate world as seeing the same ground with certain landmarks removed. Because contact must still be described in terms of the alignment of one individual's language-practice with another's, it is a ground which will seem both totally familiar and wholly strange, like the landscapes we cross in dreams. The relationship, now hardly if at all compounded with direct experience, can be forged only by the play of one man's words on another's. For the writer this is an altogether more hazardous venturing; for the reader a far more problematic encounter. And this is likely to mean a steep increase in defensive activity. On the novelist's side, the argument with the self, the 'work', is intensified, since he can have no knowledge of the language-practice of his putative readers. If his freedom of movement is that much the greater, so are the risks attending that freedom. He is offering the terms of a notional relation, while being, until it is too late, the only witness to the adequacy of the terms. The temptations are many and familiar (the stridency of tone that marks a leading-with-the-chin; the recourse to self-distancing that invites collusion in 'knowingness'; the attempt to short-circuit the difficulty by instancing verbal inadequacy within the fiction; and so on), but these are in the end merely variants of a single false hope: that one may both issue the challenge of words and, by an act of will, determine the response to that challenge. Indeed so false and yet so widespread is the hope (not only can the writer not resolve single-handed the question of reception, but the reader, who has his own temptations, may refuse to see challenge at all, preferring to take the words as a gift or an injection) that we must either assume most writers to be solipsists or conclude that there is being enacted in their words, whatever else these carry, the whole play of their desire and fear. The extent to which any given writer is aware of this may vary, but no degree of awareness will allow escape from the difficulty itself: the naming of central feelings may ease them, but it cannot resolve them. We are brought back to a final sense of 'work', of 'I' and of indirectness.

If we turn again now, before trying to suggest what that is, to the reader's side, it is less a postponing than a filling out. While it is tempting to see reading as, like swimming or riding a bicycle, an example of the kind of psycho-physical control we can, however painfully, learn (we may be more or less at ease in particular circumstances—choppy water, hilly roads, difficult words—but the exercise of the skill is natural enough). Yet even when we have allowed for the extra difficulties which words bring into the experience, we are likely to forget or play down one factor. For if in one sense reading a new book is, as we have seen, like meeting a new person, and even though from the writer's side words have to do duty for everything else in that meeting, the fact is that they also take the reader, almost from the start, far beyond the terms of all but the most exceptional first meeting. Precisely because the writer has consented to the particular kind of coherence, of finishedness, that they present; because he has, in so doing, revealed so much of his way of resolving his language-conflict, his new acquaintance—the reader—is miles behind. The 'ordinary life' parallel, indeed, might rather be that of eavesdropping on highly charged words directed at someone else. He passes, within minutes of the beginning, from unfamiliarity to intimacy. Nor is this astounding result produced by the skill he has learned: that merely puts him, so to speak, in a position to eavesdrop. We cannot therefore draw up some simple parallelism between the writer's position and the reader's, in which, say, intention would correspond to expectation, active to passive, and so on. The reader's language-practice is not simply aligned with the writer's: it has first to discover what that is and then, working from the signals generated by the discovery, accommodate the discovered practice. The challenge of irony comes readily to mind as an example, because irony is a specific testing of the capacity to accommodate; but with or without irony there will always be challenge. Even where the words carry reassuring labels (we have only to remember the force of titles like *The Body in the Library* or, for Wodehouse-lovers, *Summer at Blandings*), it is still necessary to find out: disappointment, or worse, is always possible.

And so we come to the hardest question of all: how is it possible to map together these separate worlds in a conception of fiction that will not deny or merely wish away their autonomy and their separateness? It is not, after all, possible for us to 'map' human behaviour; perhaps fiction, too, is inconceivably diverse (in a not very unusual reading experience we will have been making connections over a period of twenty years or less with Biggles and Borges, Dr Seuss and Dr Faustus). But that diversity, that unpredictability, may supply the key. For if we turn from fiction or life as wholly or partly achieved acts (totalisable, so to speak, only by the librarian of Babel or the Recording Angel) to these same as venturings, something like a general pattern emerges. It is not mere perversity that keeps us, on the whole, living, even though 'life' is unmanageable; reading or writing novels even though 'fiction' is unmanageable. Nor is the line from Biggles to Borges merely one of increasing sophistication: we are not only contemptible but wrong when we blush for our earlier enthusiasms. If all the modes of language record and enact in transposed form our hold on the world, it is fiction which, with peculiar insistence, maintains the sense of that hold as *venture*: as adventure, as journey, as exploration in time and space. It continues to do so, and we continue to turn to it, because we are endlessly preoccupied with boundaries. Early representations of these ('enemy lines', 'the edge of the forest') may be simple, but the play of our excitement is rather less so. By way of these named boundaries we are led into the pre-reflective exploration and provisional redrawing of others (fantasy/reality, tolerable/intolerable, I/he and, of course, reading/doing). Even in the immediate post-decipherment stage of reading, there is, as we have seen, room for preliminary discriminations, however inarticulate: reading itself felt as a possible adventure which in prospect disquiets some, attracts others. What is in any event set up is a possible connection between the words (written and read) and the provisional boundaries of the self; and that connection, moreover, not wholly determined by the self. The countless differences between *The Lost World* and *A la recherche du temps perdu* cannot hide their resemblance in that. For to the spatial emphasis in 'boundaries' we must add the temporal emphasis in 'exploration'. Fiction, whatever the ostensible complexities of its surface patterns (narrative direction, tonal variations and so on), can also recreate that formal continuity which is the other great feature of our venturing: that, with whatever halts or lapses, we *go on*. And it does so as experience rather than as demonstration: only by being 'in' the fiction can we know the shiftings 'in' the self, just as it is only the possibility of movements within the self which makes accessible the transpositions which are fiction. One example will perhaps serve: Alice and her looking-glass. When Alice passes effortlessly through the glass and into the other world, she is—we are to discover—in the territory of dream, a territory in which assumptions about boundaries no longer hold. But we, reading before, during and after that moment, are not dreaming; we are, *inter alia*, accommodating the vision by means of skills belonging in the non-dream world. We cannot read the dream without being awake, nor reach looking-glass country without being on the near side. And Lewis Carroll cannot write this dream without the same conditions being true. Nor will 'suspension of disbelief' help us: we are not after all experiencing or confronting an *actual* vision; we are reading some words. And these are neither reflecting surface nor magic door; they are and remain words. Whatever imaginative leaps we and Lewis Carroll are separately capable of performing, it is not those private gifts which are at issue. The point is whether we can come to terms with those words, themselves not touched by any conventional or otherwise external vision-inducing property. Even those of us who may prefer 'dreams' to 'reality' must, if we are to apprehend *this* 'dream', read these non-dream words. The venture which is reading must precede the venture which is following Alice; the words are reflecting surface *and* magic door.

In the end, one adventure must stand for all: that in which the reader, enmeshed lifelong in his attempt to verbalise 'I', meets the writer, who has issued an interim representation of his own attempt. Unable to reach any reader direct, the writer works in the area between the subject (his whole self, forever unknowable) and the 'I' that he knows (writer, reader, comparer, aspirer); the work is a dialogue across the space between; the result is his language—provisional, opaque, other. By venturing out into a ground in which his sovereignty does not run, a no-man's-land, he lays himself open to every kind of response, including indifference; he is also taking the step without which no contact is possible. His 'dialogue'—the transposed attempt to explore his frontiers, however they have been established—is what his reader reads. Challenge, invitation, confession, demonstration: it is all of these, and more. And it at once puts under stress the language-practice of his reader, bound, unless he refuses the contact, to experience it as a testing of his frontiers. Whether he is swept away, brought up short, briefly amused or gradually repelled will depend on how far, in the no-man's-land, the writer's 'dialogue' creates the conditions of a corresponding 'dialogue' in the reader. Only when each has had to forgo direct sight of the other can relation be established. To the form of one man's venture responds the form of another's: the unimaginable contact is made across the ground of fiction.

1 Stéphane Mallarmé, 'La Musique et les Lettres', in *Œuvres Complètes*, Bibliothèque de la Pléïade (Paris, 1945), 647

2 Vitality of language in nineteenth-century fiction

Rachel Trickett

It is the custom of critics today to judge novels in accordance with certain established procedures: assessment of character, consideration of structure and investigation of meaning. When these are shown in relation to the author's style, stylistic criticism commonly limits itself to noting symbols or motifs, realism of dialogue and solidity of description. This has stikingly concentrated our attention on writers – George Eliot is one of them – who are strongest at precisely those points, and left us in danger of misjudging or underestimating those who work in a different way. Critics who feel that the novel is essentially a criticism of life and experience, rather than a work of art or play, tend to confuse art with such other estimable qualities as intelligence, psychological penetration or that ambiguous condition, 'maturity'. But the art of the novel is linguistic, and the language of fiction is as proper a study as the language of poetry.

Since we read today by the eye rather than by the ear, we are likely to concentrate immediately on the visible, on description, imagery, event, and are inattentive to tempo, the movement of words and sentences and the syntax which conditions them. But our enjoyment of the arts of language is not essentially conceptual or perceptual; we ought more often to say of a passage in a poem or a novel that it 'sounds right' than that it 'seems right' or 'feels right'. Whether we recognise it or not, we are affected, as the author was, by the varied and subtle movement of dramatic or meditative or narrative discourse. Novelists must hear what they are writing, at least in the act of writing, as poets more especially hear what they imagine in the act of conceiving it. In short, most artists in language hear what they think, for language is speech, and perhaps nineteenth-century novelists who expected their works to be read aloud in the family circle were more aware of this than we are.

To think of the novel in this way – with regard to time and movement as it is conveyed through language – suggests new and profitable critical approaches. Successful television adaptations of well-known novels may recall to us how much the form derives from the drama. Vivid sequences of optical realisations match the mental pictures we make as we read (or contradict them), and the translation retains to some extent the direct dialogue which marks the connection between fiction and drama. But what they lack is the unique linguistic quality of narrative movement. Such adaptations, even, may thus help us to reconsider the distinctions between the rhythms and tempi of dramatic and narrative art.

Narrative is consciously concerned with time. It moves through time and takes as much time as it needs for its purpose. Unlike lyric or meditative poetry it does not make time stand still; it is like the drama in forcing our awareness of a temporal dimension. But the way drama does this is quite other than the way prose fiction does so. Drama takes time by the forelock and establishes certain conventions which simultaneously enable the spectators to ignore the actual passing of time in the theatre, and to believe implicitly in the temporal scheme of the dramatic action. The simplified notion that because you will be sitting in the theatre for three hours you should only witness an action that would take three hours may be easily exploded as a theory. But it has produced some wonderfully intense and concentrated plays. In that brief space, a series of climactic episodes can take place and those which are not enacted before the spectators may, to save time, be reported or described. This convention is especially attractive to one kind of imagination: the intense and ingenious, which enjoys restrictions whereby exposition, description and report, all delivered in a short time, can retrospectively enlarge the dimensions of time and space while actually appearing not to disturb the strict limits of immediate action. A peculiar counterpoint is at once set up: the actors act their essentialised drama, the chorus universalises it; the length of time of the action is strictly accommodated to the actual circumstances of the performance, but the devices of exposition and report extend the mental space and time of the drama. Such is the effect of the concentration of 'classical' tragedy. But even in 'irregular' Shakespearian plays where this convention has been exchanged for a greater theoretical freedom of time and space, elements of suspense, retrospection and resolution are manipulated within the same limits of the actual temporal performance.

In non-dramatic narrative the pace is inevitably slower. The temporal rhythm is that of our own day-to-day experience, consecutive, sequential, gradually accumulative. From the eighteenth century onwards novelists have adapted the counterpointing of drama to this wholly different context. They have made use of set-scene and dialogue, have, as it were, extended the stage directions into the narrator's exposition of what is taking place (and, in later novels, *why*); have recounted the past, or again in a flashback presented it like a dumb-show to offset or explain the present. But the narrative mode of sequence, the recounting, the act and art of telling, not to an audience of many so much as one-to-one, remains the essential condition of prose fiction.

This condition has its own linguistic conventions. The language of drama is concentrated, instantaneous, intentionally affective. The language of narrative is progressive, leisurely, connective rather than disruptive, aiming to catch the attention by a serial process which imitates the commonly experienced pattern of rational consciousness. To achieve this successfully requires a mastery of certain kinds of syntax, a command of transition and of tense, all the devices which denote the consecutive and which connect clauses and sentences by other means than the elliptical compressions that the conventions of verse to some extent require. Within this overall pattern other devices may be deployed – many others, for the novel, apparently the least artful, is certainly the most hospitable of literary kinds. Lyrical passages, dramatic moments, curious effects of stasis in the most episodic fictions, all these can be found counterpointing the basic rhythm of prose narrative in novelists from the eighteenth century to the present day. But it is with that basic pattern or rhythm and the linguistic usages it requires that we may begin to examine some nineteenth-century examples.

Undoubtedly the most linguistically accomplished of all nineteenth-century novelists is Dickens. Yet with the notable exception of Randolph Quirk's *Charles Dickens and Appropriate Language*,[1] Dickens criticism has neglected narrative style in favour of theme and symbolism, and most comments on his language are directed towards his use of imagery, jargon and the verbal mannerisms of his characters. The aspects that would be singled out in the kind of approach I am proposing are brilliantly exemplified in the following passage from *Bleak House*:

There may be some motions of fancy among the lower animals at Chesney Wold. The horses in the stables – the long stables in a barren red-brick courtyard, where there is a great bell in a turret, and a clock with a large face, which the pigeons who live near it and who love to perch upon its shoulders seem to be always consulting – *they* may contemplate some mental pictures of fine weather, on occasions, and may be better artists at them than the grooms. The old roan, so famous for cross-country work, turning his large eyeball to the grated window near his rack may remember the fresh leaves that glisten there at other times and the scents that stream in, and may have a fine run with the hounds, while the human helper clearing out the next stall never stirs beyond his pitchfork and birch-broom. The grey, whose place is opposite the door and who, with an impatient rattle of his halter pricks his ears and turns his head so wistfully when it is opened, and to whom the opener says 'Woa grey, then, steady! Nobody wants you today!' may know it quite as well as the man. The whole seemingly monotonous and uncompanionable half dozen stabled together, may pass the long wet hours when the door is shut in livelier communication than is held in the servants' Hall or at the Dedlock Arms – or may even beguile the time by improving (or corrupting) the pony in the loose box in the corner.

So the mastiff, dozing in his kennel in the courtyard, with his large head on his paws, may think of hot sunshine, when the shadows of the stable buildings tire his patience out by changing, and leave him at one time of day no broader refuge than the shadow of his own house where he sits on end, panting and growling short, and very much wanting something to worry besides himself and his chain. So, now, half-waiting and all-winking, he may recall the house full of company, the coach house full of vehicles, the stables full of horses, and the outbuildings full of attendants upon horses, until he is undecided about the present and comes forth to see how it is. Then with that impatient shake of himself he may growl in the spirit 'Rain, rain, rain! Nothing but rain – and no family here!' as he goes in again and lies down with a gloomy yawn.

So with the dogs in the kennel buildings across the park who have their restless fits and whose doleful voices, when the wind has been very obstinate, have even made it known in the house itself; upstairs, downstairs and in my lady's chamber. They may hunt the whole countryside while the rain-drops are pattering round their inactivity. So the rabbits with their self-betraying tails frisking in and out of holes at the roots of trees, may be lively with ideas of the breezy days when their ears are blown about, or of those seasons of interest when there are sweet young plants to gnaw. The turkey in the poultry yard, always troubled with a class grievance (probably Christmas) may be reminiscent of that summer-morning wrongfully taken from him when he got into the lane among the felled trees, where there was a barn and barley. The discontented goose, who stoops to pass under the old gateway, twenty feet high, may gabble out, if we only knew it, a waddling preference for weather when the gateway casts its shadow on the ground. (Chapter VII)

This long passage is entirely characteristic of Dickens, but not perhaps of the elements in his genius which attract most admiration nowadays. It is a self-indulgent flight of fancy, but the self it indulges is Dickens's inner imaginative self, and the evidence for this lies, to my mind, in the extraordinary subtlety and vitality of the linguistic devices. The rain at Chesney Wold adumbrates to Dickens's imagination its opposite – high noon in summer; the solitude of the house and estate in the Dedlocks' absence is felt both through the monotony of the rain and the recollection of still heat. The emptiness is defined through a typically populous scene, but the population is animal, not human. The present, dank and solitary, is alive with recollections of a sociable past; the use of the present tense suggests the continuum of time Dickens's narrative so often relies on, and it is through this historic present that the past is evoked and realised. A deliberate confusion of time effects is crystallised at the point when the mastiff 'is undecided about the present and comes forth to see how it is'.

The linguistic devices whereby Dickens varies the structure of his sentences bear a direct relation to the way his imagination works. His first subject – the horses in the stables – is instantly suspended while an appositional clause elaborating the stables extends our perception of the detail of the scene. Dickens's fondness for the indefinite article contrasts strongly with, for instance, George Eliot's preference for the definite article. 'A barren red-brick courtyard', 'a great bell in a turret, and a clock with a large face' are all objects we have not seen before, and their isolation is stressed by the fact that they are not defined by 'the', presupposing previous connections of which the definite article would remind the reader. The indefinite article, in contrast, endows them with an absolute quintessential existence which allows Dickens to perform his usual trick of animating the inanimate or humanising the unhuman: the clock has shoulders, the pigeons consult it – plausibly in this linguistic context.

After this brief digression the horses – now 'they' – resume their function as subject. In the next sentence they are reduced to one example, the old roan, whose hypothetical memory of a freer past is interrupted by a phrase defining him and a participle clause 'turning his large eyeball' so that we *see* him at the same time as we know his speciality. What he imagines is 'a fine run with the hounds' extending out beyond the restrictions of the stable, 'while' – at the same time as – the groom is cleaning his stable. So the descriptive detail of the present is introduced: pitchfork and birch-broom, no more real or less real than the fancied run with the hounds. Here is the time confusion – a confusion of fancy and reality, too, which is the point of the passage. The next subject, the grey, is presented entirely through a progressive series of relative connective pronouns – '*whose* place is opposite the

door, and *who*, with an impatient rattle of his halter . . .
and *to whom* the opener says "Woa grey, then, steady! Nobody
wants you today!"'. The grey is more vividly characterised
than the roan through these repeated relatives and the direct
address of the groom which epitomises the implicit desertion
of the whole situation. And that sequence of relatives is
matched by the progression in the whole paragraph of hypothetical verbs from 'may contemplate' to 'may remember' to
'may know' – the horses, the roan, the grey contemplating,
remembering and finally understanding.

But the centre of the passage is the mastiff, characterised
in his surliness more than any of the other creatures. The
second paragraph, introduced by the conjunction 'so' (thus),
continues with the present participle phrase 'dozing in his
kennel' and all the implications of infinitely boringly extended
present time are reinforced by the following adverbial clauses
'with his . . . head on his paws', 'when the shadows of the
stable buildings tire his patience' to create a backwards and
forwards movement. The nature of the dog is defined by
the first of these, the nature of the climate and season by
the second, which introduces the recurrent motif of shadows.
And how exquisitely Dickens pinpoints the imagined hot
season with that precise observation of the time of day when
the mastiff has no broader refuge than the shadow of his
own house where he sits on end! But then or now? The
vivid image of the upright dog panting and growling merges
with the dozing dog, and in the next sentence, after the
repeated conjunction 'so', this composite creature emerges,
'half-waiting and all-winking', to decide whether it is then
or now, 'to see how it is'.

The first paragraph moved from the horses to the single
horse; the third progresses from the mastiff to many dogs.
There is here a slight modulation in construction which an
inattentive ear might miss outside poetry. 'So *with* the dogs
in the kennel buildings across the park.' It extends the rhythm
reticently as the scene is extended out of the bounds of the
stables and yard with the baying of the hounds carried into
the house itself, 'upstairs, downstairs and in my lady's
chamber' – 'Goosy Goosy Gander', which not only recalls

Lady Dedlock but anticipates the last disgruntled creature of the series. A slight ambiguity varies the next sentence as its construction changes again with the general noun substantive 'they': 'They may hunt the whole countryside', meaning they may imagine themselves hunting the whole countryside, but with the additional implication that they are permitted to hunt the whole countryside – a sense of liberation which is increased by the introduction of the rabbits who 'may be lively with ideas of the breezy days when their ears are blown about' – the whole tone growing more lively and frivolous and less concentrated. But from this excursion we are carefully brought back to the house by the turkey in the poultry yard, *the* particular turkey who one day escaped into a lane to a barn where there was barley (but is now back in captivity). By this stage our ear should be attuned to the kind of variation Dickens is playing. The definite article, the demonstrative 'that' localises and identifies the bird, bringing us round to the original setting and focal point. The turkey is given importance by a variation of verb structure (a very self-conscious one that draws attention to itself), 'may be reminiscent of that summer-morning' – the passive voice emphasising the past freedom and heat, the demonstrative 'that' giving a half-comic poignancy to the occasion. The final sentence of the paragraph resolves the whole procedure as perfectly as music: 'the discontented goose', the only creature provided with a descriptive epithet (for the 'old roan' is so conventional as to have lost the clarity of adjectival definition); the discontented goose – summarising the condition of all these creatures – gabbles under the gateway of his preference for the kind of weather when the gateway casts its shadow on the ground, as had the mastiff's narrow kennel in noonday heat.

By such oblique and subtle devices Dickens indulges his own imaginative perception of the rain and the solitude of Chesney Wold, and of the detailed actual world of buildings, men and animals, a perception so complex in its range over time and season, over objects and beings, that we would hardly expect the techniques of prose narrative to accommodate it. But they do, in the hands of such a master of linguistic vitality. There are other briefer and simpler instances which reveal a similar command. In *David Copperfield*, for instance, the episode when the weary boy is brought by Mr Mell to Salem House after his sleepy dream-like experience of visiting the master's old mother, is vitalised into the sinister by a sudden movement from the active to the passive voice.

A short walk brought us – I mean the Master and me – to Salem House, which was enclosed with a high brick wall, and looked very dull. Over a door in this wall was a board with SALEM HOUSE upon it; and through a grating in this door we were surveyed when we rang the bell by a surly face, which I found, on the door being opened, belonged to a stout man with a bull neck, a wooden leg, overhanging temples, and his hair cut close all round his head.   (Chapter VI)

The observer is here observed while observing. 'Through a grating in *this* door [the door he has noted] *we were surveyed.*' The device is reticent, might almost go unnoticed, but it is a stroke of genius reflecting exactly the paradoxical comprehensiveness of Dickens's imagination.

It is possible to display a contrasting inertness of linguistic device in the most admired of nineteenth-century novelists, George Eliot, though to do this does not of course disvalue her achievement in other spheres. What we can find in her best work – unlike Dickens's – is a linguistic heaviness that sometimes reflects a confusion of imaginative vision, a lack of immediate coherence which requires extended commentary on the author's part to clarify and correct. Dorothea's return with Casaubon after her honeymoon is justifiably taken to be one of the finest passages in *Middlemarch*.

Mr and Mrs Casaubon, returning from their wedding journey, arrived at Lowick Manor in the middle of January. A light snow was falling as they descended at the door, and in the morning, when Dorothea passed from her dressing room into the blue-green boudoir that we know of, she saw the long avenue of limes lifting their trunks from a white earth and spreading white branches against the dun and motionless sky. The distant flat shrank in uniform whiteness and low-hanging uniformity of cloud. The very furniture in the room seemed to have shrunk since she saw it before: the stag in the tapestry looked more like a ghost in his ghostly blue-green world; the volumes of polite literature in the bookcase looked more like immovable imitations of books. The bright fire of dry oak-boughs burning on the dogs seemed an incongruous renewal of life and glow – like the figure of Dorothea herself as she entered carrying the red leather cases containing the cameos for Celia. (Chapter XXVIII)

It is only in contrast with the very best that this is less good. But it is worth comparing with Dickens, because here again a contrast of past and present is the centre of the imaginative meaning of the passage. A close scrutiny reveals far less imaginative confidence, a slighter degree of assurance in the management of language. What George Eliot wants to say is all-important; she translates it carefully and effectively into language, but the very effects her language creates have to be interpreted by the author herself and are not allowed to speak to the reader for themselves.

The two opening sentences are perfect in their handling of narrative, the transitions easy, the first sentence merely advancing the action, the second producing an immediate sense of climatic premonition – the use of descriptive detail to suggest atmosphere and mood that his successors had learned from Scott. The shift of time is smoothly accomplished: 'and in the morning' Dorothea's entrance into the blue-green boudoir 'that we know of' is pointed so as to require the reader to remember the first account of that room. The intimate authorial 'we' is used by George Eliot to teach her reader to be alert for the points she thinks important. But the boudoir, as yet only incidental in the construction, is the room to which Dorothea passed as she saw 'the long avenue of limes'. That strong perfect tense 'saw' throws all the weight of the sentence on to the description of the lime avenue and the sky above it which, by this emphasis, acquire a peculiar significance. The repetition of 'white' in this descriptive sentence is a device attempted again in the following sentence, where: 'The distant flat shrank in uniform whiteness and low-hanging uniformity of cloud.' The intention here is to emphasise blank whiteness and depressing flatness and monotony and it might be felt that a certain clumsiness was permissible, given this intention. But 'uniform', though an exact word, is too wide and general in its connotations to bear the precise function it is given here. 'The flat' may refer to earth or sky – presumably to the horizon where earth and sky merge. 'Shrank' is a good strong verb for recede, a physical verb, but the low-hanging uniformity of cloud again generalises – the first 'uniform' refers to whiteness; the second 'uniformity' appears to indicate formation, shape, texture, perhaps colour, but the sky has already been described as 'dun'. This slight uneasiness of connotation is reflected in the aural clumsiness of the rhythm of the sentence. A more sensitive ear would have rejected the repetition from adjective to abstract noun for its sound as well as for its ambiguity of sense, and its shift from the particular to a general which is hardly wanted at this point. The impression of an imaginative uncertainty this gives is reinforced two paragraphs later when we are reminded that outside 'there was the snow and the low arch of dun vapour'. The low arch comes as a shock of inconsistency, so strongly has George Eliot insisted on the flat monotony, the blank whiteness of the scene.

The next sentences indicate that Dorothea has entered the boudoir and enumerate what she saw and how she saw it in comparison with the previous occasion. The definite article preceding the noun is repeated from the opening of the previous sentence and occurs again in each successive subordinate sentence: 'the very furniture', 'the stag', 'the volumes of polite literature'. There is intent in this monotony which marks the similarity of the ghostly inanimate effect of the separate furnishings. But the next sentence is meant to flare up as the fire which is compared to Dorothea's youthful liveliness and glow. George Eliot underlines and comments on its figurative connotations. Only the rhythm and the construction fail to establish such a contrast. 'The bright fire of dry oak-boughs', an exact repetition of the earlier rhythm, minimises the contrast when it should be leaping into the life and intensity it purports to show. An omitted article ('Bright flames from dry oak-boughs burning on the dogs') would have given a more intuitive sense of lively transition.

But, looked at closely, this sentence reveals another and more curious factor – that the entrance of Dorothea into the boudoir, which must have been already accomplished for her to compare its furnishings and their effect with her earlier reactions, has, in fact, not occurred at all: 'The bright fire . . . seemed . . . incongrous . . . like the figure of Dorothea herself as she entered carrying the red leather cases containing the cameos for Celia.' It may be that the intention is to force the reader back from Dorothea's present reaction (through which we see the furnishings) to the earlier moment when she walked in, now recalled to make the image of the fire – representing her intrusion of youth and life – more effective. But the confusion of time sequence here is not an added subtlety, as Dickens's is; it disrupts; we suspect it was something the author hadn't noticed. This may be unfair, but George Eliot deliberately did not write: 'The bright fire . . . *as* the figure of Dorothea herself *had seemed* when she entered', and clearly from her choice of language she wants us to see this as here and now. We enter with Dorothea, but we have been in the room with her before. The shift of viewpoint is the author's, intended to move into an objective description of the heroine from a subjective sharing of her emotions. There is the same sort of uneasiness of effect here, it seems to me, as in the earlier evocation of the horizon, and to notice it is not to carp at a fine passage, but to indicate how a slackening of imaginative pressure and of imaginative coherence is reflected in such verbal clumsiness and stylistic inconsistency.

A similar analysis of the subsequent paragraphs of this important chapter of *Middlemarch* confirms that George Eliot's imagination is continually checked and sometimes confused by her conscious or didactic intention. The shift from narrative to commentary is always deliberate but not always stylistically successful. This is not to deny her other subtleties and successes: her best effects are almost always of significant gesture or incident, reflecting character which she has already realised and brooded over, as when Dorothea in this same episode 'laid the cameo cases on the table . . . [and] unconsciously kept her hands on them, immediately absorbed in looking out on the still white enclosure which made her visible world'. The impression is always of an accomplished realisation of intent. However much we are moved forward or backward by authorial reminder, or by the reactions of characters, we are always in the already achieved present of the novelist's conclusions. This is as it is, this is as I see it, George Eliot's language tells us. The achieved present, however, always and inevitably presents itself to the imagination as finished and past. Exploring experience is a meditative, analytic process in her books. In Dickens's it is a continuous instant recreation of the act of imagining.

There are other nineteenth-century novelists who might be reassessed on these principles. Chief among them is Thackeray. His reputation as an almost equal sharer of Dickens's popularity is in some sense related to his power of narrative and linguistic control. It used to be fashionable to admire his style and to mark its debt to the eighteenth century. A passage from *Tristram Shandy* shows how Sterne anticipates Thackeray's tone:

I will not argue the matter: Time wastes too fast: every letter I trace tells me with what rapidity Life follows my pen; the days and hours of it more precious, – my dear Jenny, – than the rubies about thy neck, are flying over our heads like light clouds of a windy day, never to return more, – everything presses on, – whilst thou art twisting that lock; – see! it grows grey; and every time I kiss thy hand to bid adieu, and every absence which follows it, are preludes to that eternal separation which we are shortly to make. (Volume IX, Chapter VIII)

But Thackeray learned more than a deft and elegant syntax from Sterne. Their imaginative interests, especially their preoccupation with transcience, coincide. Thackeray's club-window view of life might seem in danger of trivialising it to a passing show, but the mastery of tense and transition in his constructions betrays an imaginative seriousness that matches Sterne's.

In the passage from *Tristram Shandy* the time continuum is felt in the punctuation most obviously, where colons, semi-colons and commas followed by dashes isolate a swift succession of moments. The described detail, with one exception – Jenny's rubies – is all in motion; time flies as the pen presses on. The verbal constructions are reticently varied to draw us to the striking climax of the passage: 'whilst thou art twisting that lock; – see! it grows grey', where the whole inevitable process of time wasting happens under our eyes. 'The days and hours ... *are flying*', 'whilst thou *art twisting* that lock' – the continuous present tense here contrasts beautifully with the two strong and simple present verbs: 'every letter *I trace*' (though tracing is a gradual and continuous process), and 'see! *it grows* grey', where the exclamatory imperative stops the flow, and growing old becomes a vivid momentary metamorphosis.

Thackeray's touch is not always so sure, but this passage from *The Newcomes* shows an extraordinarily complicated but vivid use of tense and transition. Clive Newcome has seen Ethel again after a long time, in the audience listening to Barnes Newcome's oratory; it is a pretext for Thackeray to begin one of his meditations on time and change, on the burial of dead love and on picking up the strands of living again:

Do you suppose you are the only man who has to attend such a funeral? You will find some men smiling and at work the day after. Some come to the grave now and again out of the world, and say a brief prayer and a 'God bless her!' With some men, she gone, and her viduous mansion your heart to let, her successor the new occupant poking in all the drawers, and corners, and cupboards of the tenement, finds her miniature, and some of her dusty old letters hidden away somewhere, and says—Was this the face he admired so? Why, allowing even for the painter's flattery, it is quite ordinary, and the eyes certainly do not look straight. Are these the letters you thought so charming? Well, upon my word, I never read anything more commonplace in my life. See, here's a line half blotted out. Oh I suppose she was crying then – some of her tears, idle tears ... Hark, there is Barnes Newcome's eloquence still plapping on like water from a cistern—and our thoughts, where have they wandered? far away from the lecture—as far away as Clive's almost. And now the fountain ceases to trickle;

the mouth from which issued that cool and limpid flux ceases to smile; the figure is seen to bow and retire; a buzz, a hum, a whisper, a scuffle, a rustling of silks ensue. 'Thank you! delightful I am sure!' 'I really was quite overcome.' 'Excellent.' '*So* much obliged,' are rapid phrases heard amongst the polite on the platform. (Chapter XXVIII).

The direct address to the reader imposes the present tense on the passage, but the whole piece is a sequence of shifting addresses, moving from direct authorial voice to reported speech, to imagined soliloquy that turns imperceptibly into implied dialogue, and back to the novel's present in the concluding public address and the comments that follow it. It is a most skilful piece of verbal orchestration in which the deliberate time confusions are used to manipulate the reader's feelings as he responds to the general and the particular at once, and sees time passing in the single occasion. The special complexity of the fourth sentence here deserves close attention. 'With some men, she gone, and her viduous mansion your heart to let, her successor the new occupant poking in all the drawers, and corners, and cupboards of the tenement, finds her miniature . . .' There is a deliberate confusion of subject here: 'With some men' suggests that they will be the active agents in the sentence, but these are the kind of men who admit other loves into their lives to rummage in their past, and it is 'her successor' who takes over the sentence as she has taken over the man. The terse compression of 'With some men, she gone' emphasises the compression of a marvellous pun: 'viduous'—empty and widowed, though the actual rhythm of 'and her viduous mansion your heart to let' has the expansive lilt of sentimental verse. The aural contrast of such precise furniture as drawers, corners, cupboards with '*some* of her dusty old letters hidden away *somewhere*', and of the sophisticated tone of narrative with the coarse sharp direct observations, 'Well, upon my word, I never read anything more commonplace in my life' modulates into another exact verse echo with all its intenser overtones: 'Oh I suppose she was crying then—some of her tears, idle tears.' A sharp ear catches the change, too, from:

'Was this the face *he* admired so?', to 'Are these the letters *you* thought so charming?' *Some* men can be forced to take part in such an inquisition. *'Here's* a line half blotted out.' 'Hark, *there* is Barnes Newcome's eloquence still plapping on like water from a cistern.' These counterpointings create an extraordinarily deft and rapid complex of impressions and feelings, more subtle than a simple 'stream of consciousness' or interior monologue technique. They depend for their effect, too, on a continual shift of address and addressee. The concluding buzz, hum, scuffle, rustling intrudes like the real world in a simple coarser construction, to which we have been conveyed by that intervening sentence of elaborate literary irony disposing of Barnes Newcome and his 'eloquence'.

As with Dickens, Thackeray instinctively feels in terms of language. The ultimate superiority of their art, to my mind, depends on this. Different though they are in imagination and achievement, their contemporaries were right to dispute their claim, seriously, to the title of best in the artistry of the novel. Henry James, supreme stylist though he was, found less to discuss in them than in George Eliot. In this he was right. Their peculiar skills could not help him; the extraordinary linguistic density of his later novels reveals a struggle to relate conscious verbal craft to an equally conscious imaginative conception. The latter he had seen and admired in George Eliot, though repudiating her technique. But the fascination and the failure of his later works exists in the sort of deliberate efforts to adapt one to the other which produces a mandarin prose valuable to the artist but lacking the peculiar dimension of linguistic genius which derives from intuitive confidence in a traditional or instinctive vision. Such a vision finds words to embody it and can use all its energy on the task of finding because it does not need to question the original act of imaginative conception. In a sense Dickens and Thackeray start where James leaves off. They are originally convinced of their vision of experience; their task is not to explore it, fix it and find words to embody it; rather they engage the reader in the continuous enjoyment of discovering how and how variously to say what is known unquestioningly. Vitality of language flourishes in these conditions. The 'great tradition' of George Eliot, James and Conrad has many virtues, but this it lacks. It cannot play with words. That Dickens and Thackeray can—and do—given the premises I have assumed, forces us to look at them freshly and to recognise their genius in a way we have often neglected by regarding fiction in isolation from the art of fictional prose.

1   Inaugural lecture delivered at the University of Durham, 1959

3 Towards a reading of *Dombey and Son*

Gabriel Pearson

We are only the actors, we are never wholly the authors of our own deeds or works. (D.H. Lawrence, *Studies in Classic American Literature*)

Notoriously Dickens was trying with *Dombey and Son* to become for the first time a serious, self-conscious fictional artist. Most critics, from Chesterton onwards, have taken the intention for the deed and have read, whether fully consciously or not, the intention *in* the deed. Chesterton's verdict that *Dombey and Son* represents Dickens's 'final resolution to be a novelist and nothing else, to be a serious constructor of fictions in the serious sense'[1] passes virtually unchallenged save by some, like Leavis in *The Great Tradition* and more recently Robert Garis,[2] who have wished to restrict Dickens's claim to seriousness to one book – to *Hard Times* or *Great Expectations*. The Leavises' recent book on Dickens is called assertively *Dickens the Novelist* and opens with F. R. Leavis's lecture on *Dombey*. Here *Dombey's* centrality is emphatically restated: '*Dombey and Son* marks a decisive moment in Dickens's career; he offered it as a providentially conceived whole, presenting a major theme, and it was his first essay in the elaborately plotted Victorian novel.'[3] Yet in both Chesterton's statement and in Leavis's, definitive though each seems, there lurks the shadow of a reservation. In both formulations what baulks largest is Dickens's *intention*: 'his final resolution to be a novelist and nothing else'; 'he offered it as a providentially conceived whole . . .' Not only is the intention being read as the deed, but one might think that the intention is the deed, that the deed exists to proclaim the intention.

Butt and Tillotson have meanwhile documented this account of *Dombey and Son* from Dickens's own statements in his letters to Forster, his directives to his illustrator, his number-plans and his changes in proof.[4] This evidence confirms Dickens's intention to be a novelist in the new sense. Still, we should note that all this evidence is of Dickens's own providing. The basic source is Forster's *Life*, a work designed to consecrate the view that Dickens had of himself. It requires some critical scepticism to escape the mythic pressure that Dickens exerts through that work. In effect Dickens is writing through the pen of his friend, biographer and executor the novel of his life as a writer. We should be aware that we are reading a story and within that story *Dombey and Son* marks, as Leavis obligingly retails it, 'a decisive moment in Dickens's career'. From the start Dickens held that 'the general idea of *Dombey* is interesting and new.' He was now going to resist diversion and digression: '. . . so I mean to carry the story on, through all the branches and offshoots and meanderings that come up.' Dickens knew well enough how much this design must be threatened by the inspirational nature of his creative demon: 'Invention, thank God, seems the easiest thing in the world; and I seem to have such a preposterous sense of the ridiculous . . . as to be constantly requiring to restrain myself from launching into extravagances in the height of my enjoyment.'[5] Self-restraint amounting to self-repression is clearly to be one of the elements of the new seriousness. The habit of repression is built into the novel in the character and characteristic stiffness and *rigor mortis* of Mr Dombey. Extravagance often takes the form of thwarted comic initiatives. Mainly it is outlawed to the sentimental and humorous sub-worlds of the book.[6]

I remain at best guarded about this account of the change from 'great entertainer' (Leavis's phrase) to serious novelist. Literary scholarship fastens with suspicious readiness upon such satisfactory models of development. Ideas – indeed ideals – of development form a central aspect of our mythic apparatus, where they reinforce a strongly individualist ideology. This does not make them especially wicked or necessarily false: the point is that they are assumed to be utterly natural, where they are no such thing. The myth of their naturalness disguises their true nature, as ideology. In relation to the novel, which is manifestly dedicated to celebrating ideals of personal autonomy, such developmental patterns are peculiarly appealing. But I am already embarrassed by the way my own discourse has slipped unnoticed into a conventional pattern of assumptions. To do justice to my own sense of how suspect, misleading and mythic this whole complex of author/development/work is, I am tempted to put the name Dickens in quotation marks throughout. To express the impulse, however, is happily to spare its necessity.

To name the author before his work already involves assumptions about the causal priority of one over the other. Most critics seem bent on intuiting a Dickens who is the originator, the effective cause, the *sine qua non* of his works. I want to push beyond such fiddle-faddle as 'the intentional fallacy' to an actual inversion of this 'natural' assumption and suggest that it is not so much authors who create their works as works which create authors. Novels in particular seem to have got written almost to promote a myth of authorship. So natural has this process appeared that it has been applied retrospectively to such resistent anonymities as 'Shakespeare' and 'Chaucer' with gratifyingly meagre results. *Dombey and Son*, I would argue, is precisely a work designed to create its author. With *Dombey*, Dickens ceased definitively to be Boz, the old, popular 'Inimitable', with Boz's peculiar showman's gusto, his ringside intimacy, his mountebank's creative mendacity. Dickens was trying to prize himself loose from Boz as early as the first one-volume edition of *Nicholas Nickleby*, which features a portrait of the author signed 'Yours faithfully, Charles Dickens'. There is something touching about this attempt to make each reader the recipient of a personal communication. The preface to the first edition of *Dombey and Son* takes the new relationship for granted: 'I cannot forgo my usual opportunity of saying farewell to my readers in this greeting place.' Reader and author are thought of as engaged on a common journey; but the direction of flow is now reversed and moves from the reader to author ('the unbounded warmth and earnestness of their sympathy . . .').

Dickens adverts inevitably to the death of little Paul:

> If any of them have [*sic*] felt a sorrow in one of the principle incidents on which this fiction turns, I hope it may be a sorrow of that sort which endears the sharers of it, one to another. This is not unselfish in me. I may claim to have felt it, at least as much as any one else; and I would fain be remembered for my part in the experience.

In disclaiming 'unselfishness' Dickens recurs to what he has claimed to be a major theme of his previous book. Within the elaborately courteous phrasing of 'I would fain be remembered' we divine a guarded but still emphatic appeal to a veneration for the author as such – uniquely distinguished in his suffering, which effectively cancels the communal identity of Boz.

Finally, all the documents and statements and memoirs and letters and gossip and autobiography from which the author of his works is deduced are just another set of texts, no more authoritative or explanatory than the works themselves. To be sure they may well be contrived to look like especially privileged or neutral evidence, from which to deduce 'a real man'. They will be all the more suspect if addressed to one singled out as his testator and biographer. Even number-plans may be less spontaneously authentic than they look: more in the nature of a prompt-book in the theatre of artistic self-consciousness. If anything, they testify to a significant splitting, in Dickens's case, between the professional craftsman and his more capacious and public identity as mime, manipulator and performer. I am suggesting that at a certain stage Dickens began to act the part of the autonomous creative artist. The acting was no hypocrisy. He was his own most moved, most convinced, most rapt audience. In creating *Dombey*, he partly created himself as Dombey, the linear, purposive, selfish architect of a unique destiny. In little Paul, by the same token, he acknowledges a cost – the death of that innocent, childish spontaneity which was the well-head of his own common humanity. Dickens seems to feel a need to make his readership participate in this death before redeeming it by a series of master strokes. Paul Dombey's death was a carefully plotted *coup de grâce*.[7] It produces a violent rupture in the text, as it was designed to do in the flow of the first readers' expectation, with the result of decisively reclaiming the text as the author's own property. By contrast, the death of Little Nell had been a shared, public ritual. Her persecutor, Quilp (the demonic side, surely, of Dickens himself),[8] had been duly executed. Paul's death indeed succeeded in staggering the public. Jeffrey as usual responded with a gush of purging tears. Perhaps more surprisingly, Paul's death 'amazed Paris'. Thackeray, then in the thick of *Vanity Fair*, reacted with envious rage, dashing a copy of *Dombey* against a table in the *Punch* office, exclaiming with startling vehemence, 'There's no writing against such power as this – One has no chance! Read that chapter describing young Paul's death: it is unsurpassed – it is stupendous!'[9]

Dickens responded to Paul's death with a night of total sleeplessness:

When I am reminded by any chance of what it was that the waves were always saying, my remembrance wanders for a whole winter night about the streets of Paris – as I restlessly did with a heavy heart, on the night when I had written the chapter in which my little friend and I parted company.[10]

If sleep stands for natural piety then Dickens had certainly murdered it. How uncanny too, that Dickens should refer to Paul in Blimber's phrase: 'my little friend'. Thackeray had undoubtedly located an intention to be unsurpassable and unbeatable at any cost. Of course one could dismiss his reaction as no more than a paroxysm of professional jealousy. But then what is the significance of professional jealousy? What does so intense an investment in the idea of the professional life signify with respect to the idea of the creative artist? It suggests at least that division of labour has entered into the marrow of the writing process. One is forced to become increasingly suspicious about the nature and status of that 'Dickens' so blithely postulated by literary scholars as the author of his work. What significance are we to ascribe to Dickens's gusts of brutal practicality in relation to *Dombey* itself? What are we to make of a Dickens

58

who, apparently with respect to a novel specifically concerned with the evil of money and mercantile pride, decides not to end a monthly part with the spurning and flight of Florence Dombey in order 'to leave a pleasant impression on the reader' over Christmas?[11]

The new self-consciousness as a novelist does, to be sure, manifest itself partly in a greater concern for architectonics. There is the strategic surprise of Paul's death, exploding a powerful irony in the title: the firm is after all to fail of a successor. There are carefully wrought parallelisms, such as the encounter between Mrs Skewton and Mrs Brown and their two daughters Alice and Edith on the downs above Brighton. There is the careful positioning of the railway sequences and the contrasted versions of Stagg's Gardens. As Dombey's empire collapses, Sol's investments come correspondingly into their own, 'bad' business being superseded by 'good', the apparently obsolete and inept turning out to be more viable than thriving big business.[12] This new architectonics could be seen as an elaboration of the performer's old manipulative 'make 'em laugh, make 'em cry' formula rendered more subtle and persuasive. *Dombey* – as indeed Chesterton sees very clearly – is still transitional: the Wooden Midshipman inhabited by the comic spirit of Captain Cuttle represents some of the more basic elements of Dickens's traditional, performative art. The same sort of moral significance attaches to it as attaches to the circus in *Hard Times*. Cuttle is meant to be an eruptive, spontaneous play principle, dissolving rigidities and releasing a spirit of redemptive incongruity. But Cuttle is, if anything, more wilfully contrived for this role than Sleary: he is simply not handled with the anarchic spontaneity he is supposed to embody.[13] *Dombey*, the novel, is in the grip of a thematic rigour which it shares with the selfish rigidity of Dombey, the character. Ironically, *Dombey* was supposed to be concerned with Pride, whereas *Chuzzlewit* was to have been concerned with Selfishness.[14] Applied to *Chuzzlewit* this assertion of thematic unity in any case looks like the merest afterthought: it so outrageously fails to unify itself at all. Its power derives largely from its improvisational elements: the American episode, Mrs Gamp, Jonas's murder of Tigg. These improvisations are also capable of engendering morally serious matter. Nothing in *Dombey* is more telling than the married misery of Mercy Pecksniff, Jonas Chuzzlewit's wife. *Dombey* undoubtedly does exhibit a unity of design which *Chuzzlewit* lacks. The idea of unity goes hand in hand with the idea of authorial control: the one follows from the other and evidences the other.

The critical preference for *Dombey* over *Chuzzlewit* derives from a collusion between a critical orthodoxy obsessed with ideals of unity and Dickens's own attempt to enact similar ideals in his own art. There is every difference between unity actually inhering in the objective pattern of a work (as it does in that of Jane Austen) and unity which consists in a deliberated imposition of design. In *Dombey and Son* Dickens can be seen as offering his readership a sort of consolation for its own lack of autonomy through offering to share with it his own artist's autonomy and self-direction. Yet this programme implies a deliberate repression of the pleasure principle. Somehow the two must be combined. The overt statement of the novel is that spontaneous life, flickering up out of the ancient hearth of the human heart, must – indeed *will* – redeem the mechanistic will. Meanwhile that will goes on constructing railways, and slums, and money, and 'elaborately plotted Victorian novels'. The most blatant product of rigid, linear wilfulness is the railway: but in *Dombey* the railway is driven, though not actually run, by Polly Toodles's husband, gentle dandler of profuse child-life. One could say that in the very years in which Engels's *Condition of the Working Class* was written, Dickens was already intuiting the half-alliance between industrial capitalism and the new unionism of the 1850s. Within the structure of *Dombey* the consoling impression is fostered that after all severely masculine enterprise can be returned to the loving care of child-like and child-loving men. Yet our total experience of *Dombey and Son* is of a text which cries down firmness and wilfulness only to endorse them in the willed elaboration of its design. Dombey is not of course a novel about the railway boom of the 1840s. But that boom, however apparently rational, was also deeply hysterical.

Financial activity, as it often does in such a period, took on a hectic, inspirational life of its own. The authorial will which conceived *Dombey* shares (as Dickens's maniac-depressive swings of mood during its composition testify) something of the same hysteria. One has to add to the figure of Dombey the lurid ambition that finally explodes the calculated self-repression of Edward Carker.

Dickens exhibits some of Carker's need to bamboozle and divert. Dickens himself was a businessman, his whole career as an author an entrepreneurial activity. In fact his novels were more obviously his business than Dombey's lofty and remote dealings were ever his. Dombey was after all a hereditary merchant prince, unlike Dickens himself. The full title of *Dombey and Son* is: *Dealings with the Firm of Dombey and Son, Wholesale, Retail and for Export*. This title was kept as a jealously guarded secret, a trade secret, in fact, and one which Dickens was particularly anxious not to have leaked. Evidently he invested exceptional significance in it. The novel undoubtedly sets out to attack mercantile pride with its associated masculine egoism and drive to dominate and so deny the claims of womanly tenderness and natural affection. This pride is itself duly humbled and made to confess its error. Feminine values of love and generosity and feeling-ness are reinstated. The longer title punningly foreshadows this reversal: Dombey's firm is indeed 'dealt' with, in the sense of being chastised and put in its place. A jocular extension of the word 'dealing' turns author and reader into customers of Dombey, but customers providentially immune to the stringencies of real commerce. We are meant, moreover, to find the phrasing of the extended title absurdly, almost gaily, pompous. After all, so much puff and pretension can hardly be very menacing. At another level the full title implies that Dickens and his readers have embarked upon a common enterprise, where 'Dombey and Son' is the title of the book rather than of the firm within the book. But the enterprise of the novel, the reading and writing of it, is a gentle kind of anti-business, more like Sol Gills's little shop, paradoxically capable of realising large profits, but to the heart rather than to the purse, though it fills the author's too, and, in the book, ultimately Sol Gills's own. Dickens's later book, *The Uncommercial Traveller*, reminds us that Dickens was partial to this kind of title.[15] All this elaborate verbal play in the title simultaneously conceals and states what all of his original readers must really have sensed: that they were enrolled in Dickens's own trading venture, whose stock in trade[16] was his capacity to move them to laughter and tears, and this, paradoxically, with a tale that denigrated mercantile pride and mercenary intent.

I am not suggesting that Dickens *is* Dombey in any auto-biographical sense. My suggestion is that there is an analogy between the central character of Dickens's fable and his project of novel-making. Dombey is a father, that is how he mainly defines himself, and one dedicated to repeating himself through his son, who is not so much to be a new individual as a kind of repeat, effectively a clone. The novelist's enterprise is rather of the same sort, to reproduce, or author himself, through the project of novel making. The readership assumes a different relationship from that it had previously to Dickens: it becomes more passive, more recipient, more like a womb – to continue the analogy – in which the novelist's project is conceived and nourished and from which it is delivered. *Dombey* becomes Dickens's first 'real' novel, in the sense claimed for it by its critics, partly because that is the project it sets itself. To read it is not merely to be immersed in a story, but to 'read' narrative and thematic equivalents of Dickens's intention to invent 'Dickens the Novelist'. 'Dickens the Novelist' then takes his place as a powerful mythic personality in the Pantheon of Possessive Individualism.

Of course, the ideal of perfect autonomy is in fact unrealis-able. It always in the novelist's as in the capitalist's case requires for its project the co-operation of others, of an alterna-tive presence: an audience, a market, workers, readers. The autonomy of individualism is always betrayed by its own economic base, frequently feminine in its passivity, but actively female in the sense of its being the author's real author, the true ground of his design. To complete the logic of our modest Copernican revolution, it follows that if the work creates the author, then the reader creates the work, a fact that the Dombeyan author has continually to repudiate. This would establish a further parallelism between the reader and one other destroyed figure in the novel – the mother. Part of Dombey's sin is that he tries to appropriate the identity of the mother, or at best to reduce it to a mere function. Leavis is admirably perceptive about the deliberate, lingering pleasure that Dombey takes in rejecting candidates for the position of wet-nurse to the orphaned Paul. When he finally has perforce to accept one of these he denatures and mas-culinises her by insisting she be renamed Richards.[17] Some-thing analogous happens to the reader, who is transformed into a customer, a passive recipient, even a dupe of the author's (particularly with respect to the contrived death of Paul). Part-publication gave Dickens splendid opportunities for this kind of manipulation. I shall discuss this a little later. Mean-while it is worth observing that he had never before used part-publication to bring off such a contrived coup as that of Paul's dying. Up until *Dombey* part-publication had been more often a condition of Dickens's vulnerable fellowship with his audience, a medium through which he sensed its needs and sometimes abjectly catered for its cruder requirements. It is perhaps significant that Dickens first mooted the idea of public readings as a result of a private reading of the first part of *Dombey*.[18] Public reading was an attempt to recover a lost intimacy with his readership whose devotion had made him rich and famous and isolated.

His new triumphant yet guilt-ridden relationship with his readers makes the opening chapter of *Dombey* quite unlike anything he had written before, and certainly quite unlike any previous opening chapter. After *Dombey* his openings become notably strong, confident and commanding. By contrast, his previous openings had been remarkably uneasy and tentative, as though he were still groping blindly for the lineaments of his readership. In this opening chapter, in which a child is born, a mother dies, a daughter is ignored, there is a quite striking impression of authority and control. We sense, as readers, that we are in the grip of a master, who totally commands the narrative tempo, the variations in texture, the subtle shifts of key from comedy to pathos to satire to epic elevation. The only comparable opening is that of *Oliver Twist*, where likewise a child is born as a mother dies. But in that case there is a kind of desperation in the writing which comes across as hysterically heightened facetiousness. Dickens seems unsure of how to modulate between the modes of pathos and satire: only the urgency of his concern shapes and drives his prose. In *Oliver Twist* the birth of the hero seems to signal the creation of Dickens's first, wholly self-conceived work of fiction (*Pickwick* involved an inspired takeover of someone else's design). But in *Oliver Twist* there is no father present; the orphan Oliver is necessarily fathered upon the world, or the readership that constitutes the novel's world. The reader is invited to adopt the orphan, to acknowledge his responsibility for his fate, to choose between Brownlow and Grimwig, to constitute a vital partnership with the author in the creation of his novel. Hence the striking mythic resonance of so much of the work which survives the total shambles of its plot. Nothing in Dombey has the mythic resonance of Oliver's Asking For More. That incident is propelled beyond the confines of its immediate context in the novel into a kind of mythic space beyond. This kind of impersonal myth-making largely disappears with *Dombey*: there is nothing after to compare with Pickwick and Sam Weller, with Bumble, Fagin and Sykes, with Squeers, with Mrs Gamp. The only thing at all like it later is the bursting of the wine barrel in *A Tale of Two Cities*. Dickens's 'resolution . . . to be a serious constructor of fictions in the serious sense' evidently entails loss as well as gain, as Chesterton saw so clearly.[19]

The opening of *Dombey* lets us into the text at its point of production by means of a story about fathering, mothering and death. This has been true of many novels. Smollett's *Roderick Random* is a classic instance:

I was born in the northern part of this united kingdom, in the house of my grandfather; a gentleman of considerable fortune and influence, who had, on many occasions, signalised himself on behalf of his country; and was remarkable for his abilities in the law, which he exercised with great success, in the station of a judge, particularly against beggars, for whom he had a singular aversion. (p. 9 in the Everyman edition of 1927)

The grandfather's 'singular aversion' is markedly Dombeyan. As we read this paragraph we seem to be witnesses simultaneousy of the birth of Roderick Random and of *Roderick Random*, since the first person is always, at a number of levels, his own author. The question of unity obligingly comes up, but in a political context ('this united kingdom'). Smollett himself is at work acquiring a 'united British' identity through authorship. The novel and Smollett's own career as author thus work through some of the implications of the Act of Union. Besides the birth of author, work and character, this birth seems to recapitulate the whole genre of the novel, committed as that has historically been to the ideology of individualism. Novels always posit the idea of a new life, though one which often returns to its origins. Epics, by contrast, begin by taking the reader *in medias res*, where the *res* in question seem ultimately to be the substance of a whole community already constituted through a body of myth or a shared system of belief. Dante's *Commedia* seems necessarily to begin:

> Nel mezzo del cammin di nostra vita
> Mi ritrovai per une selva oscura

where the communal *nostra vita* demands priority over the first-person reflexive verb, *mi ritrovai,* that follows. The *Commedia* follows *La Vita Nuova*, graphically illustrating the deep argument within Christianity as to whether every soul has to be new born or can find salvation through the institutionalised body of the Church. Dante is poised at the unique juncture where he can envisage the individual and communal ideal as virtually identical.[20] From the Renaissance onwards, the notion of a wholly autonomous artistic career has fed into an extending ideology of individualism. With the novel this notion has become, in a disguised form, the subject-matter of the work, where it has helped to foster the idea that the only career an individual can have is that of being himself, or sometimes of finding or failing to find a self to be.

The most searching inspection of the values of *Dombey*

and Son is that of Julian Moynihan.[21] Moynihan sees the novel as schematically divided. On the one hand there is the rigid, linear Dombeyan mode, associated with money pride, character armour, railway trains, freezing decorum. On the other is a whole set of oceanic motifs embodied in such fishy characters as Walter Gay ('water'), Sol Gills, Captain Cuttle, Perch, Susan Nipper, to which one may assimilate the redeemed Miss Tox through her fishy-eyed locket. I would add on my own account that while Dombey seems wholly singular in his concentration on number one, Polly Toodles, the wet-nurse, rejoices in a Christian name that denotes plurality: hung all over with round-cheeked progeny she is made to resemble some especially fecund and prolific Hindu deity, all arms and breasts, polymorphous indeed, though not perverse. At this level of the novel the verbal play is positively Joycean: there are simply oodles of Toodles. Moynihan finally dismisses the novel as an abject sell-out to gross sentimentality, the whole aqueous and oozy ideology of tears, milk and wetness.[22] My response would be that this apparent sell-out, by virtue of its thoroughly contrived and predetermined nature, actually redresses the whole balance of the novel towards the Dombeyan mode. It requires Dombey-like powers to engineer so purposive a construct, the autonomy of the object corresponding to the autonomous self that designed it. Dombey's 'firm' promises all the required firmness: in so far as the novel does build a world, the implications of *firm* embrace a whole firmament.

Indeed the opening paragraphs deploy a cosmological imagery which seems in excess of its function as satirical hyperbole:

'He will be christened Paul, my – Mrs. Dombey – of course.' She feebly echoed, 'of course,' or rather expressed it by the motion of her lips, and closed her eyes again.

'His father's name, Mrs. Dombey, and his grandfather's! I wish his grandfather were alive this day!' And again he said 'Dom-bey and Son' in exactly the same tone as before.

Those three words conveyed the one idea of Mr. Dombey's life. The earth was made for Dombey and Son to trade in, the sun and moon were made to give them light. Rivers and seas were formed to float their ships; rainbows gave them promise of fair weather; winds blew for or against their enterprises; stars and planets circled in their orbits, to preserve inviolate a system of which they were the centre. Common abbreviations took new meanings in his eyes, and had sole reference to them. A.D. had no concern with anno Domini, but stood for anno Dombei – and Son.

He had risen, as his father had before him, in the course of life and death, from Son to Dombey, and for nearly twenty years had been sole representative of the firm.

This is, to say the least, a particularly majestic piece of scene-setting, with all the valuations fully developed. Even the facetious jocularity of 'anno Dombei' becomes positively magisterial in this context. The main device is a kind of mimetic hyperbole: Dombey's inner conviction of cosmic self-importance is rendered by the appropriate cosmological imagery. Yet the effect is not merely deflationary: this imagery also generates its own, partly independent, system of reference. It is as though the text were supplying a mythic account of its own generation. The 'anno Dombei' joke arises partly out of the reiteration of *son* and *sun*: the Son of God fuses with the earth's annual orbit round the sun. *Son* sets off a covert train of association to the Trinity, '*three* words in *one* idea', reinforced by a curious conceptual interplay between *word* and *idea*. The next sentence produces a chiastic representation of the opposition and inter-action of male and female: 'The earth (A) was made for Dombey and Son (B) to trade in, and the sun (B) and moon (A) was made to give them light.'[23] There is a further elaboration of puns in *sole* (Sol), *sun* (son) and *risen*. This imagery prepares the way for the much more conscious trope of the ocean as death with which the chapter concludes, and for the elaborated icononography of little Paul's infamous waves. Remoter connections reach to Sol Gills, who, unlike Dombey in his fallen state, does successfully rise again. Well, might not all this verbal activity arise simply from Dickens's themes and the diction appropriate to them? My modest point is that the election of this diction with its resonances and ramifications flows from the kind of project that *Dombey* wills itself to be. It evokes a creation story and takes on these theological reverberations because the novelist has assumed god-like powers to create an independent world by personal fiat. He is doing verbally, in the creation of his own novel, what he condemns Dombey for sacrilegiously believing himself to be doing in the creation of his son and his firm.

The opening chapter recalls another myth of origin. Dombey is closely identified with time in a novel fairly obsessed with it, and with the opposition between linear, clock time and natural, cyclical time. Dombey himself is naturally attached to the linear variety. 'Dombey, exulting in the long-looked-for event, jingled and jingled the heavy gold watch-chain.' When Florence enters the room she glances 'keenly at the blue coat and stiff white cravat, which, with a pair of creaking boots and a very loud ticking watch, embodied her idea of a father'. To Mrs Chick's rousing call of 'Fanny! Fanny! . . . There was no sound in answer but the loud ticking of Mr. Dombey's watch and Dr. Parker Peps's watch, which seemed in the silence to be running a race.' All readers remember Dr Blimber's clock with its reiterated question to Paul Dombey: '. . . how, is, my, lit, tle, friend, how, is, my, lit, tle, friend?' As the clock takes up the rhythm of Dr Blimber's heavy, interrogative jocularity, he clearly manifests himself as the educational limb of Dombeyism. One is touched by the picture of Paul being addressed as 'little friend' by agencies so unconsciously inimical to his well-being.[24]

The marine chronometers of the Wooden Midshipman are by contrast attuned to cyclical, oceanic time. Indeed Sol Gill's establishment is rapidly transformed by Dickens's metamorphosing prose into a ship itself:

The stock in trade of [Sol Gills] comprised chronometers, barometers, telescopes, compasses, charts, maps, sextants, quadrants and specimens of every kind of instrument used in the working of a ship's course, or the keeping of a ship's reckoning, or the prosecuting of a ship's discoveries . . . the shop itself seemed almost to become a snug, sea-going, ship-shape concern, wanting only good sea-room, in the event of an unexpected launch, to work its way securely to any desert island in the world.

Dickens effectively gives it just that—an 'unexpected launch'—

as he floats all that instrumentation on the surge of his own extravagant verbal inventiveness.

> Objects in brass and glass were in his drawers and on his shelves, which none but the initiated could have found the top of, or having once examined, could have ever got back again into their mahogany nests without assistance. Everything was jammed into the tightest cases, fitted into the narrowest corners, fenced up behind the most impertinent cushions, and screwed into the acutest angles, to prevent its philosophical composure from being disturbed by the rolling of the sea. Such extraordinary precautions were taken in every instance to save room, and keep the thing compact; and so much practical navigation was fitted and cushioned and screwed into every box (whether the box was a mere slab, as some were, or something between a cocked hat and a star-fish as others were . . .)
> (Chapter IV)

The starfish is a stroke of genius which brings the marine and celestial aspects of navigation into precise alignment. Sol Gills's watertightness and dryness, his rightness and snugness amount to a parody and reproof of Dombeyism. His shop seems odd, sharply angled, screwed down and intensely over-ordered, but these qualities acknowledge the mastery of time-less and elemental realities. One becomes grateful to the 'anno Dombei' joke which releases *dominus*, *domus* and *dominate* from Dombey, the proper noun. A paragraph above the one quoted Gills is referred to as 'sole master', but it is a mastery without domination. Dombey, however, is a devouring Chronos in the later allegorisation of his name. The syllables DOM BE spell out doom. Everything associated with him involves a repetition which seems the formula of an endless sequence of repetition, from the 'jingling and jingling of his heavy gold watch-chain' to the tolling double beat of 'Dombey and Son; Dombey and Son'. In the opening sentence of the first chapter the doubling of father and son is carefully initiated. Both are red, both are wrinkled and both are bald. But Paul is also presented as something vulnerably edible: '. . . Son lay tucked up warm in front of the fire and close to it, as if his constitution was analogous to that of a muffin, and it was necessary to toast him brown while he was very new.'

Time, we know, notoriously devours its own children, though not, admittedly, after having first toasted them. And yet, metaphorically, Dombey does devour his son's life. The christening party allows Dickens to make splendid play out of an ungenial feast, where Dombey's rigidity and egocentricity seem to turn all food into inedible anti-matter. Throughout Dickens's novels the idea of food and nurture seems closely connected to the deepest exercise of his art in its generosity or deprivation. When Oliver asks for more the power of his demand issues from a gaping hunger in Dickens himself, to be cherished, endowed with an identity, to be loved, to commune in human fellowship. Hence the significance of the wet-nurse, the breast which Miss Tox refers to in an incantatory phrase as 'one common fountain' (chapter II).[25] Dombey, as a hungry Chronos, seeks to devour his own child, if only by appropriating the timeless fecundity and bodily nutrient of the feminine principle. He is allowed within the story one clear triumph. One Toodles child is abstracted from the familial flux to become Rob the Grinder, literally robbed, ground down, to represent a permanent deformation of the life forces. Dombey comes to represent Dickens's own hunger for identity and fame. It is an intensively defensive sleight of hand that bequeaths the predatory teeth to the gnawing Carker. A similar logic seems to lead Dombey to Edith, she of the stony and sterile bosom, perpetually struck in self-repudiation. Appropriately enough, much of the bad, forced melodrama in the book surrounds Edith, and some of the bad pathos too. A sterile bosom seems to go with the bad art. Yet the married life of the Dombeys had very real force and intensity. In that marriage some of the implications of a bad relationship between author and reader seem to find their narrative equivalent, as Dickens plots their desperate struggle to dominate one another, a struggle which the feminine principle, turned defensively domineering, naturally wins. The deepest resonance in this respect is sounded by Mrs Skewton, Edith's mother, who brilliantly acts the part of artifice impersonating nature. Her dying cry to Edith–'For I nursed you!' (chapter XLI)–is the deepest, most desperate thing in the book. Her cry might stand for Dickens's own vindication and smothered guilt.

Dombey and Son, the novel, dominates the reader's own time through its control of the subdivisions of time involved in part-publication. So much of the rhythm and structure of the novel seems the result of the surprises and arrests and suspensions that part-publication makes possible. Of course we no longer read it in parts, and to that extent some of the force of that particular necromancy is disabled. But since this periodical domination remains frozen into the book's architecture, imagery and plot, it still enforces its effects. We too, though less than the original readers, remain at the mercy of the author, looking to the dispensations of his genius, as though he were some kind of providence. The author has powers of life and death over his characters and, in the original form of publication, exercises them with deliberate arbitrariness. True, Dickens remained susceptible to the pull of the market, but increasingly less so as the planned elements triumphed over the improvisational elements of his art. I am not suggesting that part-publication explains the shaping of the novel, its arrangements of climax and its timing of incidents. That hopeful thesis has long been exploded.[26] My suggestion is that the kind of authorial domination that part-publication permitted is enacted at the level of character and plot. It is no accident that Dombey is imagistically a devouring Chronos; no accident that Carker is the master of the waiting game. Florence herself is planted like a kind of time-bomb in the bosom of Dombey's house, waiting her moment to bloom and conquer. In Florence, Dickens seeks to conjure a natural time, yet I fear that her role is the most desperately planned of all. He wants us so much to believe, wants so much to believe himself, that his art is one with nature, his design part of the rhythm of spontaneous life, when just that aspect of the novel represents the supreme triumph of his contriving will.

Dickens acts out in the fable of the novel and in the act of novel-writing itself some of the implications of asserting the priority of individual values over communal values. All novels—or all classic novels—do something like this. It happens that *Dombey and Son* is a particularly pertinent example, because it represents, within the work of one author, a moment of decision between an earlier, more performative phase and a later, more professionally authorial one. Through his career as novelist he sanctioned the most developed myth of the artist as great representative individual, who vindicates, through whatever reservations of inner guilt, ideals of self-creation and personal power. Dickens joins the company of Balzac, Hugo, Dostoevsky, Wagner, the bearded and waistcoated Prometheans of the epoch of High Capitalism. Yet at many levels he retained his loyalty to communal values, which, however, as a literary captain of industry he continued to merchandise and purvey in the commercial enterprise his novels could not help being. Dickens, like Verdi, for example, is a radically impure artist, but the impurity is the source of his power, the condition of his insight. It is not just an anecdotal peculiarity to be bemusedly exclaimed over by his biographers. Again and again after *Dombey* he returns to the basis of this impurity, the demonic project of inventing the glorious, philanthropic, suffering author of his works, until, in *Great Expectations* and *Our Mutual Friend*, he comes close to dismantling him and with him the myth he was designed to serve.

The dates of the Dickens novels referred to are as follows: *The Pickwick Papers* (1837); *Oliver Twist* (1838); *Nicholas Nickleby* (1839); *The Old Curiosity Shop* (1840); *Martin Chuzzlewit* (1844); *Dombey and Son* (1848); *Hard Times* (1854); *A Tale of Two Cities* (1859); *Great Expectations*|(1861); *Our Mutual Friend* (1865)

1   G.K. Chesterton, *Appreciations and Criticisms of the Works of Charles Dickens* (London, 1911), 118

2   Robert Garis, *The Dickens Theatre: A Reassessment of the Novels* (Oxford, 1965)

3   F.R. and Q.D. Leavis, *Dickens the Novelist* (London, 1970), 2

4   J. Butt and K. Tillotson, *Dickens at Work* (London, 1968), particularly 90 and 91

5   Quotations are all three from John Forster, *The Life of Charles Dickens*. They are from 5.iii, 5.v and 6.ii respectively

6   To be sure, Dickens had promised Forster from the outset of his work on *Dombey*, 'Some rollicking facetiousness, to say nothing of pathos'.

But interestingly this is added (by way of reassurance to Forster?) to a sentence that puts the stress on the character and main design: 'I think *Dombey* very strong – with great capacity in its leading idea; plenty of character that is likely to tell . . .' (Forster, op. cit., 5.iii)

7   Cf. ibid.: '. . . shall certainly have a great surprise for people at the end of the fourth number . . .' The surprise in fact came at the end of the fifth number, for reasons explained in Butt and Tillotson, op. cit., 96–7

8   As I have argued in my own essay on *The Old Curiosity Shop* in Gross and Pearson (eds), *Dickens and the Twentieth Century* (London, 1962)

9   Cited in Edgar Johnson, *Charles Dickens, His Tragedy and Triumph* (London, 1953), vol. II, 611

10 Preface to the first edition of *Dombey and Son* (London, 1848)

11 Cf. Butt and Tillotson, op. cit., 107. 'Over Christmas' is their own very plausible conjecture

12 Indeed the architectonic intent threw up insoluble problems such as the doubling of roles for Sol Gills and Captain Cuttle. Hence improvisation acquires the new function of dissolving architectonic rigidity and as such it becomes an aspect of the feminine, unconditioned, spontaneous activity, whose values triumph thematically. (cf. Butt and Tillotson, op. cit., 99)

13 Chesterton agrees, though with an uncharacteristic show of diffidence: 'It may be a personal idiosyncracy, but there is only one comic character really prominent in Dickens, upon whom Dickens has really lavished the wealth of his invention, and who does not amuse me at all, and that character is Captain Cuttle' (p. 122). And more bracingly: 'I could never find Captain Cuttle and Mr. Sol Gills very funny, and the whole Wooden Midshipman seems to me very wooden' (p. 129). One agrees, but wonders why the rigidity of Dombey should successfully petrify the humour

14 Cf. the opening para. of Forster, op. cit., 6.ii

15 'Figuratively speaking, I travel for the great house of Human Interest Brothers, and have rather a large connection in the fancy goods way.' (*The Uncommercial Traveller* (London, 1861), Chapter 1)

16 The word 'stock' crops up in another sense in Dicken's long letter to Forster of 25 July 1846 (Forster, op. cit., 6.ii): 'I also rely on the Toodles, and on Polly, who, like everybody else, will be found by Mr. Dombey to have gone over to his daughter and become attached to her. This is what cooks call "the stock of the soup." All kinds of things will be added to it, of course.' One need not be over-solemn about authors' culinary metaphors. Kipling left his stories to drain. Still, the pun

does effect an interesting transition from commercial to culinary codes, a matter of some interest in a novel which pits milk against money

17 The name, through its popular abbreviation, Dick, connects Polly's transformation with Dickens himself. Around all Dick, Rick, Richard names there seems to be an affective halo. Is it merely fanciful to note the queer cypher provided by crossing the names of the Artful Dodger, Charlie Bates and John Dawkins, in *Oliver Twist*? Pair them crosswise and one pair gives Charlie Dawkins, a vulgar version of Charles Dickens, perhaps the 'little robber or vagabond' that Dickens felt parental neglect had nearly made him into. Little Dick in the same novel becomes the version of Oliver that could never really survive his brutal and degrading experience

18 Cf. Johnson, op. cit., vol. II, 601

19 Cf. Chesterton, op. cit., 122: 'Broadly speaking . . . [*Dombey and Son*] . . . shows an advance in art and unity; it does not show an advance in genius and creation.' This observation arises out of a brilliant comparison between Mrs Nickleby in *Nicholas Nickleby* and Mrs Skewton in *Dombey*: 'Mrs. Skewton has not so much time as Mrs. Nickleby to say [her] good things . . . she is always intent upon her worldly plans, among other things the worldy plan of assisting Charles Dickens to get a story finished.' A very acute observation that, and highly pertinent to my argument

20 Allegorically, the first shift towards salvation in *Inferno* is Dante's recognition of Virgil as his master and author:

> Tu se' lo mio maestro, e il mio autore;
>
> tu se' solo colui, da cui io tolsi
>
> lo bello stile, che m'ha fatto honore.

Dante is not his own author, and the recognition that men are not so is the first motion of faith

21 Julian Moynihan, 'Dealings with the Firm of Dombey and Son: Firmness versus Wetness', in Gross and Pearson, op. cit., 121–31

22 Moynihan compares the sell out in *Dombey* to one similar in Lawrence's *Lady Chatterley's Lover*: 'Mellors writes Connie that things would be all right if men wore tight scarlet trousers and learned to dance and hop and skip, "and amuse the women themselves, and be amused by the women".' A travesty, surely, to isolate an incidental absurdity as the final argument of the novel. On *Dombey*, however, his findings are more substantial: 'The vast resources of human energy and wit that have been trapped within an unjust and destructively orientated socio-economic system are not released or transformed but merely abandoned. So that the problem each writer set out to solve is merely perpetuated in a new, grossly sentimental form' (ibid., 130–1)

23   Cf. the original cover design (reproduced in Butt and Tillotson, op. cit., between 92 and 93). This shows at bottom right the sun rising over a ship prosperously launched and at bottom left a half-moon standing over a shipwreck. The imagery of the cover design is an assemblage of highly traditional motifs and icons. Yet is seems to me powerful and suggestive beyond Dickens's general intention 'to shadow out the drift' without giving away the story. The cover design and Dickens's own prose fit together with unusual intimacy, like the poetry and design in a Blake Prophetic Book. This certainly complicates any easy ascription of the cosmological imagery attached to Dombey's view of himself as merely satirical. The prose of the opening paragraph and the cover design seem to arise directly from the same inspiration. One would like to know more about Dickens's instructions to his illustrator Hablôt Browne. Dickens began Dombey at the end of June 1846. Butt and Tillotson assume that 'during August, Dickens had been instructing his illustrator Hablôt K. Browne about the cover design . . . for early in September he approved it as "very good" . . .' (p. 92). But whether Browne would actually have read the first chapter, I cannot discover. Dickens was dissatisfied with some of Browne's illustrations and remarked, 'I think he does better without the text; for then the notion is made easy to him in short description, and he can't help taking it in.' One supposes that the cover design came from such a short description. (Forster, 6.ii)

24   Even as late as chapter XLIII Dombey, at least in relationship to Florence, is associated with a time-piece. Visiting her injured father after he has fallen from his horse, late on in his matrimonial crisis, she finds everything 'so still within, that she would hear the burning of the fire, and count the ticking of the clock that stood upon the chimney-piece'. Dombey's sleeping face looks innocent. Dickens himself assumes the voice of avenging time with his twice-repeated choral interjection: 'Awake, unkind father! Awake now, sullen man! The time is flitting by: the hour is coming with an angry tread. Awake!'

25   An elaborate example of the transmutation of tears into food through the middle term, milk, occurs in chapter LIX. Following the tearful reunion of father and daughter, Miss Tox and Polly 'came out of their concealment and exulted tearfully'. In a beautifully handled and very British anti-climax that paragraph concludes: '. . . and they took a last cup of tea.' The reformed Rob the Grinder is then invited 'to take a little bread and butter and a cup of tea . . .'. Dickens contrives a transition from highly wrought pathos to tearful comedy with a last flourish on grinders: ' "Thankee Miss," returned the Grinder; who immediately began to use his own personal grinders in a most remark-able manner, as if he had been on very short allowance for a con-

siderable period' – as had Dickens himself, we feel, of that kind of jollity
26   Notably in Archibald Coolidge Jr, *Charles Dickens as a Serial Novelist* (Ames, 1967)

4 Reading late James

Tony Inglis

'Chaws more than he bites off,' remarked Mrs Henry Adams on reading *The Portrait of a Lady*. For the late novels in which that tendency is fully developed, James's early criticism of fiction is only distantly helpful, with its rich, subtle but broadly conventional accounts of representation, morality and 'solidity of specification'; and the still later retrospective Prefaces in which, now letting us glance into the workshop and now distracting us with genial chatter, James ruefully or complacently propounds a formal and technical account of his concerns are downright misleading. The very first Jamesians swallowed those Prefaces whole; a grittier later generation, rejecting such elaborate indirection but still reading the late novels by its light, accused James of 'castrating . . . for the sake of a particular aesthetic effect', of 'technical elaboration . . . [in which he] let his moral taste slip into abeyance' or of 'a defective procedure in style, the result of an error in theory'. Such accounts, I shall argue, overlooked an internalisation and metaphysical tightening in the late novels, whose distinctive interest lies in the number and variety of the modes in which they offer meaning, and in the intricate structures of dynamism and inhibition which operate in and between modes.[1]

Seymour Chatman's account of mentalisation, negation, obliquity and ellipsis in *The Later Style of Henry James* (1972) gives entry to one fundamental mode. Chatman notes James's striking preference for abstract 'subjects' over human ones (pp. 6–9). 'The conversion of mental acts into entities through nominalisation is an essential device for James' (p. 23); among the nominalisations, perceptions and precognitions abound but beliefs are rare (pp. 32–3). The perceptions are typically passive and recipient, not active (p. 17) and 'it is the onslaught of the impressions – not what the impression is – that is crucial' (p. 43). Performant verbs of perception 'are introduced precisely to be negated', as in 'Strether couldn't yet measure' (p. 18). Other devices negate, parallel or question the proffered substance of the novel, drawing the reader into constructive complicity with the narrative voice and the characters – the deictic 'it' of teasingly vague reference, the 'cleft' sentence introduced by 'What . . .', other suspensions ('She waited, Kate Croy . . .'), subtly out-of-place metaphors and colloquialisms which draw attention to their own dubiety. Finding virtue in the amount of work the style demands of the reader, Chatman confesses himself at a loss for the right characterising vocabulary; the words he would use for praise have already been used in censure. A little reluctantly he puts forward *intangibility* as the quality on which the various features of James's later language converge.

The analogies Chatman finds between the syntax of these novels and their treatment of perception extend also to character and plot. The paradoxical opacity and resistance of the 'intangible' prose, and its capacity none the less to lure and involve the reader, find their parallel in the characters' defending the boundaries of the self while reaching out into the world of experience. The negated perceptions and the suspended or displaced acts parallel James's endings (long before his last phase even) in suspension or disjunction: 'For life, as it were', 'Just you wait!', 'We shall never be again as we were!' I shall work by interposing an account of James's imagery of the disjoined and incomplete between the features of his language summarised from Chatman and the larger significances, ethical and epistemological, of the late novels. My essay should constitute some rejoinder to the formalism of the Prefaces, to the various accounts of James's characters as Lockean *tabulae rasae* or as lacking unconscious lives, and to Winters's challenging *obiter dictum* that 'all intelligent criticism of James is resolved inevitably into a discussion of plot'.²

I

The early tale *Madame de Mauves* (1874) readily yields a schematic summary of James's abiding substantial interests and the figures in which he repeatedly embodies them. An American girl, rich and innocent if not downright naïve, plunges herself, under manipulation and despite 'rather awful advice', into a mercenary and 'continental' marriage with the Baron de Mauves. In the course of the tale he tries (and of course fails) to manipulate her once more – into an affair, potentially her consolation and revenge for his own unfaithfulness but (*we* see) certain to compromise her in the world's eyes and in her own, with Longmore, the American visitor through whose perception the story is unfolded. She dismisses Longmore to America, where two years later, at fourth hand, he hears the outcome: Madame de Mauves withdrew into a haughty passivity which convinced her husband of her worth, kindled his love for her and, un-relentingly enforced, drove him to blow out his brains. Although there is now no specifiable obstacle to reunion, Longmore lingers in America for years, 'conscious of a singular feeling, – a feeling for which awe would be hardly too strong a name'.

Straightforward elaborations and transpositions of that plot give Daisy Miller and Isabel Archer and, more remotely, the matrix of *The Golden Bowl*. James's lasting concerns are enunciated: will exercised in successful or unsuccessful mani-pulation of the other, working through a nicely calculated appeal to interplay between the victim's sense of freedom and the cultural code; will negated actively in renunciation, or passively through submission, paralysis and death; the in-scrutability of facts, of the motivation of other people and of their messages, of their manner of apprehending cultural codes; the lonely absoluteness of personal impasse. *Madame de Mauves* introduces James's binary notation of settings and frames – the city and the country, the house and the parkland, the long vista from the terrace and the point-blank face-to-face dialogue taking place within it, the window at once inter-rupting and preserving the wall. Twice Longmore, looking through framed apertures, uncovers sexual irregularity. Once, watching a *belle brune* in a restaurant, he recognises Monsieur de Mauves in the man who leans into his field of vision to kiss her. Again, watching a clever and happy young painter outside a forest inn, he sees him summon up to the window a pretty and happy young woman; having woven a sentimental idyll round the young couple, Longmore learns to his discomfiture that she is 'not his wife'. One can't but recollect the couple who row, 'exactly the right thing', into Strether's view of the river in chapter 31 of *The Ambassadors* and so compromisingly complete the living landscape painting he had framed in imagination during chapter 30.

Other ingredients of that composition – the river, the boat and the rower with averted face – appear in Longmore's dream in *Madame de Mauves*:

He seemed to be in a wood, very much like the one on which his eyes had lately closed; but the wood was divided by the murmuring stream he had left an hour before. He was walking up and down, he thought, restlessly and in intense expectation of some momentous event. Suddenly, at a distance, through the trees, he saw the gleam of a woman's dress, and hurried forward to meet her. As he advanced he recognised her, but he saw at the same time that she was on the opposite bank of the river. She seemed at first not to notice him, but when they were opposite each other she stopped and looked at him very gravely and pityingly. She made him no motion [*New York edition*: sign] that he should cross the stream, but he wished greatly [unutterably] to stand by her side. He knew the water was deep, and it seemed to him that he knew that he should have to plunge, and that he feared that when he rose to the surface she would have disappeared. Nevertheless, he was going to plunge, when a boat turned into the current from above and came swiftly toward them, guided by an oarsman who was sitting so that they could not see his face. He brought the boat to the bank where Longmore stood; the latter stepped in, and with a few strokes they touched the opposite shore. Longmore got out, and, though he was sure he had crossed the stream, Madame de Mauves was not there. He turned with a kind of agony and saw that now she was on the other bank – the one he had left. She gave him a grave, silent glance, and walked away up the stream. The boat and the boatman resumed their course, but after going a short distance they stopped, and the boatman turned back and looked at the still divided couple. Then Longmore recognised him – just as he had recognised him a few days before at the café in the Bois de Boulogne. (pp. 190–1)

'No great ingenuity', thinks Longmore when the dream comes back to him, 'was needed to make it seem a rather striking allegory', and indeed the Baron has made Euphemia accessible to Longmore in a manner that simultaneously renders their relation impossible; he does so again in the dénouement. Rather than elaborate the marvellous tension between the indicative monosyllabic style and the condensed symbolic content, I point to the river as a regular note of boundary and separation in James's scenic vocabulary; to the look exchanged across the river (without, be it noted, any communication by word or gesture) and the Baron's averted face as recurring metaphors in James for thwarted and withheld communication, and to the boat as a common item among the vessels and vehicles with which James signals both complicity and exclusion. The metaphoric element in ordinary language assists these meanings – by the end of *Madame de Mauves* we may grant that Longmore and the Baron have indeed been more 'in the same boat' than either of them realised. The vehicles, the looks and turned backs persist into later James, diversified and enriched; the absolutely sundering river gives way, however, to the dry abyss or neutral void or knife-edged mountain ridge, often perceived as vertiginous in its danger and in the instability of state which links it with the trembling scales, taut cords and brimming vessels of the later novels.[3]

The deeply personal, yet also social, subjects already in flower in *Madame de Mauves* – the assertion, abeyance and avoidance of will and of knowledge, and the accompanying experiences of negation, boundary and suspense – develop through James's mature fiction. Interpretation, and each state's or object's symmetrical relation to its opposite, are recurrent mediating figures. The Baron's companion in the restaurant 'was a very pretty woman, and Longmore looked at her as often as was consistent with good manners. After a while he even began to wonder who she was, and to suspect that she was one of those ladies whom it is no breach of good manners to look at as often as you like' (p. 164). First the code restrains perception of the object, but when the object is sufficiently saturated with perception to be known its category changes, constraint disappears and value changes radically. To attain plenitude instead of vacancy is a mixed and unstable blessing: Ralph Touchett lives to know the effect of the wind he has put into Isabel's sails; Nanda Brookenham, impaired by the reticences rather than by the talk of her mother's set, is made to seem deficient because of evil knowledge which she is strong enough to deal with better than the adults in the circle; the completion of Strether's landscape is a cruel blow even if he can come to terms with it. Elsewhere the reciprocity appears as chiasmus in the plot, as the Monarchs and the professional models exchange roles in 'The Real Thing', as Nanda accepts 'the appearance of having changed places' with Vanderbank 'precisely in order that he – not she – should be let down easily' (IX, p. 501; p. 353) and Milly helps Sir Luke Strett to leave the prognosis of her fatal disease sufficiently vague (XIX, pp. 239–44; pp. 156–9). Again, definition-by-negation works through shocking parody: Little Aggie's innocence virtually *is* her capacity for swift and complete corruption, and Maisie's 'family', the space in which parental functions and relationships must be worked out, *is* the liaison between her father's ex-second-wife and her mother's ex-second-husband.

II

The bravura opening of *In the Cage* (1898) shows how James's continued command of the tactile and the concrete could sustain his developed psychological and epistemological concerns with vacancy, boundary and will:

It had occurred to her early that in her position – that of a young person spending, in framed and wired confinement, the life of a guinea-pig or magpie – she should know a great many persons without their recognising the acquaintance. That made it an emotion the more lively – though singularly rare and always, even then, with opportunity still very much smothered – to see any one come in whom she knew, as she called it, outside, and who could add something to the poor identity [meanness] of her function. (p. 139)

'It had **occurred** to **her early** that in **her** position' – her prompt and shrewd speculative leap is caged already by the slurred vowels and low stress of the impersonal verb-phrase. **Position**, emphasised by the following pause, enunciates a triple play on posture, status and employment that runs right through the paragraph and the tale, beginning at once with the socially placing **young person** – neither **woman** nor **lady**. The cage is both actual, material (**framed and wired**) and conceptual, attitudinal (**confinement**). The analogy from animal life will recur, and the mimicry and fragmentary thieving of the **magpie** are proleptic of the girl's conduct later in the tale. **Persons** is the most empty and impersonal of the available synonyms, and James ends his first sentence with the paradox of the unrecognised acquaintance which is yet knowledge. The rhythm of that sentence, with its sense-determined pauses, well in advance of any need for rest or breath, on **position**, **spending**, **confinement**, **magpie** and **persons**, enacts disjunction and sets the pace for the whole paragraph. The structure, a parenthesis within a parenthesis within a noun clause attributing a statement, enacts confinement syntactically as, later, the cage within a cage containing the telegraph buzzer does in the setting. The second sentence intensifies that parenthetic structure but works against it with **emotion**, **lively**, **singularly rare** – a diction more personal, less reified, than that of the opening – only to be **smothered** (a negative tactile image, suppressing both breath and utterance). The final clause, raising explicit issues of freedom and selfhood, also initiates the arithmetical concern appropriate to a shop but perverted in its relation to language in the next sentence:

Her function was to sit there with two young men – the other telegraphist and the counter-clerk; to mind the 'sounder', which was always going, to dole out stamps and postal-orders, weigh letters, answer stupid questions, give difficult change and, more than anything else, count words as numberless as the sands of the sea, the words of the telegrams thrust, from morning to night, through the gap left in the high lattice, across the encumbered shelf that her forearm ached with rubbing.

The young men are themselves nameless functions. The list of duties is vividly tinged with irritation and self-pity; the accumulated repetitions and parentheses of the last item turn our attention to the gap in the lattice, exit from and ingress to the cage, and onto the suddenly introduced bodily sensation of the aching, rubbing forearm. The duality of the screen, the intrusion of the life of the senses, and the telegraphist's willed resistance to the full acknowledgement of her physical condition round off the paragraph:

This transparent screen fenced out or fenced in, according to the side of the narrow counter on which the human lot was cast, the duskiest corner of a shop pervaded not a little, in winter, by the poison of perpetual gas, and at all times by the presence of hams, cheese, dried fish, soap, varnish, paraffin, and other solids and fluids that she came to know perfectly by their smells without consenting to know them by their names.

Without losing contact with the life of the body and the tactility of objects, James has introduced the quest for and status of knowledge, and its modes in relation to will and identity, into three of the four opening sentences. As the tale proceeds we find that the telegraphist is by no means a passive receiver of impressions; rather she pursues them, seeking 'personal identity' (p. 151) in the eyes of others, even power. She interprets the telegrams she handles, puzzling out the love-affairs and even the multiple identities which her favourite customers embody in their varying signatures:

This was neither more nor less than the queer extension of her experience, the double life that, in the cage, she grew at last to lead. As the weeks went on there she lived more and more into the world of whiffs and glimpses, and found her divinations work faster and stretch further. It was a prodigious view as the pressure heightened, a panorama fed with facts and figures, flushed with a torrent of colour and accompanied with wondrous world-music . . . she had at moments, in private, a triumphant, vicious feeling of mastery and power [ease], a sense of having their silly, guilty secrets in her pocket, her small retentive brain, and thereby knowing so much more about them than they suspected or would care to think. There were those she would have liked to betray, to trip up, to bring down with words altered and fatal; and all through a personal hostility provoked by the lightest signs, by their accidents of tone and manner, by the particular kind of relation she always happened instantly to feel. (pp. 152–4)

In the event she influences life not by distorting but by correcting a message. To help a favourite customer, Captain Everard, she calls attention to an error in a telegraphic code-system used by his fashionable mistress, and retrieves vital information when scandal threatens. The rescue of the mistress's reputation leaves Everard bound to marry *her* when her husband dies; had that affair become public, Everard would have been free to pursue his relation with the tele-graphist, in which 'everything, so far as they chose to consider it so, might mean almost anything' (p. 173). But consciousness of the mistress overshadows their only tête-à-tête, in a characteristic figure: 'By the mere action of his silence, every-thing they had so definitely not named, the whole presence round which they had been circling became a part of their reference, settled solidly between them' (p. 198).

Such renderings of the instability of category and identity, of the need to fabricate, project, interpret, conceal and renounce, echo through all James's later novels. Even through passion, negation threatens – for Kate and Densher, 'What they said when not together had no taste for them at all' (XIX, pp. 65–6; p. 46). Characters read interrupted or frag-mentary volumes, decipher codes or foreign languages, play games of bluff and conceive their own lives and relationships in such terms. The structure embraces not only the characters' perception of the world but also James's concern with the use and abuse, the gain and loss, of significant freedom. By pitting individual drives for fulfilment against the inescapably connected and conflicting rights of others on the one hand, and against the scandal of vacancy, transience and death on the other, James forestalls over-simple ethical judgements; he makes his interest fully moral by exploring the conflicts through his characters' most intimately personal experience in the areas of marriage and parenthood. Only Richardson, in English, treats with comparable intensity the half-suppressed irresoluble rivalries within a family. In *The Awkward Age,* love-making serves only to conceal the sterility of the relationships (e.g. IX, p. 173; p. 138); marriage is seen explicitly as that which makes adultery possible (IX, pp. 428, 442; pp. 306, 315); wisdom consists in marrying the rich man who loves you, keeping your penniless sweetheart for afterwards (IX, p. 295; p. 218), and in making due provision for your unportioned child by displaying your full awfulness as a parent before a compassionate and wealthy spectator (IX, p. 455; p. 323). The plot combines the impasse of *Andromaque* (A loves B who loves C who . . .) with the Oedipal motifs of *Phèdre*: indeed *What Maisie Knew, The Awkward Age, The Ambassadors, The Wings of the Dove* and *The Golden Bowl* all include pairs of women actually or notionally related as mother and daughter and in competition for the same man. At a high 'vertiginous' moment in *The Golden Bowl* (XXIV, pp. 257–8; p. 480) Maggie manages to sustain the 'exquisite tissue, but stretched on a frame', 'their thin wall [that] might be pierced by the lightest wrong touch' – manages, that is, not to acknowledge her father's intuition of her suspicions concerning her husband and her stepmother. Maggie's struggle is elsewhere described in a sentence which anticipates now Kafka, now Sartre: 'To be free to act, other than abjectly, for her father, she must conceal from him the validity that, like a microscopic insect pushing a grain of sand, she was taking on even for herself' (XXIV, p. 142; p. 396).

James's later art enacts with intense particularity the onto-logical and epistemological quest for being and meaning – the 'struggle into being' in Lawrence's terms, a struggle in which James involves his properly attentive reader through his whole range of stylistic and structural devices and educates him by the varied athleticism of reading and attention that he demands.

III

Selective discussion of a longer passage may build up some general application, where mere inventory of membranes, webs and tissues, games, abysses, brimming cups and taut ropes, books, telegrams and theatre scripts, negations, significant silences, imagined but unuttered speeches, imagined but non-existent spectators, vehicles and cages, looks and turned backs, all reft from their contexts and grouped analytically, could at best compel recognition of a point partly made. I choose chapter 17 of *The Golden Bowl*, beginning at the fourth long paragraph with its typically suspensory 'The fact that time, however, was not, as we have said, wholly on the Prince's side . . .' (XXIII, p. 293; p. 224). (A text, or a fresh memory, of the novel will certainly be needed: readers lacking both may pick up the argument in the next section.)

The Prince has only his thoughts to **fill** his hours or his house (an expansion towards plenitude) although they do not suffice to fill a single room (concentric confinements, including the space left by the 'loose fit' between his thoughts and the saloon). He **looks** into a **room** for the Princess, but 'though the fireside service of the repast was shiningly present the mistress of the table was not' – her absence is doubly defined by the account of her appurtenances and her function. 'He had waited, if waiting it could be called . . .' – the already empty 'activity' of waiting is questioned and drained, declared too aimless to count even as waiting. 'Her not coming in . . . became in fact quite positively, however perversely, the circumstance that kept him on the spot'(vacuity becomes a positive motive). He walks **to and fro** like Kate Croy awaiting her father and Densher awaiting Mrs Lowder (*Wings*, XIX, pp. 4 and 76; pp. 6 and 53), rhythmically pausing at one of the **windows,** feeling 'quickened throbs of the spirit' which 'scarcely expressed, however, the impatience of desire, any more than they stood for sharp disappointment' (they fell short of expressing either of two postulated responses to his deprivation). They do image the appearance of **light** ('fine waves of clearness through which . . . dawn at last trembles into rosy day'), but the clarity, withdrawing first into that hesitancy, shrinks again – 'The illumination indeed was all for the mind, the prospect revealed by it a mere immensity of the world of thought.' There is no real dawn ('The March afternoon, judged at the **window**, had blundered back into Autumn') and the colours of rain, mud and houses, of the air and of life, are brown. The Prince fails to see significance in the visual detail of the approaching **cab** and postulated 'person within' until the passenger **crosses** the 'wet **interval**' of the pavement and enters the Prince's house. 'The recognition kept him for some minutes motionless' – perception checks action. The visitor is named twice (and by her superseded maiden name) in the first sentence of the next paragraph:

Charlotte Stant, at such an hour, in a shabby four-wheeler and a waterproof, Charlotte Stant turning up for him at the very climax of his special inner vision, was an apparition charged with a congruity at which he stared almost as if it had been a violence.

The triple suspension of forward movement, including an enclosure within an enclosure for Charlotte, breaks into a restatement of that 'subject entering the picture' motif noted already; the reciprocity of the invited and given look (**apparition, stared**), brimmingly infused with force in **charged**, prefigures the way in which the scrutiny and identification of **congruity** modulates into the antithetic **violence**. The apparently abstract, hesitant, conceptual writing resonates with tension from the incipient moral conflict.

Then, James tells us, the intensity drops – other possibilities crowd in, she isn't visiting *him*,

merely leaving a message, writing a word on a card. He should see, at any rate; and meanwhile, controlling himself, would do nothing. This thought of not interfering took on a sudden force for him . . .

We have the possibilities of misunderstanding, of mediated proximate communication, the intention to **see**, to exercise self-control, **do nothing** – then the nothing-intention itself

takes on **sudden force**, the negative one of letting Charlotte
exercise her own will. 'Taking no step, he yet intensely hoped.'
The deep and the superficial conditions of her coming are
in contrast: 'he neither heard the house-door close again nor
saw her go back to her cab', and from these negatives he
infers a provisional certainty as he hears her foot, behind
the butler's, on the landing. The renewed pause would have
heightened his tension if it could have been heightened. She
enters, the butler's presence imposes restraint as the man
particularly deals with the kettle and the fire and answers
questions (or rather in **high blankness** doesn't answer them).
Then come the rocket image, 'from the form to the fact'
and another suspensory sentence, a question cast in the rhythm
and tone of passion and without clear boundaries to its field
of reference and implication – 'What else, my dear, what in
the world else can we do?'

Knowledge, rich yet qualified, internal and external, breaks
at once on the Prince. Leaving out of the account the 'as
if's and the suspensory parentheses of time and qualification,
we follow him into knowledge of 'why he had been feeling . . .
as he had felt', of things he had *not* known even while
Charlotte was vividly **panting** at his door, of Charlotte's
greater knowledge of **signs and portents** and his **vision
of alternatives** (undefinable **solutions**, **satisfactions**) discerned in the **tangible truth** of her look and her domesticated
yet alluring posture. 'He couldn't have told what particular
links and gaps had at the end of a few minutes found themselves renewed and bridged', for the past offered no visual
link with the circumstances of her present arrival (which
are restated in order to deny them) and her **Bowdlerised**
hat is an expurgated message stressing age and morality in
ironic contrast to the play of 'her handsome rain-freshened
face'. *There* of course, at the end of the sentence, we do
have, long withheld, the link sought a dozen lines before.
The past revives and interlocks with the future 'before his
watching eyes, as in a long embrace of arms and lips', negating
the present until 'this poor quantity scarce retained substance
enough, scarce remained sufficiently *there*, to be wounded
or shocked'.

IV

The significance of the look is already explicit in late James, though full articulation of it was left to Sartre.

And the truth of it had, with this force, after a moment, so strangely lighted his eyes that, as for pity and dread of them, she buried her own in his breast.

Thus, in the last sentence of *The Golden Bowl*, Maggie evades her husband's look. She has waited agog, on the preceding page, in a passage of extraordinary nervous terror, tension and wild speculation, for the 'payment' of her husband's exclusive attention, restored by Charlotte's departure for America. Adroitly averting any embarrassing confession on Amerigo's part by her allusion to the strength they will draw from Charlotte's poise and reticence, she elicits from him the avowal ' "See"? I see nothing but *you*.' Enough, one might think – but Amerigo's look conveys perhaps *too* complete a betrayal of Charlotte (after which, could Maggie continue to value him?), perhaps some sense that the limitation now enforced on his field of vision is not entirely welcome. In this realm of experience in which victory is in principle hollow, Maggie 'buries' her eyes. Her flinching from light and sight, the suspensory grammar, the wholly unexpected resonance from Aristotle, decisively qualify Maggie's achievement. In so far as she has triumphed, her triumph is muted; in so far as she has sinned, punishment is assured.

The documents and the messages, too, and the acts of interpretation and response which they elicit, participate in the moral substance of the novels as well as in their figural and metaphoric texture. In *The Golden Bowl* the text of Amerigo's telegram to Charlotte, opening with a gnomic French proverb and necessarily ambiguous even to her, is kept from the reader for four chapters (XXIII, pp. 239 to 90; pp. 189 to 222). Adam assumes it to be a funny telegram from Maggie; he learns it is a grave, a very grave, one from Amerigo. Adam's not asking to read it shows his delicacy towards and trust in his bride; if he had read it, it would have compromised Charlotte certainly, Amerigo possibly. Charlotte's offering the telegram to Adam counts, in retrospect, as evidence of her straightness; her not again mentioning it to Amerigo implies, even acknowledges, a nuance in her consciousness of the relationships among them (XXIII, p. 290; p. 222). The telegram precipitates and embodies characters' judgements of each other. It contributes to the reader's grasp of the situation, incomplete with an incompleteness different from any of the characters' understandings; but by setting the reader too an interpretive puzzle, it draws him into the novel beside the characters.

In *The Wings of the Dove* the two letters around which the final chapters are organised help substantially with the critical problem of the competing claims of the Milly material and the Kate and Densher plot to be the centre. The point of Milly's letter from beyond the grave, and of her lawyer's letter announcing the fortune bequeathed to Densher, is that their content is of no importance – what matters is the fact of their existence, and what the living characters make of them. Densher does not need to open either letter; he discusses the seals and postmarks, the handwriting, the method of delivery. His surrender of the personal letter is the finest tribute he can offer Kate – the chance to know first and thoroughly the tone Milly adopts with him therein. After a tense exchange of looks and short utterances concerning will, knowledge, desire and mutuality, she tosses it still unopened into the fire. The lawyer's letter, which Densher would have returned unopened in lofty renunciation of the bequest, he forwards to Kate, this time as a test; opening it, she ensures for herself the poisoned gift of Milly's legacy without Densher. Each stage in the handling of the letters is an occasion for widening the breach between the lovers, until, in the last paragraph, Densher withholds his crucial declaration. Kate's 'We shall never be again as we were!' leaves flux and irrevocability, the altered and the emptied, as the final note, sounded in connection with the lovers and not with the absent Dove.

V

In this account of the overlapping and converging movements towards complexity and tentativeness in James's language, imagery, conceptual habits and ethical interests, I have sought to acknowledge the fine cohesion of his later novels without acquiescing in the formalism by which in his Prefaces James deflected recognition of his achievement. In late James the solidly specified and the nervously vital are found in the characters' movement towards a fullness of understanding which includes a grasp of boundary and limitation, and in the novels' struggle, through a mounting pressure of perception, resolution and decision, towards ethically significant action, or significant inaction.

James's later development springs not from *Adam Bede* or *Madame Bovary*, but from Gwendolen's paralysis of choice and Deronda's sense of the futility of English social life in *Daniel Deronda* – akin to Wrayburn's malaise in *Our Mutual Friend*. If those novels acknowledge in an English setting the apathy and indolence, the reflection without passion, by which Kierkegaard had characterised the Denmark of his day, James's later characters typically face the dynamic corruptions of a plutocratic, post-Darwinian jungle of sexual and social *arrivisme*. James sharply renders the crucial intellectual and emotional difficulties in their dealing with experience: truth, groped for in struggle with its negation, is irrefragable, and may be shockingly or even murderously alien when you grasp it. In necessarily interpreting the implications of others, we leave it open to them to manipulate us – he who controls the code controls the interpreter, and Isabel walks into Osmond's web, Tony Bream (in *The Other House*) confesses to murder in advance of the false accusation that has been devised against him, Mrs Brookenham, hypocritically naïve, can ask just the set of questions that will most compromise her daughter before her other guests (*The Awkward Age*, book 8, final chapter). A mythic dimension suggests that it was ever thus: Mrs Brook had 'pulled us down – just closing with each of the great columns in its turn – as Samson pulled down the temple' (IX, p. 439; p. 313); in *The Ambassadors* Marie de Vionnet is presented as Cleopatra mourning Anthony (XXII, p. 286; p. 368); Dido's ghost inhabits *The Golden Bowl*'s 'pale, unappeased faces . . . deprecating, denouncing hands' (XXIV, p. 74; p. 350). The experiencing consciousness, with its voids aching to be filled, now presses painfully and unevenly against a world of epistemological uncertainty. Without imputing anything like genuine solipsistic fear to James and his characters, I do offer 'epistemological' in a stronger sense than the fairly simple relativism associated with James's own discussions of point-of-view.[4] The co-presence and convergence in the later novels of definition by negation, that vertiginous sense of abysses, disjunctions and voids, the impingement of the Other through the Look, inhibitions about language and interpretation, and plots turning on renunciation and disjunction define a dimension of offended consciousness and existential terror in James's work which links him with the lines of reaction and influence that run from Hegel through Kierkegaard to Sartre – and, of course, through Bradley to Eliot.

James's late characters remain inside experience, like the characters of Proust and Kafka, instead of meditating on cultural questions, like those of Dostoevsky, Lawrence and Forster, but they cut no less directly close to the nerve for that. Emphasis might well shift from the important truths beneath the joke about 'chawing more than he bites off' to the perception of the pre-Freudian reviewer who wrote 'Mr James has learned how to make repression a factor of art instead of an impediment.'[5]

Page references for quotations from *Madame de Mauves* and *In the Cage* are to volumes 3 and 10 respectively of *The Complete Tales of Henry James*, ed. Leon Edel, 12 vols (London, 1962–4). References to the novels give first the volume and page of *The Novels and Tales of Henry James: The New York Edition*, 24 vols (London, 1908–9), with the page in the current Penguin reprints following after the semicolon

1   Mrs Adams is no 47 in Roger Gard (ed.), *Henry James: The Critical Heritage* (London, 1968). The critics quoted are E.M. Forster, *Aspects of the Novel* (Harmondsworth, 1962), 163; F.R. Leavis, *Scrutiny* 5 (1937), 404–5; and Yvor Winters, *In Defense of Reason* (Denver, n.d.), 341

2   The endings are from *Washington Square*, *The Portrait of a Lady* and *The Wings of the Dove*. For the Lockean James see J.H. Raleigh, 'Henry James: The Poetics of Empiricism', *Publications of the Modern*

Language Association 66 (1951), collected in Tony Tanner (ed.), *Henry James: Modern Judgements* (London, 1968). For the missing unconscious see F.O. Matthiessen, *Henry James* (New York, 1946), 23; Winters on plot is op. cit., 306

3 Notes drafted to substantiate this account emerge as long lists of page numbers for the accumulating minor instances, and further elaborated commentary and analysis for the major ones. Readers will just have to check my account when next they turn to James's novels; some gathered apposite material – approached from other directions than mine – may be found in articles by J. Kimball (on the abyss) and M. Beebe (on the turned back) in Tanner, op. cit.; by R.W. Short and P. Gibson in *Publications of the Modern Language Association* (1953, 1954); by J.C. Roe in *English Literary History* (1973); and in A. Holder-Barell, *The Development of Imagery and its Functional Significance in Henry James's Novels* (Bern, 1959)

4 The famous 'house of fiction' paragraph in the preface to *The Portrait of a Lady* (III, x-xi; ix); Tanner, op. cit., 268, 277 and chapter 15; M. Walters, 'Keeping the place tidy for the young female mind: *The Awkward Age*', in J. Goode (ed.), *The Air of Reality* (London, 1972), 188–92

5 *Academy* (May 1899), collected as no 132 in Gard, op. cit.

5 Taking a nail for a walk: on reading *Women in Love*
Gāmini Salgādo

In his British Academy lecture C.S. Lewis drew attention to the odd state of *Hamlet* criticism, with hardly any two critics agreeing as to what the play was actually about, and with not a few disagreeing as to whether it was a very good play or a very bad one. *Women in Love* has not of course accumulated anything like the Great Barrier Reef of interpretation and commentary which *Hamlet* has, yet critical discussion seems to have resulted in much the same state of affairs.

Until recently, most published criticism of the novel, when it was not gossipy or merely biographical, was shaped by the massive authority of Dr Leavis. *Women in Love*, he pronounced, was a novel in the mode of a dramatic poem, undoubtedly Lawrence's greatest, as it was also one of the outstanding achievements of English (or any) fiction. It celebrated 'spontaneous-creative fullness of being' and the continuities of communal living. It did this by presenting, in scenes of vivid and varied dramatic life, the conflict and interplay between figures who stand for 'life', 'creativity' and 'spontaneity' (principally Birkin and Ursula) and those who stand for the opposites of these (principally Gerald Crich, Gudrun, Hermione and Loerke). The struggle between these is conceived not only as a psychic conflict between individuals but also as the death throes of a corrupt civilisation. Such blemishes as the work does have – chiefly an occasional over-explicitness born of uncertainty and leading to jargon – are decidedly minor when set beside the originality and achieved mastery of the whole. Though Birkin himself is by no means to be taken merely as a mouthpiece for the author, it remains true that: 'In Birkin's married relations with Ursula the book

95

invites us to localize the positive, the conceivable and due – if only with difficulty attainable – solution of the problem; the norm in relation to which Gerald's disaster gets full meaning.'[1]

Leavis's skill in selecting those passages from the novel which lent most support to his view of it, as well as the frequent subtlety of his analysis, certainly led to an upgrading of *Women in Love* in the Lawrence canon (though privately most admirers confess to a sneaking preference for *The Rainbow*). His criticism certainly illuminates much of the novel, though the enormous shadow cast by it has equally certainly led to some darkening of counsel. Within the last few years the Leavisian view of *Women in Love* as 'making for life' has been sharply challenged by critics like Frank Kermode, who emphasise the doom-laden apocalyptic vision (ultimately deriving from the author's experiences during the period of the First World War), and others such as George Ford and Colin Clarke who (taking their cue from Middleton Murry) point out the related feature of corruption and degradation conceived as essential elements in the redemptive process.

This is broadly how the battle lines have been drawn, but the main conflict has led to critical skirmishes regarding virtually every important character and episode in the book, as well as widely contrasting evaluations of it. I choose a few of the more notorious examples from a richness of embarrassments. One of the questions which has excercised the critics has been – which character in *Women in Love* is closest to the author? The favourite candidate has been Birkin ('that Birkin is substantially Lawrence there can be little temptation to deny', according to Leavis), but Gerald Crich has been put forward as being Lawrence himself 'in important ways'[2] while even the 'wizard rat' Loerke has been put on a pedestal as a 'Lawrentian saint'.[3]

Again, there has been a remarkable divergence of opinion as to the significance of the African (or West Pacific – Lawrence dithered about this for fear of a libel suit from the composer Heseltine, the original of Halliday) statuettes which figure so prominently in the chapters 'Totem' and 'Moony'. To one critic the statue was, for the author of the novel, 'perhaps the most important figure in the book', because: 'She is positive, concrete, the perfect representative of life as opposed to the imperfect human beings surrounding her . . . In all four characters, male and female, the statue sets the standard, never fully realized by any of them.'[4] Another critic finds this point of view 'extraordinary' and goes on to affirm that 'the African statues signify for Birkin a whole process of decline and fall', and 'however aesthetically pleasing they evoke for him the impurity of a degenerated civilization'.[5] Leavis himself is sure that 'the West African statuette . . . represents something that we are to see as a default, a failure'.[6] Finally, we may contrast Middleton Murry's view that the characters of *Women in Love* have no individuality ('as indistinguishable as octopods in an aquarian tank')[7] with Leavis's own claim that 'the power of making human individuality livingly present [is] undeniably there in *Women in Love*'.[8]

Now if I had to choose between one of the two broad ways of looking at *Women in Love*, I should have very little hesitation in choosing the one deriving from Murry rather than from Leavis. Leavis's reading is persuasive while one is reading his essay, but when we return from it to the novel we have the sense that too much that forces itself on our attention has been left out. But that is less important than my main point, which is based on my perception that every single critical comment quoted above is substantially true, *including the most flagrantly contradictory ones*. *Women in Love* is not merely a novel that accommodates contradictory readings, it positively invites and even compels them. It beckons us towards both sorts of reading and frustrates both, and it does this on such a scale and with such 'consistency' that we are justified in calling it the novel's intention. It is, to use a recent critic's useful term, a Janiform novel, that is 'a two-faced novel: morally it seems to be centrally or importantly paradoxical or self-contradictory. Not merely ambiguous or complex, but paradoxical or self-contradictory.'[9]

Thus I begin and end with what the experience of reading the novel is like. And I am heartened by a remark of Leavis whose significance has, I think, been insufficiently pondered: with the honesty which is just as characteristic as his acerbity, he begins his account of *Women in Love* with the remark: 'I have not always thought *Women in Love* one of the most striking works of creative originality that fiction has to show',[10] and goes on to say that he saw no reason to protest either at Murry's original review of the book or at the amplified account which appeared ten years later in *Son of Woman*. In *For Continuity* (1933) Leavis tells us that to get through *Women in Love* requires great determination. And I would not believe anyone who told me that his first reading of the novel was easy or wholly enjoyable. If a sensitive critic could be so radically mistaken for so long a period about a novel, it is at least possible that some of the things he first saw in the book really are there. At any rate there is a certain piquancy in the realisation that no one, Leavis himself not excepted, saw in the novel 'those immediately impressive aspects of the book which should make it *at first reading* an unquestionable and astonishing work of genius' (my italics).[11] It seems to me therefore that critical attention could be usefully directed not so much to 'interpretation' as to the difficulties which face the reader in getting through the novel.

One of the most obvious ways in which the novel defeats a schematic reading is the arrangement of the two pairs of central characters. As far back as 1906, when Lawrence was thinking of his first novel, he felt that this arrangement was in the 'great tradition' of the English novel: 'The usual plan is to take two couples and develop their relationships. Most of George Eliot's are on that plan. Anyhow, I don't want a plot, I should be bored with it. I shall try two couples for a start.'[12]

Gerald and Gudrun, Ursula and Birkin (why does it seem natural to use the surname?) seem at first to stand in a relation of simple opposition. Ursula, dissatisfied with her life, waits expectantly for a new birth: 'Her spirit was active, her life like a shoot that is growing steadily, but which has not yet come above ground' (p. 57). She is drawn towards Birkin, who appears to embody that fructifying richness for which she is yearning (although the thinness and the pallor add their qualifying note):

Ursula was watching him as if furtively, not really aware of what she was seeing. There was a great physical attractiveness in him – a curious hidden richness, that came through his thinness and his pallor like another voice, conveying another knowledge of him. It was in the curves of his brows and his chin, rich, fine, exquisite curves, the powerful beauty of life itself. She could not say what it was. But there was a sense of richness and of liberty. (p. 48)

Of Gudrun we are told: 'Her look of confidence and diffidence contrasted with Ursula's sensitive expectancy' (p. 8), and at her first sight of Gerald she feels an intense and inexplicable affinity with him: 'Am I *really* singled out for him in some way, is there really some pale gold, arctic light that envelopes only us two?' (p. 16). Gerald himself is presented in terms that appear to endorse Gudrun's first response to him: '. . . about him also was the strange, guarded look, the unconscious glisten, as if he did not belong to the same creation as the people about him' (p. 15).

But it is not long before what look like oppositions turn out to be variants. The terms in which Ursula is 'characterised' (that is clearly the wrong word), or at any rate very similar ones, are often applied to Gudrun and even to Hermione, and the same is true of Birkin and Gerald. Both girls feel the same sensations of deadening isolation. 'She [Gudrun] was so alone, with the level, unliving field of water stretching beneath her. It was not a good isolation, it was a terrible, cold separation of suspense' (p. 203), while Ursula's 'passion seemed to bleed to death, and there was nothing. She sat suspended in a state of complete nullity, harder to bear than death' (p. 214). Like Hermione, Gudrun shrinks from the life about her and both girls seem outwardly self-possessed yet are inwardly vulnerable. (This is of course, one of the points we are meant to take even on the Leavis reading.) When Ursula feels 'bright and invulnerable, quite free and happy, perfectly liberated in her self-possession' (p. 295) Gudrun feels closest to her: 'It was at these times that the intimacy between the two sisters was most complete, as if their intelligence were one. They felt a strong bright bond of understanding between them surpassing everything else' (p. 296). There is a strong parallel between Ursula's response to Birkin and Gudrun's to Gerald. If we did not know the exact context of a sentence such as: 'There was a certain hostility, a hidden ultimate reserve in him, cold and inaccessible' (p. 22), we might suppose it applied to Gerald rather than to Birkin, and be forgiven for imagining that the possessor of the 'subtle, feminine demoniacal soul' (p. 142) was Gudrun or Hermione rather than Ursula. It has often been remarked, too, that the sexual experiences of the two pairs of lovers, with their peculiar combination of obliquity and explicitness, are virtually indistinguishable. It is not only Gerald whose love-making has the smell of the grave about it. This would not matter if some general point about the connection between love and death were being made; what disturbs us is that at one level similar or identical experiences are being given radically different evaluations. It is of course true that it is the dialectic of relationships that interests Lawrence, not 'the stable ego of character'. But the appearance of consistency and distinction at the level of character (an appearance which at one level is a quite genuine 'reality') is one element in the novel's janiformity. It is possible to resolve this contradiction by invoking the famous letter to Garnett in which Lawrence says: 'You mustn't look in my novel for the old stable *ego* of the character. There is another *ego*, according to whose action the individual is unrecognisable, and passes through, as it were, allotropic states which it needs a deeper sense than any we've been used to exercise, to discover are states of the same single radically unchanged element.'[13] But this is not as helpful as it may appear, for what is in question is not merely identity (persistence in time) but individuality, which appears to exist only at that 'social' level where it is explicitly condemned, though the novel's emphasis on a proud singleness of being leads us to expect it at a deeper level. We find ourselves agreeing both with Leavis, when he says that the characters of *Women in Love* are completely and significantly differentiated, and with Murry, who can 'discern no individuality whatever in the denizens of Mr Lawrence's world'.[14]

The way the novel is put together is also designed to get in the way of a consistent growth of understanding and illumination on the reader's part. One should be wary of making too much of the argument from design, given the very confused textual history of the novel,[15] but though the novel grew out of and to a large extent alongside the novel that became *The Rainbow*, it almost entirely lacks the earlier work's majestic progression through large tracts of generational time alternating with the intimate rhythms of time subjectively experienced. Narrative sequence is not of course abandoned in *Women in Love*, but it is treated with the utmost casualness. Some chapters are clearly continuous in time with others, but many indeterminate and connective phrases such as 'the days went by' and 'one afternoon' are fairly typical. The 'events' of the novel are loosely structured round five locales – Beldover, Shortlands, Breadalby, the Cafe Pompadour and associated London scenes and the Tyrol. But sequence is not nearly as important as ebb and flow and in this the novel's structure seems to figure the typical psychic states of the characters. Yet these ebbings and flowings seem unrelated to any real progression in time. The contrast with *The Rainbow* is striking. Time passes, things happen in the inner world as well as the outer, yet the inner events seem to move in a circle and the outer ones to stand in a relation of indefinable obliquity to them. For much of the novel, Lawrence's characters seem to have no memory. Even the catastrophic climax of Gerald's death in the snow is not the end of the book. The actual ending, in contrast to the paradisal tremors at the close of *The Rainbow*, is tentative to the point of off-handedness. It contrives to be both an assertion and a kind of interrogation mark, in effect if not in grammatical form; yet it bears on one of the central points in the book's apparent 'message'.

The vexed question of 'symbolism' in the novel adds to the general sense of doubleness. It is perfectly true, as Leavis says, that Lawrence's art is never a matter of a mere intended 'meaning' symbolised,[16] but no reader can fail to be aware of the tremendous contrast between the brilliant vividness of the 'symbolic' scenes (Gudrun dancing to the cattle, Gerald curbing his mare, Birkin stoning the moon) and the uncertainty as to their direction and tendency. One-to-one correspondence and the consequent reading off is not of course the point. ('There is just the one fact to emphasize' [p. 39].) These scenes, through the sheer immediacy of their presentation, develop a life and authority of their own, which are unlike the heightened realism of *Sons and Lovers* on the one hand ('that hard, violent style full of sensation and presentation', as Lawrence himself called it) and yet are devoid of anything we can fairly call symbolic meaning except by ignoring some part of the total effect. The incident of Gerald and the mare stands out as a striking exception. We may adapt Lawrence's words about the African statuette to describe the effect of the Lawrentian 'symbol'. At its heart it is abstracted almost into meaninglessness by the weight of 'sensation beneath' (p. 87).

There is in fact a good deal more of the 'hard, violent style full of sensation and presentation' in *Women in Love* than is generally allowed. A passage like this, from near the novel's beginning, could be matched many times over:

The sisters were crossing a black path through a dark, soiled field. On the left was a large landscape, a valley with collieries, and opposite hills with cornfields and woods, all blackened with distance, as if seen through a veil of crape. White and black smoke rose up in steady columns, magic within the dark air. Near at hand came the long rows of dwellings, approaching curved up the hill-slope, in straight lines along the brow of the hill. They were of darkened red brick, brittle, with dark slate roofs. The path on which the sisters walked was black, trodden-in by the feet of the recurrent colliers, and bounded from the field by iron fences; the stile that led again into the road was rubbed shiny by the moleskins of the passing miners. (p. 12)

But brilliant though it is, this kind of writing does not strike us, either in reading or in retrospect, as the staple of the novel's style. There seem to me to be three aspects of Lawrence's language which point to the radical indeterminacy which is the novel's principal effect. All of them are in some degree characteristics of Lawrence's later prose style, but they are found with greater frequency, or at least with a peculiar intensity of effect, in *Women in Love*, as any reader who comes straight to this novel from, say, *The Rainbow*, will notice. The first is the persistent tendency of the prose to hanker for an idea or an attribute and its opposite at the same time – the antithesis being usually qualified by the rhetoric of 'and yet', 'but also' as well as 'odd', 'strange' or 'curious'. Extensive quotation would be tedious, but the reader will be able to collect several examples in five minutes of random reading from the book. Hermione 'like the fallen angels restored, yet still subtly demoniacal' (p. 24) and the mining village 'uncreated and ugly, and yet surcharged with this same potent atmosphere of intense, dark callousness' (p. 129) are instances of the sort of thing I have in mind. The passion for inclusiveness results in a language that is always hovering on the edge of paradox and sometimes thrusts beyond it into contradiction. A man and a wife can know each other 'heavenly and hellish, particularly hellish' (p. 327). Gudrun 'could not believe – she did not believe. Yet she believed' (p. 372). Gerald feels 'a mordant pity, a passion almost of cruelty' (p. 88).

Secondly there is a pervasive contrast between vehemence of tone and something which appears variously as either tentativeness or cloudiness of utterance. This occurs not only in situations where we may fairly assume that it is the character, not the author, who is in a state of uncertainty, as when Ursula feels Birkin's power: 'A strange feeling possessed her, as if something were taking place. But it was all intangible. And some sort of control was being put on her' (p. 145). It is also characteristic of such a celebrated and crucial moment as that in which Birkin tells Hermione what he 'gets' from copying the Chinese drawing:

I know what centres they live from – what they perceive and feel – the hot, stinging centrality of a goose in the flux of cold water and mud – the curious bitter stinging heat of a goose's blood, entering their own blood like an inoculation of corruptive fire – fire of the cold-burning mud – the lotus of mystery. (p. 99)

The Romantic paradox – life and beauty rooted inescapably

in corruption – is asserted with a convoluted violence, which seems to cast doubt on itself. The single opposition between Hermione's desire to 'know' (intellectually understand) and Birkin's 'knowing' (realising and responding to with one's whole being) is undercut by a sense that language is being used as a deliberate defence against communication, or at any rate with an overwhelming sense of its inadequacy, which seems to be the source of the vehemence.

Finally, there is hardly any other modern novel in which argument figures so prominently, and in which at the same time argument is so persistently devalued – summarised, parodied, dismissed, interrupted and trivialised. It would be only a slight exaggeration to say that discursive argument exists in *Women in Love* mainly in order to show its inadequacy as a mode of ordering experience, and to suggest that those most committed to it – Hermione, Sir Joshua, Gerald – are guilty of dangerous psychic self-deprivation. This would certainly account for the way in which what many would want to call Lawrence's message is at least twice parodied – in the *Telegraph* editorial and the Cafe Pompadour letter – as well as being echoed by, of all people, Hermione, in her diatribe against self-conscious knowledge (p. 44). It could be argued that Birkin's attack on her for bad faith points up precisely the defects of knowledge in the head. But this is to ignore the inescapable fact that Birkin, in his own way, argues more than anyone else in the novel, and that his 'arguments' appear to be an important element in his total impact; he does not convince only by his presence. It is true that in a neurotic civilisation people will tend to do too much talking about their ailments, yet it is not merely the quantity but the self-cancelling tendency of the argument that affects the reader. The way in which discursive argument seems to take on a serious importance ('It is because he had the genius of a great creative writer that he has been capable of this thinking,' Leavis tells us)[17] and then deflate itself is not unlike the way in which certain crucial scenes (notably the one where Birkin stones the moon in the water)[18] seem to cry out for 'symbolic' translation and then mock it, as the attempt to 'symbolise' a daisy in socio-political terms mocks itself in the conversation between Ursula and Birkin (p. 146). 'I don't mean anything, why should I?' says Birkin at one point (p. 446). And it is not only Birkin whose authority as a commentator is undermined. 'I don't trust you when you drag in the stars,' Mino tells him. But the 'starry' rhetoric is often used by the author in his own person.

If we glance briefly at the circumstances in which Lawrence produced *Women in Love*, as well as at the wider Romantic tradition to which it in part belongs, we may also find factors which account for the novel's janiformity. Though it grew out of the same rich fictional raw material as *The Rainbow*, most of the later novel was written when Lawrence was in the throes of his agonised experiences of the First World War. In his preface to the American edition he wrote: 'It is a novel which took its final shape in the midst of the period of war, though it does not concern the war itself.' The sense of universal catastrophe is palpable enough as we read and it is not difficult to understand why Lawrence seriously considered calling the novel *The Latter Days* or *Dies Irae*. Often in the novel we have the sense that the perspectives opened up imply a reader who is something other than a human being, something more like an impersonal life force:

. . . But what if people *are* all flowers of dissolution—when they're flowers at all — what difference does it make?'

'No difference – and all the difference. Dissolution rolls on, just as production does,' he said. 'It is a progressive process – and it ends in universal nothing – the end of the world, if you like. But why isn't the end of the world as good as the beginning?'

'I suppose it isn't,' said Ursula, rather angry.

'Oh yes, ultimately,' he said. 'It means a new cycle of creation after – but not for us. If it is the end, then we are of the end – *fleurs du mal*, if you like.' (p. 193)

Again:

'No, death doesn't really seem the point any more' says Birkin. 'It curiously doesn't concern me. It's like an ordinary tomorrow.' (pp. 228–9) and even more explicitly:

Birkin looked at the land, at the evening, and was thinking: 'Well, if mankind is destroyed, if our race is destroyed like Sodom, and there is this beautiful evening with the luminous land and trees, I am satisfied. That which informs it all is there, and can never be lost. After all, what is mankind but just one expression of the incomprehensible. And if mankind passes away, it will only mean that this particular expression is completed and done. That which is expressed, and that which is to be expressed, cannot be diminished. There it is, in the shining evening. Let mankind pass away – time it did. The creative utterances will not cease, they will only be there. Humanity doesn't embody the utterance of the incomprehensible any more. Humanity is a dead letter. There will be a new embodiment, in a new way. Let humanity disappear as quick as possible.' (p. 65)

I am aware that this is a passage from fairly early on in the book and that the focus of Birkin's anti-humanity narrows to something like mere anti-Englishness. But one is a development from the other only in the case of Birkin, not in the novel as a whole, where the larger anti-humanity seems to me as persistent as the more human concern for dying so that one may be truly reborn. Birkin's occasional indifference to humanity and its fate seems to be endorsed by his creator: 'I cannot touch humanity, even in thought, it is abhorrent to me. But a work of art is an act of faith, as Michael Angelo says, and one goes on writing, to the unseen witnesses.'[19]

On the other hand the novel was finally called *Women in Love*, which suggests a more affirmative note as well as a less anti-human perspective. Further, although the positives of pure singleness of being and fulfilment within the chosen community are both part of the Romantic tradition,[20] there is a gap between the importance attached in that tradition to *yielding* to experience ('a wise passiveness' or a passionate abandon) and the prophet's assertiveness. *Women in Love* demands at least two incompatible things of Birkin. Put in their simplest terms, these are that he should both dramatise and assert the virtue of an abandoment to the depths of experience so that he may be renewed by the contact. In so far as the novel shows him doing this (by dying out of the world and returning to it in 'the freedom together' of his relationship with Ursula), we are wholly convinced. As a vehement and even violent spokesman for passivity he also evidently has the best of most of the novel's arguments, even when he turns them to mockery. But the second stance is incompatible with the first, and the incompatibility is surely more than a matter of the man who shouts about the value of silence being suddenly embarrassed by the sound of his own voice. That Lawrence himself was aware of the problem is shown by his description of Birkin in the abandoned prologue to the novel:

In his most passionate moment of spiritual enlightenment, when like a saviour of mankind he would pour out his soul for the world, there was in him a capacity to jeer at his own righteousness and spirituality, justly and sincerely to make a mock of it all. And the mockery was so true, it bit to the very core of his righteousness, and showed it rotten, shining with phosphorescence. But at the same time, whilst quivering in the climax-thrill of sexual pangs, some cold voice could say in him: 'You are not really moved; you could rise up and go away from this pleasure quite coldly and calmly; it is not radical, your enjoyment.'[21]

Finally there is the problem of finding a language in which to communicate the incommunicable. Throughout *Women in Love* we come into contact with a perfectly conventional 'novel of character and circumstance' as identifiable in dialogue, description and event as the evidences of dissatisfaction with it. This dissatisfaction shows itself when, for instance, Birkin is described in terms which suggest the conventional novelist:

He affected to be quite ordinary, perfectly and marvellously commonplace. And he did it so well, taking the tone of his surroundings, adjusting himself quickly to his interlocutor and his circumstance, that he achieved a verisimilitude of ordinary commonplaceness that usually propitiated his onlookers for the moment, disarmed them from attacking his singleness. (p. 22)

Or when the effort of ordering one's life is contrasted with the 'formlessness' of the picaresque novel (p. 340), or in Birkin's weariness with the life at Breadalby because of its tedious familiarity:

... how known it all was, like a game with the figures set out ... the same figures moving round in one of the innumerable permutations that make up the game. But the game is known, its going on is like a madness, it is so exhausted. (p. 110)

The 'conventional novel' intermittently coming up against all that which is resistant to it admirably mimes one theme of *Women in Love*, which is new life urgent and struggling to grow out of old forms. A novel in which character is vividly related to environment and in which a central theme — say, the implications of modern marriage and its relation to the possibility and necessity of companionship between men — is included within a larger whole which appears to cast doubts on the entire enterprise. 'A fate dictated from outside, from theory or from circumstance, is a false fate,' wrote Lawrence in his foreword to the American edition of the novel.[22] But in the nature of the case, this 'false fate' manifests itself as the 'conventional novel', while the 'promptings of desire and aspiration' which the 'creative, spontaneous soul sends forth', and which are 'our true fate, which it is our business to fulfil', not only follow a different pattern, but are presented with an awareness that the very presentation is a kind of falsification.

It is not enough, though it is certainly true to say that Lawrence's novel deals with the theme that: 'Love is a thing to be learned, through centuries of patient effort. It is a difficult, complex maintenance of individual integrity throughout the incalculable processes of interhuman polarity.'[23] It is not enough, though it is certainly true to say, with Colin Clarke, that the reductive process of corruption is a necessary part of the regenerative and redemptive process. Corruption and regeneration, orgiastic abandonment and liberating freedom, insane will and necessary self-discipline, proud singleness and egotistic separateness, perverse anal intercourse and the healthy purging of sexual shame, homosexual abomination ›

108

and satisfying love between man and man – almost any pair of apparent contrasts will do – are constantly losing their distinctiveness, under the pressure of an urgent necessity to cry out the truth, and an equally resolute determination not to preach expressing itself in janiformity of idiom and structure. 'Art speech is the only speech', but at the same time it is 'indirect and ultimate' and the times seemed to demand directness and the fictional world specificity. Characters are described in ways which seem to make their inner lives interchangeable and their external selves vivid but unimportant; events seem both to affirm and to deny any symbolic or representative meaning; and a whole range of key terms – 'obscene', 'mindless', 'mystic', 'dreadful', 'will', 'single', 'corrupt', 'unspeakable' are a few of them – point in opposite directions. The reader is constantly challenged to make a range of discriminations of the kind which I have catalogued earlier but which cannot be made consistently from *within the novel itself*. If we go outside the novel, of course, to the Romantic tradition in European and English literature or to Lawrence's discursive writings, we can make a convincing case for either reading of *Women in Love*, depending on whether we want mainly to use (with Leavis) *Psychoanalysis and the Unconscious* or (with Clarke) *The Reality of Peace* and *The Crown*. But this brings us to the question of the relation between the novel and discursive prose which, I have implicitly argued, is in this case a peculiarly baffling one.

No one who has read *Women in Love* is likely to feel that he has wasted his time or 'got nothing' out of it. But he will be more than usually at a loss to say what it is he has got, not because of the meagreness of the experience but because of its abundance. Working through the novel leaves one reader at least with the sense that its 'message' or 'messages' are snares and delusions: the final effect is the typically 'modern' one of having the experience and missing the meaning. One remembers Lawrence's own words: 'If you try to nail anything down in the novel, either it kills the novel, or the novel gets up and walks away with the nail.'

There is a perfectly ordinary sense in which this observation could be true of the relationship between any creative work and any 'message'; the significance of the one could not be derived from that of the other. There is a more complicated, even paradoxical, sense in which Lawrence's remark is relevant to janiform novels, for we could say that the tension between the 'messages' vivifies the novel instead of killing it. In the end one has to say that *Women in Love* is not janiform merely because its 'messages' point in opposite directions; one could, at least in theory, reconcile the two with some such formula as: 'Spontaneous-creative fullness of being includes corruption and degradation as phases rather than as opposites', though the synthesis leaves something out of each. Lawrence's novel does not merely deploy a series of paradoxes and contradictions in the service of a larger unity. It is centrally paradoxical because it is shot through with the continuous and continuously felt tension between the necessity of articulating a vision and its impossibility, and sometimes its undesirability. The defensiveness with which Lawrence writes of *Women in Love* in the American preface is to me both revealing and touching:

Any man of real individuality tries to know and to understand what is happening, even in himself, as he goes along. This struggle for verbal consciousness should not be left out in art. It is a very great part of life. It is not superimposition of a theory. It is the passionate struggle into conscious being.[24]

Revealing because it points to the novelist's inescapable function (and intermittently that of some of his central characters) and touching because at one level (as when it is localised in Hermione, for example) it is the great modern sin. But it is not so modern, after all. Set against the passage just quoted these words from Lawrence's review of Trigant Burrow's *The Social Basis of Consciousness*:

At a certain point in his evolution, man became cognitively conscious: he bit the apple: he began to know. Up till that time, his consciousness flowed unaware, as in the animals. Suddenly his consciousness split.

110

... The true self is not aware that it is a self. A bird as it sings, sings itself. But not according to a picture. It has no idea of itself.[25]

Women in Love attempts to articulate a vision of paradisal singleness-of-being-in-relatedness both negatively and positively. The measure of its success is also the measure of its failure. The reader's fascination and his frustration have the same source.

To my colleagues Bernard Harrison and Cedric Watts I owe an enormous debt of gratitude for their copious comments on an earlier version of this essay. They saved me from many blunders and confusions; the least I can do by way of token repayment is to absolve them entirely of responsibility for any that remain

All references to *Women in Love* are to The Penguin edition (1974)

1 F.R. Leavis, *D.H. Lawrence, Novelist* (London, 1955), 174
2 W.W. Robson, 'D.H. Lawrence and Women in Love', in B. Ford (ed.), *The Modern Age* (London, 1961), 296
3 Nathan Scott Jr, *Rehearsals of Discomposure* (New York, 1952), quoted in George Ford, *Double Measure* (New York, 1965), 195
4 Horace Gregory, *D.H. Lawrence: Pilgrim of the Apocalypse* (New York, 1933), 45–6
5 Ford, op. cit., 192
6 Leavis, op. cit., 167
7 J.M. Murray, *Reminiscences of D.H. Lawrence* (London, 1936), 233
8 Leavis, op. cit., 182
9 Cedric Watts, 'Janiform Novels', *English* 24 (July 1975), 40–1
10 Leavis, op. cit., 146
11 ibid.
12 From a letter to Jessie Chambers quoted in Harry T. Moore, *The Priest of Love* (London, 1974), 73
13 D.H. Lawrence, *Letters*, ed. Aldous Huxley (London, 1932), 198
14 Murry, op. cit., 223
15 See the essay by Mark Kinkead-Weekes in Maynard Mack and Ian Gregor (eds), *Imagined Worlds* (London, 1968)
16 Leavis, op. cit., 180
17 ibid., 156

18 Critical dissension over the interpretation of this celebrated scene is instructive and relevant. Most commentators, noting Birkin's reference to Cybele, 'the accursed Syria Dea' who emasculated her acolytes, interpret it as the male's attempt to annihilate the insatiable female. Mark Kinkead-Weekes and Colin Clarke see the scene, more plausibly in my view, as dramatising how 'the individuality of the ego gives way to a true individuality, though a precarious one' (Clarke, *River of Dissolution* [London, 1969]). The first group of critics, maintain that the moon's image finally re-forms, and that Birkin is defeated. For the last two critics, Lawrence's art shuts from our minds the idea of the moon's final re-formation, so that we are indeed left with a sense of 'precarious' individuality.

But the text gives us: '. . . until a ragged rose, a distorted, frayed moon was shaking upon the waters again, reasserted, renewed, trying to recover from its convulsion, to get over the disfigurement and agitation, to be whole and composed, at peace' (p. 280), where the rhythm and language of the earlier part of the sentence suggest the activity and agitation and the final cadence suggests rest and wholeness

19 Lawrence, *Collected Letters,* ed. Harry T. Moore (London, 1962), vol. 1, 449

20 Clarke, op. cit., 88ff. My debt to this book, even where I disagree with it, is overwhelming

21 Lawrence, *Phoenix II,* ed. Warren Roberts and Harry T. Moore (London, 1968), 103

22 ibid., 275

23 Lawrence, *Psychoanalysis and the Unconscious* (London 1923), quoted in Leavis, op. cit., 149

24 Lawrence, *Phoenix II,* 276

25 Lawrence, *Phoenix* (London, 1961), 377

6 His master's voice? The questioning of authority in literature

Jeremy Lane

'The question is,' said Humpty Dumpty, 'which is to be master –
that's all.'

It seems fair to begin with what is in an important sense
preliminary: a relationship between the writer and the written.
Such a relationship exists *a priori* for the reader, a necessary
premise, antedating his own relationship with the written
work both chronologically and logically, implicit in what he
reads. However, it may be difficult to define the nature of
that initial relationship, particularly because it is so naturally
assumed, so unconsciously taken for granted. Our habitual
terminology secures us a simple and straightforward definition,
that of 'authorship'. 'X wrote Y' or 'X is the author of Y':
such, essentially, is the writer's relation to the written. There
may be superficial complications in some cases, a pseudonym
or degrees of anonymity, but there is no lasting difficulty.
A name, a designation is attributed where it is lacking or
insecure, and we have Homer and Shakespeare, El Greco,
the *Gawain* poet, and *in extremis* the familiar of the anthology,
Ignoto or Anon. We find set above or below the title of
the work the certainty of a name, another title, and we rest
assured in the appropriation.

An age of European art and literature, roughly definable
as post-Renaissance and humanist, notably substantiates such
an assurance, such an appropriation. Its basic tendency is
mimetic, despite frequent irruptions testifying to other possible
modes of experience and representation and despite the continual straining of mimesis itself, at times to breaking-point,
which characterises some of the greatest works of art in this

kind. Mimesis implies a one-way passage between the writer and his work, his world and his readership – a *sens unique*. The world is *there* to be imitated and the artist is *here* to imitate it. The mimetic directive controls in principle the relationship between writer and written, written and read, and consequently determines that between writer and reader (and, more particularly, critic – for the act of critical reading as it is usually conceived is itself an expression of that relationship). These relationships are viewed as essentially unilinear and catenary, links in a chain or stages in a movement whereby, as Roland Barthes has perhaps somewhat crudely put it, 'l'*auteur* est toujours censé aller du signifié au signifiant, du contenu à la forme, du projet au texte, de la passion à l'expression; et, en face, le *critique* refait le chemin inverse, remonte des signifiants aux signifié'.[1] Literature becomes a kind of 'snakes and ladders' in which the writer descends (more or less sinuously) from the height of his 'idea' to the level of its expression, while the reader or critic ascends, step by exegetical step, from that expression to the 'idea' from which it derives.

We are all heirs to this conception of literature, which is both the fullest consequence and the clearest expression of a certain world-view – the view of a world asserting itself as modern and yet renascent, involved in an immensely complex and ambivalent relation with both ancient and medieval worlds. It is a world, humanist, Cartesian, which is engaged in basing on quite new premises its self-certification, progressively humanising, demythologising the imagination and replacing a symbolic world with one that is largely semantic. Of course this world's self-conception is, like any other, both active and passive, both creative and contemplative. Yet it tends in principle to enforce a basic dichotomy, to separate these two qualities or moods, subordinating one to the other, by virtue of the kind of relationship which it establishes between viewer and viewed, possessor and possessed. It leads to the empiric world of Locke, for whom the mind is a blank page, a *tabula rasa*, upon which the world, as it were, writes itself (though a divine hand may be supposed to steady the pen). Or, conversely, to the world of Bishop Berkeley, who adopts the Lockean vision to subvert it. For the bishop all things become signs – here is our semantic world–and existence is confined to representability, so that God is understood as 'the Author of nature'[2] in precisely the sense that the writer is deemed the author of his work. For Locke, experience authorises the idea, while for Berkeley the idea authorises experience; for both, however, the same kind of relation pertains, a relation which is fundamentally unequal and divisive.

That relation originates effectively with Descartes, however reluctant to acknowledge the fact he might be. For Descartes, to whom credit is most often given for originating modern philosophy and the whole modern cast of thought, does two seminal things. First, he asserts, no matter how cautiously, the primacy of individual authority over experience[3] – that conservatively individualistic authority which is most fully characterised, one might claim, in the traditional novelist. In his metaphysics, moreover, Descartes begins, like the novelist, with the finite self, the separable individual, not with God or the world, the inseparable totality. Second, he enforces a division (a division of labour, one might say) between mind and matter, subject and object, creative spirit and created world. He describes mind and matter as two different kinds of substance, the one without extension (thinking substance), the other with extension (corporeal substance, which includes of course the human body); and it is mind (which is, in essence, uncontaminated by the will, infallible) which precedes and commands existence: 'Cogito, ergo sum.' The separatism implicit in this formulation (however valiantly Descartes himself attempts to mitigate it) is reflected at large in post-Renaissance literature, in the various relationships among writer, reader, and written. The writer, for example, assumes in consequence an extraordinary and unprecedented individual importance. He becomes the creator, the inventor, the shaping spirit, in short the *author*, while the written work in turn becomes his creation, his invention, a form bearing the stamp of his individuality, in short his possession. Correspondingly, the relationship between writer and reader becomes strongly dualistic, as the former develops increasingly into the active principle, projecting a certain fictional world which to varying degrees both forms and conforms with the prevailing ideology of the age, while the latter grows increasingly passive, the recipient or, in a developing capitalist society, the consumer. This passivity of the reader tends to reduce the dynamic capacity of the fiction which, seen more and more as merely an article for consumption, becomes at its worst inert and lifeless. Conversely, not only the work but in a sense the reader too – 'dear reader', 'my reader' – is reduced to being the author's possession.

We might claim, however, that, so far as narrative fiction is concerned, it has been the achievement of about the past century – the period of modernism – to question and to fragment this structure of relationships, in which the terms 'narrative' and 'fiction' themselves undergo radical review. In this, modernism reveals itself as the contentious heir to the Romantic Movement which, however, for many reasons concerned itself with poetry and drama rather than the novel or tale. Like the Romantic, the modernist has sought, though with fundamentally different emphases, to destroy the myth of 'possessibility' and replace it with the idea of 'possibility'. This latter is perhaps no less a myth, but fundamentally distinct in that it requires the abolition of all particular myths (though with Georges Bataille we may suggest that the claim to have no myth is itself the central myth of our age). The replacement sought by the artist is no simple matter, however, for possibility enters intimately into possessibility, and not merely anagrammatically. The writer no doubt in some sense owns his work, producing novel, poem, or play, which he has an obvious right to claim as his creation – the possessive adjective has an evident justification. But there is another and equally important sense in which the written work ceases to be the possession of either writer or reader. Their recognition of this paradox provides an identifying link among many modern writers who in other respects are remarkably diverse.

Consider, for example, Joyce's novel, *A Portrait of the Artist as a Young Man*, whose very title interposes its ironic barrier between would-be possessor and supposed possession, writer or reader and fiction. Here the difficult association of the author, Joyce, with Stephen Dedalus, his protagonist and persona in the novel, is at once a confirmation and a denial of his authority, his 'authorship'. For while Joyce in one sense 'writes' Stephen, creating and authorising him, giving him the right to exist, as a character delineated – penned, one might say – in a narrative, in another sense the roles are reversed. Stephen, as subject and perceiving, feeling consciousness, importantly creates his world, the world of the fiction, and thus authorises his author, James Joyce. May we not claim that the same essential process constructs the fictions of Franz Kafka, despite the immense tonal distance that separates Kafka's world from Joyce's? (Though Dublin, via Trieste, is not perhaps so far from Prague.) The pervasive consciousness within the fiction (the K figure of the two major novels and the various personae of the stories) permits no alternative viewpoint, no balancing or opposing perspective whereby any reassuring synthesis or centrality may be gauged and gained. All we know and, more importantly, all we fail to know, is all that this consciousness knows or fails to know. Yet at the same time this consciousness is also seen from the outside, intensely exteriorised and often radically objectified (seen as an animal, investigating dog, burrowing mole, as an insect, the louse which is Gregor Samsa), placed in a third-person narrative whose tone is of an extraordinary, almost extra-human detachment, or displacing itself in a first-person narrative whose 'I' is continually undermined. As Joyce writes his Stephen, so Kafka, in a sense perhaps more intrinsic, certainly more anguished, writes and seeks hopelessly to right his K, enabling K doubtfully to justify him.

This is but another, perhaps extreme, way of suggesting that this kind of fiction claims a fundamental autonomy. The fiction is, in a double sense, the writer's experience in writing, but it is not simply his to write. It is essentially the writer's search for self, Proust's *moi profond*, a search which must, however, be conducted by means of an alterity, at base that necessitated by language itself. It is a search which, though it requires a kind of self-possession – an awareness of the self's potentiality, its potency–on the writer's part, precludes by definition that self-possession which is merely presumptive, a complacency based on the conviction that the self, like the world, can be contained and more or less fully construed. The belief in such a self-possessibility marks the limitations of the humanist-Cartesian model of reality, limitations which are most fully described in the realist novel. This, assuming reality to be graspable and truth to be a kind of precious substance (prizeable, priceable) which, if one only goes deep enough down, may be mined (made mine), is the most extensive idealisation of the bourgeois culture of 'having'. But the writer who doubts – radically but by no means simply – the adequacy of such a model subverts the certainty of 'having' and affirms paradoxically the uncertainty of 'becoming'. The fiction itself is that process of becoming, a being with no security in the assumed possession of truth but incessantly in search of truth and, further, aware that where, in Joyce's words, 'today's truth' becomes 'tomorrow's trend'[4] (becomes, that is, a becoming), truth lies only in the search, a pursuit *pour soi* demanding the dispossession of self and world, a quest which is a questioning, denying truth's possessibility, perpetually affirming its possibility.

Moreover, as itself that quest (the search embodied in the title of Proust's immense novel, in the Odyssean theme counterpointing Joyce's *Ulysses*, in the 'process' which forms the baseless base of Kafka's narratives), the fiction is its own self-dispossession, releasing itself from containment, evading consumption. Yet though the fiction is affirmed as process, it remains in some sense a product and must be recognised as a possession. It is the possession of all, potentially, and of none, actually. As an object, *chose*, the fiction may be possessed by anyone; as a subject, *être*, it may be possessed by none. It belongs to the illimitable posterity of its readership but, by virtue of its being an imaginative artefact in the medium of language, to no individual exclusively, neither reader nor writer. Through the mediation of a singular and a plural genius, the writer and his language, the particular fiction – more and yet less than the immeasurable totality of the singular, less and yet more than the infinite multiplicity of the plural – emerges. It is vital for both writer and reader to acknowledge that the work contains its own dynamic principle within itself and thus asserts itself as uncontainable *ab extra* – without content, in more than one sense. As Maurice Blanchot has remarked: 'It is always necessary to remind the novelist that it is not he who writes his work, but that his work seeks itself through him.'[5] In a real sense the fiction may be said to make itself and, in that process, to make the writer, its maker. The work, an object made, the elaboration and realisation in language of the writer's own search for self, remains still an exploration, a 'making' which is also a 'seeking', a search for an absolute or universal self, the possibility which persists beyond its particular achievement. Such a tendency is not explained or satisfied by the possession of the writer's name or by the concept of authority, of 'authorship' which such possession implies.

If the work seeks itself through its writer, though it assumes no prior and extrinsic truth it nevertheless presupposes its own discovery, or at least the possibility of discovery, and so claims to be in a sense pre-existent. Is not this pre-existence of the work itself one of the most important discoveries made through the whole process of *A la Recherche du temps perdu*, a culminating insight? Such is Marcel's self-realisation in the alterity of Proust's lifework: 'Je m'apercevais que ce livre essentiel, le seul livre vrai, un grand écrivain n'a pas, dans le sens courant, à l'inventer, puisqu'il existe déjà en chacun de nous, mais à le traduire. Le devoir et la tâche d'un écrivain sont ceux d'un traducteur.'[6] The etymological and original sense of 'inventer' (from the Latin *invenire*), which Marcel here tacitly contrasts with its current meaning, is 'to come upon, to find'. The work is a discovery rather than a creation in the usual sense, 'puisqu'il existe déjà en chacun de nous'. The writer abdicates the claim to creativeness, to the role of originator, inventor, *auctor*, acknowledging himself as translator or compiler, compositor, arranger, scribe. 'I am quite content,' writes Joyce in a letter of 1931, alluding to the composition of *Finnegans Wake*, 'to go down to posterity as a scissors and paste man for that seems to me a harsh but not unjust description.'[7] Refusing adherence to external systems of order, a classical mode of certification, the writer also denies the claim to originality which is the Romantic bequest (though an aspect of Romanticism which finds its origins perhaps in the Renaissance) and surrenders the pretension to authority, whether externally acknowledged or, as Shelley would maintain, unacknowledged, entailed in such a claim.

In reaction to the Romantic cult of self, the artist *qua* artist seeks anonymity, the escape from personality. We have now become familiar with the aesthetic of impersonality, perhaps most explicitly proposed by the poets of modernism, but as strongly though, in the nature of the genre, more obliquely reflected by the narrative prose writers too. The means of attempting to gain and secure anonymity are richly diverse, but broadly they may be characterised as either negative or positive, as abolitionist, so to speak, or 'overkill'. They involve either the removal from the narrative of personalised authorial intervention, judgement, commentary, or on the contrary the repletion of the narrative with more or less explicitly parodic or implicitly ironic forms of authorial presence, controlling or intrusive. Are not such processes intended, however, to substitute for traditional forms of authorisation, social or personal, another which, because it is impersonal and anonymous, is therefore most totalitarian in its ambition and implications? There have been arguments to this effect and they merit consideration. But I think the cult of anonymity may be misconceived (even by the artist himself when he is concerned to assert it explicitly or polemically) if it is supposed to grant the artist himself a quasi-divine and apparently incontrovertible impersonal authority.

This is certainly the assertion of Joyce's Stephen Dedalus, for example, in the *Portrait*, defining the artist in almost word-for-word Flaubertian terms: 'The artist, like the God of creation, remains within or behind or beyond or above his handiwork, invisible, refined out of existence, indifferent, paring his fingernails.'[8] Almost, yet not entirely – and the difference (that final phrase) reveals the glint of irony by whose light Stephen himself is placed. Stephen, as so often, is excessive in his claim and the excess makes apparent the

120

limitations of the authority which it asserts. For the artist is not a god but a man, a man moreover in a world without gods, and, while he seeks to the utmost the abstraction of his personality in the fiction (by means of a plethora of techniques – interior monologue, multiplicity and inconsistency of narrative stance, stylistic and rhetorical plurality, parody, pun, verbal play of every kind) he is continually brought back, with the reader, to the recognition that the subjective consciousness is ineluctable, given. The fundamental dilemma persists. While the writer is unable to rely upon the security of a general, social, classical code of authorisation, he is equally unable to project with any confidence an individual, personal, Romantic voice which again may authorise the world and himself. The alternatives, no longer exclusive or synthesisable, offer no solution and yet cannot be ignored, and so the writer is pitched between extremes. 'Everyword for oneself but Code for us all,'[9] as Joyce pithily phrases the dilemma in the *Wake*'s nightlanguage – and it is the disjunctive which demands emphasis. The writer is compelled to acknowledge the impersonal authority of the work, which is a denial of his own, and yet at the same time and in the same work to admit, to affirm his own 'authority' as merely personal – to objectify his subject (himself in relation to the world) and to subjectify the object of his contemplation (the world in relation to himself). An agonising paradox results: the work, in which impersonal authority resides, can come into being only through the writer, who lacks real authority, both general (socially accredited) and individual (asserted in opposition to conventional norms). Whether or not the work may prove itself and so authenticate its maker cannot be known *a priori*, but that both he and his world lack initial authenticity is the writer's prime awareness – it is the realisation, more or less dolorous, that drives him to write.

We may claim that this paradox admits of a solution, but one that the paradox itself contains—neither assured nor final, therefore, but itself partaking of the paradoxical. The writer is authorised and justified by the work, if at all; to the extent that the latter succeeds in gaining authority, so does the former. But achievement and attempt need to be rigorously distinguished. The writer seeks authority, justification, but achieves these only in and through the work. Therein he may discover his self, but only in the other, in the alterity of the fiction, in its language, its posterity, its autonomous life. If the self is irremediably divided, it is not, however, without the possibility of mediation. For it is thus that writer and reader come into contact – not an immediate contact but one mediated precisely by and in the fiction. The limitations of subjectivity are transcended, not by technical means viewed in a mere sense as ends in themselves, but by means of the relationship which those techniques help to bring about – the relationship which is the essential mean and meaning of the imaginative work, that between writer and reader, in which each plays a reciprocating part. (Thus the aridity of so much recent fiction which, rich in technical resources, lacks any real sense of this relationship. I am thinking, for example, of the gimmickry which seems to me to be prevalent in John Barth's cycle of fictions, *Lost in the Funhouse*, and which contrasts with the force of the title story itself; of the dry crackle of novels such as Susan Sontag's *Death Kit* or Christine Brooke-Rose's fictions, works which seem to me largely 'critical' in a restrictive sense; or, different and markedly inferior in intelligence, the stale and sterile surrealism of a William Burroughs.) The authentic relationship of writer and reader to written, and thus to one another, is felt to be not unilinear, not a *sens unique*, but dual and mutual (a sharing but not, therefore, as will be seen, simply an agreement). To use a spatial metaphor, it is circular, an orphic movement of quest and return (involving gain and loss) which holds writer and reader circumscribed, as it were, within the sphere that the work forms by itself.

Such, I suggest, is the movement presented dramatically in the pilgrimage or odyssey of the two principal figures in Joyce's *Ulysses*, Stephen Dedalus and Leopold Bloom – especially as this reaches its 'conclusion' in the penultimate chapter of the novel. The circumscription here is in a sense of the work itself, for it is the meeting and conversation between the two protagonists (in almost every respect so hopelessly unalike) which provides the potential for self-realisation

– in the necessary alterity – by means of which and to which end *Ulysses* may perhaps be written. The discovery of one another by Stephen and Bloom, however pointlessly, even ridiculously slight its implications may overtly appear, is a paradigm of the artist's discovery of the self in the other, which provides the impulse and the justification for the work of art. Such a discovery is inevitably partial and uncertain; for in this work of becoming discovery is as much a 'making' as it is made. His art is not given to the writer, nor the other to the self, as truth, as totality and certitude: there is no prescription. 'There is no route map of the way to truth. The only thing that counts is to make the venture of total dedication. A prescription would already imply a withdrawal, mistrust, and therewith the beginning of a false path.' These are Kafka's words, as reported by Gustav Janouch,[10] and though we may feel that their tone, too flat and formulary, betrays the reporter, we can, I think, accept the admonition as Kafka's own. While in one sense his is a movement of abdication, from the petty pomp and circumstances of personality, in another sense it is, as Kafka remarks, a movement of dedication – to his office *ex officio*, that of writer, which consists only in the written. The writer dedicates himself totally to his work, even as his work, whatever its nominal dedication, becomes a consecration, to himself, his self, that is, discoverable only in otherness.

The writer therefore cannot know *a priori* the nature of his art and may not even be certain that it exists. He certainly cannot prescribe it. (Joyce's Stephen, would-be artist, attempts in the *Portrait* to secure assurance in critical theory, his pseudo-Thomist definitions of art, and this too is 'the beginning of a false path', to be 'corrected' *via* the odyssey – itself a moment of error, necessary error – of *Ulysses*.) His search, being for self, must be for something unknown and in a sense always unknowable. Indeed his art depends upon the search, yet this dependence does not make him master of what he seeks but on the contrary profoundly subservient to it. Or, more precisely and paradoxically, the writer is both master and servant, in that it is his quest which dictates the nature of his work while, in turn, he is subject to that quest and to the work which is its pursuit and issue. A similar paradox evolves so far as language, *modus* and *materia* of the written work, is concerned. The writer and his language must suffer and enjoy a reciprocal authorisation, mastering and serving one another. While the writer seeks to master language, moulding it according to his individual vision, he is compelled to accept its government, its general decree. His exploration is conducted in and through language and the mode of search dictates, literally, the nature of what may be found. For while the self may exist in the absolute, in itself (such an essential being, such an impossibility, always the fiction's lure), it can be known and revealed only in another, in a related form – that of the fiction, the verbal construct, and in particular the character who is contained within but also in an important sense contains the narrative, the protagonist-persona, that figure almost endemic to the modern novel.

The self of the work, then, can be neither absolutely itself nor absolutely other. Discoverable only through the mediation, the 'journeywork' of the fiction, it must comprise a relation between self and other, a self viable only in the form of another, another approachable only through the self. This is no comfortable mutuality, however, but an interaction of great intensity and difficulty. It demands the uttermost distancing – 'othering' – of the self at the same time as the most intense intimation – 'selving' – of the other, and these contradictory requirements raise various and acute problems of narrative form, perspective, and tone. They perhaps account for Joyce's tonal ambivalence, for instance, the continual shift between distance and intimacy; between the 'play' of the impersonal executant, the writer who with entire mastery holds language (the English which is foreign to him) at a certain distance, the distance which separates the virtuoso from his instrument, and the absorption of the singer, whose 'instrument' – his voice – is interfused and identified with his whole person in the act of music-making.

The fiction which at once both recognises and embodies this contradictory interrelation necessarily founds itself upon paradox. Indeed the very mode of apprehension is paradoxical

124

in its duality, since recognition and embodiment are themselves incompatible means of adopting reality. The relationship between the written work and both writer and reader is, in turn, paradoxical and dynamic, incorporating sympathy and hostility, agreement and opposition, connection and disjunction. The reader, like the writer, is at once absorbed in and held at arm's length – the length of the writing, reading arm – from the fiction. The degree of intimacy and distance may of course vary considerably – how far off the voice and world of Kafka may appear and yet how close! Joyce, though – indeed perhaps because – he pushes us back with the pen, never achieves that kind of extremity. Even in the penultimate chapter of *Ulysses*, where a sidereal distance seems attained by the narrative eye, the voice still 'pushes', rhetorical, virtuoso, and reminds us of the presence not too far behind its insistency. In comparison, the remotenesses of Kafka's China are galactic, almost inconceivable, distances so vast that, like those of outer space, they conflate space and time and still, being not merely material but spiritual too, exceed even notional measurement. Nonetheless, with Joyce too we move between nearness and distance, the subjectified and objectified self, the self-communing and confessing minds of Bloom and Stephen and the cityscape of Dublin, in which with all the other paraphernalia they appear as figures, principal no doubt but still drawn from without. While we *feel* with both Bloom and Stephen (and the complexity of feeling involved is itself tensely productive), we also *see* them with their creator's cold eye – an eye both microscopic and telescopic. In the same way, though more anguishedly, we shift with Kafka between outer and inner in a perpetual *va-et-vient*, moving dislocatingly (and yet without the comforting possibility of interruption) between the subjective fears or anxieties of the protagonist to his (or its?) variously appalling, fantastic, or merely animal objective condition. To take perhaps the most extreme but also most familiar example, Gregor Samsa in 'The Metamorphosis', man and insect, is perfectly acceptable and entirely repulsive. There is a complete continuity at the same time as an unbridgeable gap (inexplicable, unjustifiable) between the two aspects, subjective and objective, of his situation. As readers we have to move simultaneously in two opposing directions, with Gregor and as far from him as it is possible to be.

This movement is the expression of the fiction's own paradoxical dynamic, which involves the polar tensions of self and other, extremes of attraction and repulsion. The personae of the fiction, Joyce's Stephen and Bloom, Proust's Marcel, Kafka's K, in themselves both attract and repel. Yet because they at once compose and are composed by their narratives, the principle of attraction–repulsion becomes co-extensive with the fiction itself, authorising and simultaneously authorised by its central figure. This is a deeply self-subverting principle of authorisation, however. The work, a search for self whose goal can never be secured in advance and may never be secured at all, is also a movement into and out of the self – into the self out of the other and into the other out of the self. While Joyce in the conventional sense authorises (is the author of) his Stephen – as Proust his Marcel, Kafka his K – at the same time Stephen authorises Joyce, and this is a movement to and fro between fiction and reality, a reciprocation but also a contradiction. No absolute, incontrovertible authority is obtainable in these, the ineluctable conditions of fiction. The authority of the writer is reciprocated but also contradicted by the authority of the fictional self who is his persona and, more extensively, by the fiction as a whole. The same holds true with regard to the relationship between writer and reader, which can be established only through the medium of the work. The writer is authorised by the work, which in turn demands the authorisation of the reader (unread it has no real existence) – an authority 'in opposition'. As the writer is in an obvious respect the work's creator, so too, less obviously, is the reader, from the other side – its re-creator, whose re-creation the fiction is. There is thus no final authorisation, no simple authority, no single author; but a relative authorisation, the sanction of relation whose dual principle seeds plurality, admitting and containing its contrary.

That containment, such as it is, remains the work's achievement, the repose it enjoys for all its restlessness. True to its paradoxical nature, the movement of in-and-out, of for-and-against, creates a kind of stasis. Its polar tensions form a global entity, a situation, the space of the fiction, and it is in this metaphorical sense that we may speak of the fiction being itself a 'world', a world of relations, of *rapports*, dimensionless, not of material substance, *mundus* not *terra*. Understood in this sense, it may be conceived as a kind of sphere wherein both writer and reader are contained and content to be so enclosed. A surrender, an obedience to the work's authority, a subordination of self takes place and makes the fictional 'place'. Such is the true passivity of both writer and reader, the condition in which both disappear so far as possible into the work. A total *disparition* is impossible, the total abdication of the self's authority being no more attainable than its total imposition – both requiring a paradisal cosmos in which self and other, reality and fiction, world and imagination, are merged in absolute identity and so annihilated.

The absolute remains, however, the impossible goal, the perpetually tempting lure of the writer and his fiction. It manifests itself spectrally, luminously, a kind of halo about the structure of the achieved work (which, though infinite in its implications, is necessarily finite in other respects) – a relationship of infinite potentiality, a relationship which therefore absolves itself of its relative condition. It is the movement, in which utter stasis is implicit, from the work as a whole, containing both writer and reader, to all that is beyond – the other which is inexpressible, unrelatable, which cannot be said or shown. That is the ultimate authority, 'the centre of the silent Word',[11] the unsayable which cannot be gainsaid, but which must remain the fiction's constant aspiration precisely because it can never be attained.

Here, however, is the zero and infinite zone beyond words, and, while all the rest is literature, literature is necessarily the province in which both writer and reader must pursue their search. In this province capacity falls short of desire, the absolute desire in which there is absolute content – *satietas insatiabilis*, to use a term favoured by mystical writers. But it transcends the usual limitations of subject and object, composing a world (the world of the fiction) which, though in absolute terms deficient, is in relative terms (the terms of relation) excessive, extravagant, *de trop*. This is a world of both stasis and kinesis, the reflection and intimation of a world beyond and within, 'both a new world and the old made explicit' in which there is 'neither arrest nor movement'[12] (or, as Octavio Paz more positively echoes, 'quietud y movimiento son lo mismo'),[13] from which the fiction is a falling away, toward which it incessantly aspires. In it contraries are brought into relation but fail to be absolutely identified with one another: an irreducible interval, the interval of relation itself, of language, holds them apart. There is reciprocation but equally contradiction. An order, an authority is established in the very composition of the fiction, but it is an order conversant with chaos, an authority complicit with anarchy. Joyce's *Ulysses* proposes, in Umberto Eco's words, 'an order set in doubt',[14] self-undermining in the very process of self-assertion; Kafka's clarity and precision evoke endless enigma, his 'authorities' threaten a meaningless justice beyond the scope of any law; even Proust's exhaustive inquiry, the astoundingly patient unravelling of self and circumstances, includes the recognition that the analysis pursued is, though obligatory, ultimately inessential, and it ends with the acknowledgement of interminability. The only final authorisation, all recognise, is death, but therein lies the extreme irony, the acutest paradox. For death, the seal that is opened and closed, cannot be apprehended except in relation, except in another, and yet, known to the other, it is unknown to the self. The fullest possible realisation of death in life, the imaginative work, is at once the highest authority and also, being the most determined 'othering', utterance, least able to authorise the experience which is unrelatable and so, in fiction's terms, unjustifiable, the act of dying.

1 R. Barthes, *S/Z: essai* (Paris, 1970), 180
2 George Berkeley, 'Essay towards a New Theory of Vision', in *Works*, ed. A.A. Luce and T.E. Jessop (London, 1948), vol. 2, 231
3 'I argued to myself that there was no plausibility in the claim of any private individual to reform a State by altering everything and by

overturning it throughout, in order to set it right again. Nor, again, is it probable that the whole body of the sciences, or the order of teaching established by the Schools, should be reformed. But as regards all the opinions which up to this time I had embraced, I thought that I could not do better than endeavour once for all to sweep them completely away, so that they might later on be replaced either by others which were better or by the same when I had made them conform to a rational frame.' René Descartes, *Discourse on Method*, in *Descartes Selections*, ed. Ralph M. Eaton [New York, 1927], book 2, 12

4   James Joyce, *Finnegans Wake* (London, 1939), 614

5   M. Blanchot, *Le Livre à venir* (Paris, 1959), 199

6   M. Proust, *A la recherche du temps perdu* (Paris, 1954), vol. III, 890

7   Letter to George Antheil, 3 January 1931, in *The Letters of James Joyce*, ed. S. Gilbert (London, 1957), 297

8   James Joyce, *A Portrait of the Artist as a Young Man* (Harmondsworth, 1960), 215

9   James Joyce, 'Scribbledehobble Notebook', quoted in Thomas E. Connolly, *James Joyce's Scribbledehobble Notebook* (Evanston, Ill., 1961), 138

10 G. Janouch, *Conversations with Kafka* (London, 1971), 196

11 T.S. Eliot, 'Ash-Wednesday', *The Complete Poems and Plays of T.S. Eliot* (London, 1969), section V, 96

12 Eliot, 'Burnt Norton', ibid., 173

13 Octavio Paz, 'La Poesía', *Libertad bajo palebra* (Mexico, 1949), 13

14 Umberto Eco, *Opera aperta* (Milan, 1962), 289

7 Difficult language: the justification of Joyce's syntax in *Ulysses*

Roger Moss

Here all is clear. No, all is not clear. But the discourse must go on. So one invents obscurities. Rhetoric. (Samuel Beckett, *The Unnamable*)

Confronting a difficult book the reader resists it by insisting that the difficulty stands in the way of his reading and must be disposed of before he can proceed. As knight errant, the critic assumes that what he has to say must vanquish the dragon Difficulty, and in this spirit he produces a 'reading' of the book: a way through and past the 'difficult bits'. Faced with *Ulysses* the common critical reading has hitherto depended on identifying the 'difficult bits' (if at all) with a technique called 'stream of consciousness' or 'interior monologue'. In speaking here of the 'difficult language' of the book I am at once reducing a technique to the level at which we apprehend its difficulty, and allowing us to recognise at the same level a *real* – and therefore indisposable, indispensable – difficulty. Such recognition is a part of the meaning of *Ulysses*; it leads the reader from a detailed attention to the significance of Joyce's particular syntactical deviations to a more general understanding of what is difficult, deliberately so, about *Ulysses*.

If we are not to dispose of the difficulty, and clearly cannot immediately understand it, we can only ask: where does it come from? From the first paragraph of 'The Sisters' (and so from the very beginning of his fiction) Joyce insists on the difficulty of fitting language to perception: this is one root of his 'difficult language'. But in 'The Sisters' it is a difficulty to which the response in language is inadequate.

130

Joyce is 'in difficulties' rather than being justifiably difficult. The second half of that earliest paragraph reads:

Every night as I gazed up at the window I said softly to myself the word paralysis. It had always sounded strangely in my ears, like the word gnomon in the Euclid and the word simony in the Catechism. But now it sounded to me like the name of some maleficent and sinful being. It filled me with fear, and yet I longed to be nearer to it and to look upon its deadly work.   (p. 7)

This concentration on one word, the concentration of the preceding scene into it, has a strange effect. Language, with its natural linearity – especially apparent in a narrative as syntactically conventional as this one, in which 'it' ('paralysis') merely replaces 'I' as the active subject of three successive sentences – is asked to do something it cannot quite achieve: to turn that linearity back into itself and create from one word, part of its linear progression, a separate action and direction. The phrase 'the word paralysis' becomes a kind of fulcrum, belonging both to the active narrative world and to a descriptive perceived one. It is important that Joyce did not write: 'Every night I gazed up at the window I said softly to myself, "Paralysis".' To single this one word out as 'the word' punctuates it: we are made conscious of its different status, of it begging questions about its status – like the miniature of a cathedral held in the hand of the builder-bishop, sculpted on its own west wall. But it is not therefore to the *content* of the word that our concentration is turned, rather to what it portrays of the narrator's consciousness ('writerliness' at such a moment is a condition shared by the author and the narrating hero, even if that hero is strictly incapable of writing: 'consciousness' and consciousness of language become one): we turn to 'the word' as an active principle rather than to 'paralysis' as an idea.

But, as I have said, narrative language cannot quite achieve this precision. 'The word paralysis' is set apart from any other unit of language in the paragraph, yet without any distinguishing features. In the last of the three sentences: 'It filled me with fear, and yet I longed to be nearer to it and to look upon its deadly work . . .', the activity of 'the word paralysis' pushes the pronoun to an extreme where few readers will follow and most will be enabled by the forward impulsion of the narrative not to notice their own waiving of the syntax in referring 'it' in the final clauses to 'the window' or the scene behind that window as much as to 'the word paralysis'. The difficult phrase is swallowed up in the story's too simple continuity and can be put into prominence only by a falsely self-conscious critical exercise which has little to do with the actual reading.

The radical solution to this problem is to be found on the first page of *Ulysses*, at the point usually recognised as the start of Stephen's 'interior monologue':

He peered sideways up and gave a low whistle of call, then paused awhile in rapt attention, his even white teeth glistening here and there with gold points. Chrysostomos. Two strong shrill whistles answered through the calm. (p. 1)

The single word stops and is separated from the action which surrounds it, a separation underlined by the length and un-familiarity of the word. That simple syntactical break does, successfully, what the first paragraph of 'The Sisters' fails to do. It is as if we read: 'As I gazed at him I said softly to my-self the word Chrysostomos . . .', without losing that word in the linear determinism of the language from which it is sepa-rated. We naturally read 'Chrysostomos' as a parenthesis, and as such as a comment or commentary on the rest of the text. We naturally refer that comment to the 'even white teeth' of the previous sentence and the 'he' which was its subject; they are the only substantives available to which it can stand in apposition. A description and a comment on a description are thus fitted syntactically into a moment of time, a moment created by the gap implicit between the active verbs 'gave a . . . whistle' and 'answered' as much as by the verb which describes the gap: 'paused'. The language as a whole (again the contrast with the first paragraph of 'The Sisters' is apparent) contrives the breakdown of its linearity. Our concentration is focused in a pause created by Mulligan's own concentration ('He peered . . .' which starts the paragraph) and this closeness of perception, seen in such fine details as 'He peered sideways up . . .' and the contrast

132

between 'long low whistle' and 'strong shrill whistle' demands the inference of a perceiving consciousness capable of the comment: 'Chrysostomos.'

In a third-person narrative like this such a consciousness would conventionally be the author's. A Dickens who had the reference to hand would explicate it perhaps with 'A second Chrysostomos!', and the syntactical variation (loss of the main verb) would be justified by the noun-phrase and the exclamation mark as the intrusion of an author's *voice*. (One can parallel this with the continuous references, for example, in *Dombey and Son* to Carker's own 'even white teeth'.) The reader would register the moment, the relationship in it between linear and intrusive language, as *rhetorical* – 'intrusive language' would in fact stand as a definition of 'rhetoric' within the terminology of the conventional novel – that is, as a distortion of the novel's conventional allegiance to showing things to be true without direct telling. Joyce has resigned his right to evaluative intrusion of this kind; but, more important, the Joyce of *Ulysses* has asserted a right which the Joyce of *Dubliners* did not fully realise: the right of literary language to attend to itself, a preliminary recognition of the inadequacy of any fixed boundary between 'telling' and 'showing' in the book.

A price is paid, we might think, for the radical refinement with which 'Chrysostomos' is delivered: for, unlike 'paralysis', it remains unclear which consciousness is the source of the comment, imprecise in what way 'Chrysostomos' 'acts' in the narrative, and the word itself remains valueless in *content*. With 'paralysis' we lose the power of the word as such in chasing its meaning, and in chasing the narrative despite the word, whereas with 'Chrysostomos' a word-making, word-conscious facility within the language is asserted – within, in that the moment for this 'writerly' consciousness is made apparent by the gap in the narrative's consecutive action. This is not so much a technique ('interior monologue', 'stream of consciousness') as a further level of language beyond narrative through which a non-linear approach to consciousness and interiority are resolved in the language of the fiction itself. That is the full extent of the 'meaning' of 'Chrysostomos': it is more than a difficult *word*, reflecting a young poet's pleasure in learned allusion; it is also a word as a sentence, a piece of difficult *language*. To read it as such exemplifies our proper response to this language: accepting it at its fundamental level of difficulty – the syntax – and accounting for that not as a pre-established technique[1] but as a sign of the developing perception of language in the book.

The next stage in the development of this occurs a few pages later. Mulligan hands Stephen a mirror:

Stephen bent forward and peered at the mirror held out to him, cleft by a crooked crack, hair on end. As he and others see me. Who chose this face for me? This dogsbody to rid of vermin. It asks me too. (p. 5)

The same separation from action as before, the same controlling verb 'peered': closeness of observation and concentration are the gestures analogous to this language. The narrative begins conventionally; a minimal shift occurs when two adjectival phrases ('cleft by a crooked crack, hair on end') qualify in succession the two bare objects of that narrative, 'the mirror' and 'him': the man and the mirror are held together as one image. The significant syntactical difficulty, however, occurs in the noun-phrase which follows and the wider comment it generates on what Stephen sees directly, 'telling' and 'showing' bound as one. It is with such observations that an analysis assuming the prior availability of a 'stream of consciousness' begins and ends. It sees the gap as logical, the 'stream' waiting to be tapped, and ignores the fact that there is no typographical gap at all.

To ask, 'Why *here* the syntactical difficulty?' is to see this less as a 'stream' and more as a reaction to the particular moment in the narrative. Briefly, there has to be a gap for the thing to make sense: with the intervention of a mirror in which Stephen can contemplate himself, we choose between syntactical convention necessitating an epistemological breakdown, as if it read: 'What he saw there was him as Mulligan saw him . . .', when the point is that what he saw was not *him*, but *me*; or an epistemological accuracy requiring syntactical breakdown. The very objectivity of the narrative guides us to the impossibility of intruding a narrator's voice and point of view at this moment, writing with the head of the writer visible over the (reflected) shoulder of the onlooker. Language bends with the point of view of its subject. The disjointed noun-clauses take their syntactical form from the fact that they stand, as perceived objects in consciousness, in opposition to the *act* of looking in a mirror.[2]

The forms taken in these early examples from *Ulysses* do not resolve themselves as some kind of unpunctuated dialogue, or precise imitation of the workings of the mind. They lead the reader instead to a realism which incorporates among its proper objects the language applied to reality. The justification of the difficulty of *Ulysses* by this point is that the two difficult things – language and perception – justify each other and so make for a way of reading (not a 'reading' of) the book which coheres around a distinctive perception of language as well as a distinctive language of perception.

We learn, in coming to terms with the difficulty, that the shape of language and the shape of the world are distinct, that there is a realistic art whose realism insists on bending language or reality, one to fit the shape of the other. This is art in so far as we remain aware of the artifice of the bending. It is a realism of moments, what Joyce called 'epiphanies'. As we have seen in *Dubliners*, such intense perceiving can create a language in difficulties. Of *A Portrait of the Artist as a Young Man* the same charge is implied when Harry Levin says[3] that 'it is not easy to visualise' the following passage from the book: 'Her bosom was a bird's, soft and slight, slight and soft as the breast of some dark-plumaged dove. But her long fair hair was girlish: and girlish, and touched with the wonder of mortal beauty, her face' (p. 175). I can find no basis in the book for deciding between a resolution of the difficulty of that and like passages (a difficulty in awareness – ours, as Levin, indicates, but also Stephen's – before it is a difficulty in language itself) in terms of a continuity of the book's imitative, 'generic' language (where the objection would be met by saying that the language 'belongs' to Stephen's adolescent fantasising) and a resolution in terms of the moment itself. But I am sure that to transfer the first of these options uncritically to *Ulysses* and to say that the difficult language there responds vaguely to the same sort of generic modes, 'imitating' Stephen's emotional intensity or Bloom's patterns of thought, is inadequate to the difficulty and needlessly undermines the understanding we have already taken from two short passages in *Ulysses* of its clear distinction between the shape of language and that of the world.

If that language is 'not easy to visualise' in this instance from the *Portrait* it is not therefore enough to say, as Levin goes on to: 'This is incantation, not description. Joyce is thinking in rhythms rather than metaphors . . .', treating the breakdown of referability as Joyce's fault and not, as it surely is, his intention. That intention, more radical still than that behind the breakdown of linearity, makes a space for the writing consciousness to work. We are forced to face the gap between language and perception, rather than to fill it out with a borrowed iconography. When Stephen turns away and walks across the beach, we read: 'Her image had passed into his soul for ever and no word had broken the holy silence of his ecstasy' (p. 176). The 'incantation', words separated from narrative responsibility, has narrated a *silence*. It is a moment of ecstasy comparable to the moments of concentration which gave rise to single words – 'paralysis', 'Chrysostomos' – but giving rise in its more extreme emotion to the two extremes of 'difficult language': 'no word' at all, and the over-writing of the passage itself. The language belongs not to Stephen, nor to Joyce, but to a 'writing moment' which intervenes between the experience and our moment of reading.

It is without doubt a clumsy and partial solution to the problem it proposes (or perhaps ecstasy is simply too clumsy a state of mind for the attempt). But it need not be read as if it were unaware of the problem it proposes – how to render the mind's intensest perceptions – though the in-adequacy of the solution should make us beware of trying to resolve the 'difficult language' of *Ulysses* as the purple passages of the *Portrait* shorn of their main verbs and periodicity.

The fifth section of the *Portrait*, compared to the surviving fragments of *Stephen Hero*, achieves its form by taking Stephen's extended contemplations out of the one-dimensional generic modes of academic life into a conversational *milieu* where they play against the replies and interruptions of Lynch, Cranly and others; or against the contingency and appearance of the world itself, as here: 'A crude grey light, mirrored in the sluggish water and a smell of wet branches over their heads seemed to war against the course of Stephen's thought' (p. 211). The detail here, as elsewhere, requires the inference of a perceiving consciousness; and so we place not merely the world as a narrated 'setting', but the world perceived as 'crude', 'grey', 'sluggish', 'wet', in Stephen's ambit, within which he is meanwhile attempting the lucid definition of another adjective—'beautiful'. But the language and life 'of the marketplace' is not simply testing, or ironically teasing, Stephen's intense aesthetics; quite as much the facts of a perceived world are testing the writer's ability to concentrate rightly, conceive, and create. Writing—as much as the perceptions rendered here by writing — wars 'against the course of Stephen's thought'. In the 'epiphany' itself (and the book's fifth section may be seen as a conceptualised version of that mode) writing 'wars' more radically against the event.

The 'Proteus' episode on Sandymount beach, *Ulysses*'s third chapter, provides the radical extension of, and solution to, these problems. Stephen's 'concentration', which we have seen is the condition of Joyce's 'difficult language', here approaches a ratiocinative version of the ecstasy of the *Portrait*'s epiphanies. His self-contemplation, more than that demanded by the mirror, here plumbs the problem of the very nature of self-awareness. Joyce's syntax bends, we have seen, at precisely the point where the contemplation of these two facets, articulability and interiority, overwhelm whatever claim narrative objectivity may have to accuracy. That being so, we would expect 'Proteus' to contain the most difficult language in *Ulysses* yet; it does. 'Contain', though, is not exactly right: here is no 'containing' narrative to generate the 'difficult language', for if 'peering' or 'looking in a mirror' can be narrated, 'thinking', 'perceiving' and (we can add, with the *Portrait* behind us) 'writing' itself, present a different problem.

The commonest syntactical units in 'Proteus' are the noun-clause and noun-phrase ('Chrysostomos'; 'This dogsbody to rid of vermin'), which we understand through their development in 'Telemachus' and 'Nestor' as objects in consciousness free from the narrative restraints of time, sequentiality and so of a constructive meaning. The relationship of such units to the narrative is 'rhetorical' in the sense in which I used it above: they 'tell' before they 'show', as in: 'Cranly's arm. His arm . . .' (p. 6), whose two noun-phrases make the narra-tive act of Mulligan clasping Stephen's arm secondary to the 'telling' of an associated memory. Joyce avoids the naturalistic diction of: 'Mulligan clasped him by the arm and Stephen remembered Cranly's identical gesture', because the unit of language 'Stephen remembered' is in that moment strictly imprecise, the parallelism the syntax enforces between it and the action 'Mulligan clasped' is false.

But 'Proteus' is as much the source from which such recognitions develop as it is the achievement towards which these smaller instances point. We sense in 'Proteus' Stephen's own relief in solitude, away from the unsatisfactory 'home' with Mulligan and the egregious Haines, from the unsatisfying 'work' and the inane Mr Deasy; and through this to Joyce's authorial release from naturalism, the commitment to a balanced interweaving of people, thoughts and places. The tilt towards Stephen in the antithesis of the nouns 'Cranly' and 'him', replacing their laxer hypothetical alternatives 'Mulligan clasped' and 'Stephen remembered', is of course justified by its context, but also implicitly by the 'higher objectivism' which Stephen himself is to discover in 'Proteus'. It is in this dynamic way that we can call the difficult language of the first two chapters a *preparation* for the language of 'Proteus': the achievement of that 'higher objectivism', which the earlier chapters have witnessed in passing, is the unnar-rated action of the chapter, and 'contains' its difficult language. It is because of this that we attend to the act of 'telling' for itself, for the significance of the way it works, rather than to it as an oblique 'showing' and so through it to the content. The act of telling continues the portrait of the artist and shows in its development the artist's ability to portray.

The opening of 'Proteus' builds on the limits imposed by the perceptual capabilities of Stephen, by the stuff of Sandymount beach and by language. Stephen's walk is a conscious experiment in the relationship of perception to the perceived object. It produces the literary experiment of Joyce's account. The thoughts which open the chapter – noun-phrases, objects in consciousness: 'Ineluctable modality of the visible: at least that if no more, thought through my eyes. Signature of all things I am here to read. . .' – are equated in the syntax with simple objects: 'seaspawn and seawrack, the nearing tide, that rusty boot' (p. 45). The separation of nouns from adjectives, as in the 'mirror' passage (where 'cleft by a crooked crack, hair on end' was closer to a conceiving consciousness than the simple objects 'the mirror' and 'him') is re-enacted: 'Snotgreen, bluesilver, rust: coloured signs.' Adjectives line up parallel to the objects they qualify; but here the syntax makes the adjectival sentence as clearly substantive overall as the sentence of substantives it is supposed to qualify, and the novelty of the adjectives themselves has a decidedly 'perceived' quality: the nouns they compound, 'snot', 'silver', 'rust'. 'Coloured signs' are no more clearly 'added' conceptually to objects than their names, so Stephen argues and the writing demonstrates. From the first word the visible world is 'thought through my eyes' (Joyce is alive to the ambiguity in 'thought' as a noun and as a past participle). In effect writing accretes object on top of object; language, belonging to the perceiver, has a distance from the object implicit in the very idea of 'perceiving' – it does not move us appreciably nearer perceptions (nor farther away, we might add, by contrast with Beckett) but multiplies words in a line parallel to perception.

The 'difficult language' here is not an achievement of style, or of technique, but the development of a rhetoric fit for its own immediate content. It is above all 'the artist' who is asserted here as the central figure – it is *his* language, not the beach's. It mimes perceptions in the only way true to it, imitative not of a *voice* (as is often the case with Bloom or Molly) but of the way of perceiving which the discussion arrives at. That, involving Joyce as much as Stephen, goes beyond both to involve the reader in the 'moment of writing'.

What follows is even more insistently a literary experiment. Suggested by the imperative: 'Shut your eyes and see . . .', it goes on to see if the exclusion of the visible world might clarify Stephen's understanding – 'seeing' – since it is the visible which creates the terminology and situation in which perceiving and conceiving cannot be separated. The experimental paragraph begins in a conventional syntax, and its yielding is brought about by the same kind of contemplation which demanded more accuracy than conventional syntax provides when Stephen looked in the mirror. We read: 'Stephen closed his eyes to hear his boots crush crackling wrack and shells . . .', and it is at the point at which Hopkins-like alliterative pressure makes us aware of the *sound* of the language over its sense that Stephen's own narrated awareness shifts to a world of sound.

As a self-contained literary experiment it has much in common with one ideal reading of the whole book, a *Ulysses* fragmentary and relative. The conclusion of the passage ('There all the time without you . . .') could well be spoken by the reader of *Ulysses* to the world he has excluded during his reading. Seen like this it is less of a responsibility for the book to reflect life 'through the prism of a language many-coloured and richly storied' – a possibility rejected by the Stephen of the *Portrait* (p. 171), though still the core of many critics' explanations of the language of *Ulysses* – more to contemplate the 'inner world of individual emotions mirrored perfectly' in prose, even where the perfection of the mirroring demands that the prose be not 'lucid supple |and| periodic' but, as we have seen, difficult, pressured and syntactically crabbed. But Stephen opens his eyes, and the simple fact of continuity (the world that has been there all the time without him, with which the writing resumes contact) makes this passage as inadequate as any other as a model for the whole.

The last time we see Stephen alone, we see the promise of a release from the privacy of his position:

... For the rest let look who will.

Behind. Perhaps there is someone.

He turned his face over a shoulder, rere regardant ... (p. 64)

If, in the moment of its enactment, the gesture is motivated only by embarrassment and yields only a ship, in the 'writing moment' it is to reconstruct time, space and point of view in the creation of Leopold Bloom.

'Mr Leopold Bloom ate with relish the inner organs of beasts and fowls. He liked thick giblet soup, nutty gizzards, a stuffed roast heart, liver slices fried with crustcrumbs, fried hencod's roes. Most of all he liked grilled mutton kidneys which gave to his palate a fine tang of faintly scented urine' (p. 65). This opening paragraph of 'Calypso', in the very conventionality both of its syntax and of its form as the introduction of a new major character and 'plot' into the novel, gives the reader the new source of difficulty in the language which is to extend its hold in the rest of *Ulysses*, as it extends the perceptions of literary language of the first three chapters. We see again how far, and now with what significance, the reader accepts a general meaning that does not correspond to the given syntax. The paragraph, conventionally read, places the character in a convenient and characteristic generalisation. But, in the context from which the reader has come, with its unvarying specificity of language, there are no resources for such an interpretation. For this reason it is at first hard to avoid reading it as an active description: Bloom eating there and then this Gargantuan meal. Of course we 'correct' that reading; but Bloom is never quite rescued from the gigantic sensuous geniality of the original misreading – nor should he be.[4] Moreover in 'correcting' it thus, we make a conscious choice of the kind of *Ulysses* we go on to read, seeing Bloom as a fresh start, rejecting the context developed through our understanding of Stephen's chapters. Joyce's sense of the inadequacy of this rejection is, I believe, the main cause of his development of literary parody in *Ulysses*: consistently floating thereby 'the writer' and the 'writing moment' into this more diffuse world; Bloom's 'touch of the artist' (p. 302) in this respect – thrown off by Lenehan and caught unfailingly by the critics –

is surely only a further ironic hint to the inadequacy of Bloom as the sustaining 'dimension' of his own book.

The second paragraph also opens conventionally with a syntax which presumes to know of Bloom what is 'in his mind', as it does (and the parallel syntax reinforces the idea, in the *same way as*) what is 'in his kitchen'. But it ends with a minimal syntactical compression, which is enough though, tied as it is to what Bloom 'feels', to be interpreted as the start of his 'interior monologue', despite the third person:

Kidneys were in his mind as he moved about the kitchen softly, righting her breakfast things on the humpy tray. Gelid light and air were in the kitchen but out of doors gentle summer morning everywhere. Made him feel a bit peckish.

As a comment 'Made him feel a bit peckish' demands a causal relationship with something that precedes the missing 'it'. It would logically spring from his thoughts about kidneys if the temporal connection (which gains weight in such conventionally linear narrative) did not inexplicably relate the feeling to the weather 'in the kitchen |and| out of doors'. On the other hand, if the missing subject is intended to create a syntactical link over the top of the intervening description, then we are unable to infer – as we automatically do – that the description was some part of Bloom's awareness of things that morning, if not exactly the cause of his hunger; and that is supported by the intrusiveness of the word 'gelid' and of the diction of the entire middle sentence, set against the homely 'humpy' and 'peckish'. But if this is not part of Bloom's awareness, *his* language, then the author's intrusion of it into the sequence makes any idea of deliberate bathos between the heightened description and the idiomatic 'Made him feel a bit peckish' an unreasoned stacking of the ironies against Bloom, and still implies a gap in the consecutive narrative, an empty space in Bloom's consciousness out of which an uncaused result is created. With so much digging the sentence begins to totter and require another implied subject: not 'it' but 'I' – 'the writer . . . made him feel a bit peckish.'

We rightly protest that the very conventionality of the narrative which causes these lacunae also impels us to read on and over them. But just to read on does not do justice to the new difficulty presented. We accept this language only by ignoring, paradoxically, the fact that it was written – by rejecting, in effect, the perspective and perceptions of the Telemachy; for if we accept that it was written we accept also the deliberately chosen fictional status of Bloom and the doubly fictional nature of an attempt to write out his mind.

The new difficult language which develops from this situation is multiple rather than complex. In 'Nausicaa', for instance, Gerty MacDowell's narrative is a parody of romantic fiction; but it is parodic in the sense in which Ravel's 'La Valse' parodies waltz rhythm: by distortion, by imperfectly holding to it, the parody reveals its own reliance on the limitations of the parodied form, as well as revealing those limitations. And like 'La Valse' also it derives creative freedom from the parody. The 'process' of reading it leads us, moment by moment, not to a moment of 'meaning' but to the momentary intersection of mutually exclusive positions – the positions occupied by Gerty and by Bloom in a world (the world of fiction) where language and experience are equated. The language of Gerty's narrative yields by degrees to that of Bloom's, releasing him with gentle irony from the ideal position he has occupied in the linguistic limitations of her story: 'He was leaning back against the rock behind. Leopold Bloom (for it is he) stands silent, with bowed head before those young guileless eyes. What a brute he had been! At it again? A fair unsullied soul had called to him, and wretch that he was, how had he answered?' (p. 478). And releasing her with a similar quashing of the ideal while still holding up the limited language:

She walked with a certain quiet dignity characteristic of her but with care and very slowly because Gerty MacDowell was . . .

Tight boots? No. She's lame! O!

Mr Bloom watched her as she limped away. Poor girl! That's why she's left on the shelf and the others did a sprint.   (p. 479)

It is only by predetermining that what is central to the book is real that Bloom's language locates him for the reader in a dominant, central reality. Without that assumption Bloom's narrative, far from writing out his mind, can be seen only as a further distortion. Stephen's language provided a reconstruction of reality, perceived experience, according to a refined epistemology. This language provides an anagram of experience, of 'experience', that is, as the novel conventionally defines it: what I called above a balanced interweaving of people, thoughts and places; except that in the anagram the balance has been upset in favour of experience filtered through the point of view of one man on one day, and the interweaving has therefore been replaced by a vigorous but systematic substructure of quibbles and verbal associations, no longer a perfect mirroring of the inner world but a prism irresponsibly set between the action and the reader. In its usual form this becomes a quasi-rhetorical exercise: each paragraph opening gives the reader the narrative material which pushes the action forward, and the body of each paragraph descends into a chasm of associative material based on this opening. At its extreme the anagram becomes absolute, incantatory, and describes (like the *Portrait*'s 'incantation') a *silence*, here Bloom dozing:

O sweety all your little girlwhite up I saw dirty bracegirdle made me do love sticky we two naughty Grace darling she him half past the bed met him pike hoses frillies for Raoul to perfume your wife black hair heave under embon *señorita* young eyes Mulvey plump years dreams return tail end Agendath swoony lovey showed me her next year in drawers return next in her next her next. (p. 498)

Understanding this as such is not difficult for the reasonably careful reader; the difficulty is understanding its rationale. The *product* of an anagram is always the thing in the 'right' order: here, assuming the 'stream of consciousness' as the means of that production, the 'right' order would be the redundant one of a broadly conventional paragraph, a broadly conventional novel. But to understand the *process* of an anagram is a different problem. Here it leads us to an equation

between language and mind, the working of one indicating –
not imitating – the working of the other; and to do that
it rests on a prior equation: the less action, the more words.
This equation is one logical result of recognising the distinction between the shape of the world and the shape of
language – words constituting their own form of action in
the world, the 'writing moment'.

The contrast of this difficulty with the one we have already
encountered is plain: we are stopped by the breakdown of
Stephen's narrative to assess its underlying coherence; we
stop Bloom's narrative imperilling its breakdown. The
conclusiveness and significance of the whole depends on our
willingness to make the language secondary to a reality which
only the reality asserts. The claim that the meeting of Stephen
and Bloom is climactic and unifying is made wholly within
the person of the passive fiction-maker, Bloom. From the
detail of the fiction (which includes the texture of its parodies,
all the richness of its language, as much as what is enacted
through the language – 'invention', 'disposition' *and* 'elocu-
tion' in the jargon of classical rhetoric) we infer an active
fiction-making consciousness, the absolutism of the 'moment
of writing'; and we go on to choose in the correlative 'moment
of reading' a *Ulysses* which is the fragmenting, specifying
process of that moment, or its generalised, aesthetically unified
product.

I have so far tried to limit myself to an account that, in
relating mainly local difficulties to the whole, also relates
our empirical sense of what is 'difficult' (what is hard to
read) in Joyce's language to the conceptual difficulties (what
is complex to understand) undergirding it. In doing this I
have tried to show the tension between process and product
in Joyce's work, between what is and is not yielded through
a 'reading' based on a once-and-for-all *justification* of the
syntax (which must finally be stated in terms of theories,
'stream of consciousness' paramount, and the symbolic
structures used by Joyce as armatures), and what is yielded
through a reading which is also a constant *'justifying'* of
the syntax – using the word perhaps in the printers' sense,

a process of pulling and pushing, widening and narrowing the gap between our ideal and what is on the page; accepting that the final resolution of that gap is necessarily a false aim, and content instead with the creative 'moment of reading' parallel to (and percipient of) a 'moment of writing'. This attempt has entailed forgoing until now any coherent theoretical base for such an account, though a vocabulary demanding explanation has crept in. A sketch for such a base may now be given.

The syntax of rational, probative prose – borrowed in the narrative of most fiction – while flexible, is nevertheless based on limited criteria which underpin some key 'perceptions of language'. In conventional fiction 'plot' is the keystone of an edifice of meaning whose construction (at once linear and unitary, 'process' and 'product') makes that meaning *clear* (as a 'product' of the reading) by *controlling* the pace (our 'process' through it). Clarity and a controlled pace similarly govern the kind of 'main clause with sufficient relative clauses' structure learnt as the basis of all public discourse. On this basic model each sentence may also be said to yield, through a controlled 'process', a clear 'product'. Transferred to fiction, the probative nature of this prose is retained in that such fiction can be said to prove its meaning by 'showing' it[5] – clearly and controlledly. In such fiction 'syntax' can have no part in serious discussion; 'style', which takes its place, may be defined syntactically as a particular recurrence of conventional structures (antithesis in Jane Austen,[6] for example) or a controlled deviation from them (the authorial exclamations of Dickens, mentioned above): in both cases 'style' is seen to be a personal signature – we say, voice – put upon a public language, thought to exist prior to its artistic 'personalisation', 'vocalisation'. The illusion of the fiction can thus be said to depend on the illusion that the form of the language is 'natural'.[7] Another word losing, as a consequence of these assumptions, any part in the public discussion of literature is 'rhetoric'. The conditions of this ban are complex; but they surely owe something to the idea that public discourse is not dependent as it was hitherto on a 'rhetorical' stance (something *seen* to the public, pre-existent, preceptive and so not unmentionably 'natural'), since it merely *clarifies* and *controls* 'natural' quotidian speech. And literary language, based on the same broad assumptions, is said to be 'rhetorical' when it contravenes these criteria: ceasing to be clear (Virginia Woolf); losing control (Dickens); ignoring the decorous proportions of everyday (D.H. Lawrence).

Joyce, in *Ulysses*, does all three. For many that has been a sufficient justification for the more or less disparaging description 'rhetorical', amplified and balanced with kinder, vaguer words like 'exuberant', 'playful'. I have tried to show that the coherence behind, as well as the prevalence of, such unconventional literary behaviour can alert us instead to a broader rejection of the conventions and rationale behind such literary language. The divergence of 'process' from 'product' in the whole work has its counterpart in the syntax: 'meaning' in *Ulysses* ceases to be a product of clear sentences, and becomes a process of fitting together the difficult structures, seeing meaning in that *act* (we perform 'meaning' in the same way as we 'justify' the syntax rather than finding its justification); these difficulties work directly against our received expectations of controlled pace, creating a narrative not of action only, but of consciousness and writing themselves. 'Plot' is no longer the pitch to which 'meaning' is attuned. The ratio of plot to meaning in *Ulysses* is radically unconventional, because something else takes up the meaningful space of the fiction: words, rhetoric – words seen to be separable from action. Conventionally, language and action present one seamless fact to the reader: in *Ulysses* language, for a great part, constitutes that action.

Critical attention to this aspect of the book, perhaps largely because of Joyce's own seemingly careless iconoclasm, his increasing reliance as the book develops on larger armatures of literary self-awareness (parody rather than the syntax of the early chapters), has been slapdash. Detailed attention to *Ulysses* must always be difficult: the book's bulk, and the weight of its reputation, make criticism of it a process without product – like painting the Forth Bridge – and take it in a sense out of our hands; they certainly preclude any 'conclusive' readings, and create conditions in which to approach it at all is almost to submit to it. Perhaps this is why the book's third great obstacle, and the one most 'inside' the book itself – its language – is the most appealing to turn to at this time: its curiously fragmenting, but rich, surface promises nothing more than the fragments of an assessment, but that under such conditions is something.

Page references in brackets refer to the following editions:
James Joyce, *Dubliners* (London, 1954)
James Joyce, *A Portrait of the Artist as a Young Man* (London, 1956)
James Joyce, *Ulysses* (London, 1960)

1 As Anthony Burgess does; see *Joysprick* (London, 1973), 55
2 It hardly need be said, I hope, that this discussion – with that of the words 'paralysis' and 'Chrysostomos' – far from detracting from the more conventional discussion of their 'symbolism', in fact solidifies a base for that discussion beyond the arbitrary whim of the writer
3 Harry Levin, *James Joyce: a Critical Introduction* (London, 1944), 43
4 Joyce's own cartoon of Bloom, above which is scribbled the opening verse of the *Odyssey*, confirms this unlikely, mythically conceived Bloom; and says more than a dozen pages on the stale theme of whether the 'Ulysses' analogy is 'mock-heroic' or 'universalising' symbol. It is reproduced in Richard Ellman, *Ulysses on the Liffey* (London, 1972), frontispiece
5 The same idea is expressed forcefully by Jean Ricardou, *Problèmes du nouveau roman* (Paris, 1967), 92ff
6 Mary Lascelles, in *Jane Austen and Her Art* (Oxford, 1939), writes: 'From Johnson she may have learnt . . . a liking for antithetic phrasing, coming to perceive his antitheses closing in on his subjects as large hands may close on a creature which must be held before it can be set free; coming to distinguish this formality as one congenial to English idiom . . .' (p. 109). This seems to me both exemplary as a piece of stylistic criticism, and informed in an exemplary fashion by the kind of preconceptions I have described
7 An assumption perhaps traceable to, or merely in, the word 'language' itself: for of course the *words* are pre-existent (though *Finnegans Wake* breaks through that assumption as well) – their 'naturalness', however, is a point best left to the philosophical debate in and after the *Cratylus* – but the forms they take in a particular kind of discourse cannot be said to be 'pre-existent' in the same way, and rhetoric defines them as 'pre-existent' at the clear expense of their 'naturalness'

8 Figures of desire: narration and fiction in *To the Lighthouse*

John Mepham

I

The traditional novel is a form of representation which involves the creation of an imaginary but well-ordered fictional space. Within this space are represented the relationships, the dramas and the destinies of individual lives. There is thus concretised within the fiction the play of forces and values in terms of which, it is assumed, the apparently confused and chaotic accidents and demands of human life can be rendered intelligible. The orderliness of the fabricated story, of the human adventures which take place within the fictional space, consists for example in the consequentiality of fictional objective and subjective events and processes (i.e. that one thing leads significantly to another); and in their conclusiveness (that they come to a meaningful end).

But the orderliness of the fiction involves not only this internal orderliness but also an orderliness of its telling. For a story to be told there must be, implicitly or explicitly, a teller of it, a narrator, or a narrative voice, the voice of one who knows. The narrator who tells the story does so in order to speak his knowledge. The story is thus teleological both formally and substantially. The fiction has an end in terms of which its beginning and middle make sense. And the telling of the story has a purpose, a purpose which is prior to and independent of the fiction itself.

But what if we lack this sense of epistemological security? What if our experience seems fragmented, partial, incomplete, disordered? Then writing might be a way not of representing

149

but of creating order.⌉This would be a specifically literary order and would not be parasitic upon any belief in an order existing prior to it. For example think about the memory one might have of a person one has loved. It is possible, quite independently of literature, to give shape to, to fill out, this memory. It might be assimilated into some religious vision of life. Or it might be brought into relation with one's commitments to some very elaborated system of values, concepts and symbols (concepts and symbols which provide one with a means of expression, which enable one to say what it is to be a man or a woman, a mother, a political leader, a priest). But without such frameworks, without such means of thought and expression,⌈we might have the feeling that the remembered person escapes us, is ungraspable, cannot be contained in our minds except as a disordered flow of particular fragments of memory—we might have a sharp but all the more poignant memory of some particular scenes, some images, gestures, a tone of voice, haunting phrases, perhaps particularly significant colours and sounds.⌉These memories might be experienced as suggesting some unity which we cannot grasp, as raw materials which we might work on, condense, assemble into a form of speech worthy of their object.⌉Then we would feel, as it were, that there is something that needs to be said but that we lack the means of saying it.⌈If writing could be the means of completing the half-finished phrase, or bringing together and thereby enriching the fragments, then writing would not be primarily the telling of a story but the search for a voice.⌉Narration would not be the embodiment of some pre-existing knowledge, but the satisfaction of the desire to speak with appropriate intensity about things of which our knowledge is most uncertain.

In this essay I shall examine Virginia Woolf's *To the Lighthouse* in the light of these considerations. I shall focus on the relationship between the story that is told and the telling of it, between fiction and narration. Locating and identifying the function of the narration will help to clarify the notion of 'finding a voice', of relieving the pressure of things needing to be said.

II

How are we to distinguish between fiction and narration? The fiction is the totality of all implicitly and explicitly narrated events and processes taking place within the imaginary spatio-temporal continuum of the novel. The narration may not actually give an explanation of the fictional events but it will implicitly refer us to the kinds of causes operating in the fictional space as explanations of fictional events. When it is narrated that Mrs Ramsay died suddenly one summer we do not need to be given a medical report by the narration to know that it is implicitly attributing her death to (fictional) natural causes.

That there is an order of the narration which is different from that of the fiction is clear, even though it may not be immediately clear just what this order is or how it is functioning. ' "Yes, of course, if it's fine tomorrow," said Mrs Ramsay. "But you'll have to be up with the lark," she added' (p. 5).[1] This event opens *To the Lighthouse*. It is the first in the order of the narration. But it is not the first in the fiction—there are narrated later (in narrative time) events which precede this one (in fictional time). The narration of a novel differs both in content and in sequence, rhythm and manner of organisation from the fiction. The narration of *To the Lighthouse* includes the words 'said Mrs Ramsay', whereas the fiction does not.

Moreover the narration can bring fictional things and events into relations which they do not have in the fiction. For example it can figuratively relate them to one another. Of course figurative relations can also exist in the fiction, in the fictional subjective order, in which case the narration attributes this figurative connecting together of things to a fictional subject. But there does not need to be, and there usually is not, a complete coincidence between the figurative relations established by the narration and those established within the fiction. The order of narration is an independent order. Just what relation exists between the order of the narration and the orders of the fiction depends on the purposes of the narration.

The *telos* of the narration is expressed by the specific constructions of the narrative order. It may be, and this has usually been the case in the traditional novel, that the *telos* of the narration was to represent a *telos* in the fiction, and in this sense the order of the narration was determined by the orders of the fiction. But this does not have to be so. When this is so one could say that it is the general structures of objective or subjective reality as they are represented in the fiction which are dominant. It is there that meaning is located and will unfold, reveal itself. Real time, the time of human life, is taken to be teleological. 'Time may give you the right key to all.'[2] Narrative time, the temporal structure of the telling of the story, is determined by this presumed teleology of represented time. The story is the appropriate form for the representation of the emergence of meaning in a human life if a life itself has the form of a story. 'I thought I should die. The tale of my life seemed told. Every night, just at midnight, I used to wake from awful dreams – and the book lay open before me at the last page, where was written "Finis".'[3] But if life is not like a story then the novel should not be so either.

The main explicit play of the narration in part 1 of *To the Lighthouse* is between the fictional subjective order ('streams of consciousness') and the fictional objective or interpersonal order. The conversation with which the narration opens seems to take very little (fictional) objective time, but the narration of the first half-dozen of its spoken utterances takes place over twenty-five pages of text. The actual conversation is narrated in direct speech, and these few short sentences punctuate or interfere with the longer, more leisurely and expansive passages of subjective reflection. It is as if these spoken sentences were markers along the objective time axis, a background rhythm which marks the slow but steady progress of the fiction through time, an arrow pointing in the direction of the basic tendency of the narrative movement. Textually these markers take the form of the appearance of particular graphic devices (quotation marks) and syntactical forms ('. . . ,' said Mrs Ramsay) which contrast with the narration of inner thoughts and feelings. There are, as it were, two sequences of pulses, the one multiform (the great variety of verbs of attribution and other syntactic devices used in the narration of 'indirect speech'), expansive, irregular (some short but many very long contorted sentences), a kind of surging movement of different durations and degrees of intensity; the other more ponderous and uniform (syntactically, graphically and phonetically), the pulse of the passage of interpersonal time making itself heard, a rather dour but regular and dependable kind of sound.

The narration has transitions not only between these two orders but also, within the order of subjectivity, between the point of view of one subject and that of another. These transitions in point of view are always, as it were, internally (in the fiction) motivated. One point of view gives way to another as a result of subjective or objective movements in the fiction itself. That is to say the transitions are managed by the narration 'metonymically'. There are two main variants of this transition mechanism. In the first case one flow of subjective thought arrives, via its own internal momentum, at some other person as an object of thought or reflection. This other person can then change from being the object to being the subject of the narrated thoughts. In the second there is a physical movement in the space of the fiction which brings someone into the field of perception of the carrier of the narrated discourse, and the narration, as it were, takes the opportunity to pass the burden from the one to the other as if there had to be some excuse for doing this, as if the narration were afraid to appear in its own right, to show itself powerful enough to make up its own mind who should speak and who remain silent. There is thus achieved a kind of smooth passage from one subject to another, from one point of view to another, the narration never lifting itself out of the fictional space, being always generated from within it.

For example Mrs Ramsay is sitting at the window. She is thinking about the meaning of her life, about her son and her husband. She hears her husband, who is outside on the terrace, burst out with a dramatic recitation of some poetry. Hoping that no one has heard him she turns to see who is in the vicinity, and seeing Lily on the lawn remembers that she had promised to sit still so that her portrait might be painted. The line of her thought has thrown up and related, kept in subjective proximity, her husband and Lily Briscoe. The narrative plays with this conjoined pair (they are physically contiguous now as well as subjectively), holds them together with Mrs Ramsay in one narrative sentence that seems to be in flight across the gap between them and has not yet decided where to land, and then settles on Lily, adopts her point of view and begins to establish a new train of thought. Not only is the narrative passed across space from subject to subject; it is also about to go off on something of a tangent, away from both the space and the themes of the conversation which has been its basic home until this point. This it will achieve by having Lily actually walk away from the scene. She goes down to the beach, carrying the narration with her. This is therefore something of a major transition; it is marked by the narration starting a new section. This is how this shift is achieved:[4]

... but she |Lily Briscoe| was an independent little creature, Mrs Ramsay liked her for it, and so remembering *her* promise, she bent *her* head.

4

Indeed, *he* almost knocked *her* easel over, coming down upon her with his hands waving, shouting out 'Boldly we rode and well', but, mercifully, he turned sharp, and rode off, to die gloriously *she supposed* upon the heights of Balaclava. (p. 21)

Mrs Ramsay's thought has passed on from her husband to Lily Briscoe. So when he appears in the first sentence of the new section as the grammatical subject ('he'), it is as if he hovers in the narrative, an object waiting to be picked up in somebody's attention; or a pronoun waiting to be bracketed, to be brought within the scope of some attributive verb. The word 'her' announces the impending arrival of the fictional subject whose turn it is to do the work. The syntactic continuity between one section and the next ('her head'—'her easel') prepares and metonymically motivates a transition, a transition which is at last accomplished as the 'she' of Mrs Ramsay's attention becomes the subject of the thought about Mr Ramsay ('she supposed'). The new section can now settle down to its new sequence and its new point of view.

It is worth noting a particular feature of the management of narrative sequence in part 1 of *To the Lighthouse* as contrasted with that of part 3. In part 1 we find two short sections (sections 2 and 15) which have the function of re-establishing continuity after a narrative diversion in space and time. And we find one whole section (section 14) bracketed with round brackets and narrating a flashback. The episodes in the flashback are objectively and subjectively related to episodes narrated in surrounding sections. The round brackets fold these distant but related events back into the causal order in which they belong and emphasise, as it were, that any discontinuity has been in the narration and not in the fiction. In part 3 matters are quite different. As we shall see in more detail below, in part 3 there are short sections in *square* brackets which narrate events simultaneous in time but in no way causally or subjectively related to the events narrated in the surrounding sections. With these short sections the narration contrives to establish a *metaphoric* relationship between events which are not objectively related. So whereas in part 1 we find metonymic transitions and the narration of non-simultaneous but causally related events in round brackets, in part 3 we find metaphoric relations established by the narration of simultaneous but non-related events between square brackets. Instead of the flashback in fictional time we find a kind of flashpoint of figurative intensity in which narration of one event comes to assimilate, to hold within itself, that of a distant event in figurative, and no longer causal, unity.

So, to sum up, we have seen how the flow of the narrative in part 1 of *To the Lighthouse* from one point of view to another and from one point in fictional time to another is carefully motivated by the narration by its arrangement of continuities of thought between subjects, and by its arrangement of constellations of movement of the fictional characters in and out of one another's fields of attention. The transitions are solicited from within the fiction itself by the interpenetration of fictional objective and subjective orders. The narrative order never clearly and explicitly emerges in its own right, even though it is in fact very much at work. It covers its tracks by projecting into the fictional space the causes of its passage from episode to episode. It seems to achieve thereby a multiplicity of internal, intra-fictional perspectives which gradually fill out and enrich the portraits of the Ramsay family. But in fact this filling out would remain very partial, incomplete and disorganised were it not for the fact that the narration is, in a disguised way, also having its say, continually adding its own ordering and enriching powers to the play of forces at work in the text.

III

Who speaks in *To the Lighthouse?* The dominant narrative technique is that of indirect speech, or more accurately, of indirect bracketing or attribution. The content of narrated sentences is attributed indirectly to fictional subjects, it is narrated as meant by them. In the language of phenomenology it is their 'intentionality' which is the source of the meaning narrated. But the use of indirect attribution gives rise to an infiltration of meanings which do not have their source in the fictional subjects themselves. It is as if in the narration of fictional consciousness the narration has, so to speak, a double source; there is a contribution by the narration itself and a contribution by the fictional subject. Using direct speech there is a clear demarcation (quotation marks) between these two contributions; they can be clearly identified. A space always opens up for the narration to occupy with its commentary. It can have its say. For example if *To the Lighthouse* were more conventional and used direct speech with narrative commentary we might have found something like the following on the opening page: ' "It is settled", thought James, "the expedition will take place", his boyish mind rushing impetuously into the future, his wishful imagination allowing no obstacle to form in reality to the satisfaction of his desires.' With indirect attribution, on the other hand, there is no such space automatically provided. We remain within the fiction and the contribution of the narration can be disguised, hidden away. Let us examine some of the ways this indeterminacy of attribution is operative in *To the Lighthouse*, always bearing in mind that the basic, underlying principle involved is that of the duality between the partial, fragmented, manifest subjective order and the semantic unity and density of the latent narrative order.

Consider the following example of 'indeterminacy of scope'.

All the way down to the beach they had lagged behind together, though he bade them 'Walk up, walk up', without speaking. Their heads were bent down, their heads were pressed down by some remorseless gale. Speak to him they could not. They must come; they must follow.   (p. 185)

The suppleness of attributive technique is such that the narration can, as here, accomplish a transition from one subject to others (from Mr Ramsay who gives orders to his son and daughter, who feel obliged to obey) with no recourse to new explicitly attributive verbs, but via the continuity of reference of the pronouns ('them', 'their', 'they'). From being the objects ('them') they become the subjects ('they') via a transitional sentence ('Their heads were bent down . . .') which is not attributed to anybody in the fiction but which yet seems to begin to speak on their behalf. There is a suppressed attributive at work ('*They felt that* they could not speak to him') which could equally be taken to have this transitional sentence within its scope ('They felt that their heads were bent down . . .'). But since this attributive verb is both suppressed and ambiguous in scope there is also another possibility; that this transitional sentence might be attributed not to a fictional subject at all, but to a narrative voice, a narrative voice which is so close to the fiction, so intimately identified with fictional points of view, and which so seldom emerges in its own right explicitly to carry the burden of intentionality, that it is as if its existence were a closely guarded secret. The indeterminacy of attribution is exploited throughout the narration in the services of the narrative order. It allows the *telos* of the narration to be quietly at work, working on and through the consciousness of the fictional subjects, and through the flow from one to another of them, while appearing merely to be reporting what they think.

Indeterminacy or ambiguity in the scope of an attribution is very commonly used, as in the above example, as a means of inserting into the narrative a figurative description. One might see the description as conflating a contribution by the fictional subject (whose attention selects the object and determines the outlines and tone of the thought) and a contribution by the narration which performs a figurative elaboration of the thought. The narrative contribution not only adds force to the description but allows it to be articulated, in ways to be examined below, with descriptions elsewhere in the narration, to be placed within the general semantic space of the text.

. . . this sound . . . which for the most part *beat a measured and soothing tattoo to her thoughts and seemed* consolingly to repeat over and over again as she sat with the children the words of some old cradle song, murmured by nature, 'I am guarding you—I am your support', but at other times suddenly and unexpectedly, especially when her mind raised itself slightly from the task actually in hand, had no such kindly meaning, but *like a ghostly roll of drums remorselessly beat the measure of life,* made *one think* of the destruction of the island and its engulfment in the sea . . . (p. 19)

This passage is extracted from one long sentence (which lasts for nearly a full page) of extraordinary craftsmanship. The sentence begins in typical 'stream of consciousness' manner, narrating what Mrs Ramsay could hear at a particular moment one afternoon. In the section extracted here it slips effortlessly into the iterative mood, no longer narrating a singular stream of consciousness but giving the narration of the moment depth by locating it in the context of the generality of the subject's experience and its contrasting moods. The narration fills out, provides extra dimensions of meaning and association on behalf of the subject and from her point of view, in this case by expanding the temporal scope of the experience, putting it in touch with its history. There has been a repetition of experience resulting in a pattern of traces with which, each time, the renewed experience can resonate.

The attributives within the subordinate iterative clauses are 'seemed' and 'think'. Each of them *explicitly* brackets the immediately following relatively prosaic expression (repetition of some cradle song, destruction of the island), Mrs Ramsay's own contribution to capturing the meaning for her of the sound of the waves. And each attributive *implicitly*, ambiguously brackets an immediately preceding, highly charged figurative account of the meaning of the sounds ('beat a measured and soothing tattoo to her thoughts', 'a ghostly roll of drums remorselessly beat the measure of life') in which the narration speaks for Mrs Ramsay, saying, as do the poems she hears later that day, 'quite easily and naturally what had been in her mind . . . while she said different things' (p. 127).

Sometimes it is a matter of indeterminacy of subject. In this case the attribution, while suggesting that the intention has an intra-fictional and not a narrative source, does not unambiguously identify this source.

Mrs Ramsay, who had been sitting loosely, folding her son in her arm, braced herself, and, half turning, *seemed* to raise herself with an effort, and at once to pour erect into the air a rain of energy . . . (p. 44)

In this passage, which will be examined in greater detail below, an attributive verb, 'seemed', floats free. To whom did Mrs Ramsay seem thus? The word 'seemed' locates the ensuing intention within the fictional space (in a way the alternative 'raised herself' would not; if there is some seeming going on there must be someone in the fiction to do it), but does not provide a subject for it. The nearest candidate for the role of subject here is James, who is the subject of the immediately preceding passage and who is physically appropriately located in fictional space. Is the absence of explicit attribution here, then, merely a stylistic variation that poses no problem, since the search for a fictional subject to be the bearer of this thought can readily find James to hand for the job? In fact, however, one would hesitate to believe of James that he was the sole author of such a complex figurative response to his mother's movement.

. . . a rain of energy, a column of spray, *looking* at the same time animated and alive as if all her energies were being fused into force, burning and illuminating . . . (p. 44)

This is not just a matter of psychological realism but of recognising a general principle at work in the narration whereby the narration, as in the above examples, both speaks from the point of view of a fictional subject, occupies his place, and gives expression in its own words to what is for him too dense a feeling to be captured in words. The narration provides him with his own voice, makes available to him, for example, images which he would recognise as expressive of the force and content of his experience. And in fact, in this case, there is a repetition of these same images, only this time grammatically attributed explicitly to James. '. . . James *felt* all her strength flaring up to be drunk and quenched by the beak of brass . . .' (p. 45). But this explicit grammatical attribution hides an indeterminacy of another kind. 'Felt' has two meanings. In 'James felt X' there is an ambiguity as to whether X is the object of his consciousness ('James felt a stabbing pain in his back'), or the cause of the feeling ('James felt the gamma rays penetrating the epidermis in the lower dorsal region'). This duality of meaning is certainly being exploited in the quoted passage in order to leave open the implicit gap between consciousness and expression.

It is also worth noting briefly an example of indeterminacy of mode. In this case the narration attributes meanings to a subject while remaining indefinite about the mode of consciousness involved. It may even be suggested that it is not consciousness that is involved at all, but something deeper, less accessible.

Mrs Ramsay felt . . . some disagreeable sensation. Not that . . . she knew precisely what it came from; nor did she let herself put into words her dissatisfaction when she realised . . . how it came from this: she did not like, even for a second, to feel finer than her husband. (p. 46)

The narration accomplishes the seemingly impossible task of

putting into Mrs Ramsay's words a thought that she herself did not put into words; of making precise connections and at the same time denying that the connections had been made. The contradiction is, of course, not a fault of narration but its skill in capturing the subjective contradiction involved in what Sartre would call 'Bad Faith'.

'. . . she had had experiences which need not happen to everyone (she did not name them to herself)' (p. 70). This involves an indeterminacy of mode in that we are told that although Mrs Ramsay did not name to herself her past experiences she nevertheless somehow had them in mind. The narration enters with her into a conspiracy of silence, while at the same time pointing in a certain direction (by virtue of what we have heard that 'people said' about her).

We have examined some of the features of the narration of *To the Lighthouse* in order to reveal the presence of a narrative order and its modes of operation. This narrative order is an order of meanings, meanings which cannot be attributed to fictional subjects. It imposes order and density. We can now examine in more detail just how this order and density of meaning constitute a framework within which each fictional subjective intention is located. Let us take first one particular fictional subject, James, and examine the form of unity, of coherence, of the narration of his experience and development. Later we shall see how this unity transcends each individual subject, how it embraces them all. Moreover we shall see that the narrative order creates density of expression not only by providing a trans-individual framework of meanings, but also by virtue of the fact that this framework is constructed simultaneously at many different *levels* of meaning. That the narration adds density of *metaphor* we have already seen. But the elaborate framework of metaphor is consolidated by the simultaneous exploitation of other means of expression in a way that is characteristic of poetry. The narration is expressive at the levels of figurative, phonetic, metrical and rhythmic meaning. The intensity of the narration thus has its source in a double unification: the unification of the voices of the various individual fictional subjects, and the multiple over-determination of many levels of meaning.

161

IV

James, the Ramsays' youngest son, is represented in part 1 as, at the age of seven, tied to his mother. He spends his time physically close to her, lives in the world of play, imagination and fairy story, and is emotionally dependent on her. The tense triangle of James, his mother and his father is one of typical Oedipal geometry. He hates his father, yet already bears within his body a potential and competitive identification with him. In fictional episodes where he is present he moves between sitting on the floor with his mother, holding scissors, cutting out pictures from a catalogue or listening to her read the story of 'The Fisherman's Wife', and '*standing* between her knees, very *stiff*' (p. 44) as his father tends to stand, rigid, straight-backed, when expressing bodily the male heroism of his lonely struggle from A to Z. James's world of joyful fantasy, into which falls his mother's promise of a trip to the Lighthouse, is contrasted with his body's foreshadowing of his future in a man's '*stern*' world, in law, politics or business, so that 'he appeared the image of *stark* and uncompromising *severity*, with his high forehead and his fierce blue eyes' (p. 6). His father joins them, '*standing*, as now, lean as a *knife*, narrow as the *blade* of one', and (the narration slipping into the iterative to emphasise the general significance of his posture) 'Mr Ramsay would *straighten* his back and narrow his little blue eyes upon the horizon' and contemplate 'the passage to that fabled land where our brightest hopes are extinguished, our frail barks founder in darkness' (p. 6). The drama of these contrasts leaves James insecure; his mother at one time 'transferred to him what she felt for her husband', only later to abandon him when Mr Ramsay's demands become imperious.

These early (in narrative time) descriptions of James's position in the triangle with his mother and father are already firmly tied in to a whole system of expression that we are not yet in a position to recognise. As we read, traces form. Around them, as the narration proceeds, will gradually crystallise a series of marks, points of resonance. I have italicised just some of these nodal points in the preceding paragraph. There are significant bodily postures, images (the knife, the sea journey), contrasts (brightness/darkness) and sounds in the narration (picked out here in bold type): **st**ark, **st**raighten, **st**ern, **st**and.

In the key episode, as far as James is concerned, Mr Ramsay pokes his son's leg with a stick, demands and receives emotional support from his wife. James's hatred of his father increases in intensity.

Standing between her knees, very **st**iff, James felt all her strength flaring up to be **dr**unk and **qu**enched by the **be**ak of **br**ass, the arid scimitar of the male, which **sm**ote mercilessly, again and again, demanding sympathy . . . James, as he **st**ood **st**iff between her knees, felt her rise in a rosy-flowered fruit tree laid with leaves and dancing boughs into which the **be**ak of **br**ass, the arid scimitar of his father, the egotistical man, plunged and **sm**ote, demanding sympathy.   (p. 44)

In this and in the surrounding passages and paragraphs we suddenly hear the narration transformed into poetry. We hear repetitions of metrically striking phrases ('standing stiff', 'beak of brass', 'the arid scimitar of the male', 'plunged and smote' and so on). It is as if narrative space and time are multiplying themselves. Things which are singular and short-lived in the fiction become multiple and protracted in the narration, as if their fictional intensity were forcing an expansion of narrative dimensions. Repetition slows down fictional time for us, and opens up its pores and allows its full force to swell through into the narration.

We can hear also in these pages the sudden extra significance of rhythm and of contrasts of rhythm. There is an alteration or intercourse between long, breathless, even sentences (the female, giving, the fountain of sympathy):

. . . to be taken within the circle of life, warmed and soothed, to have his senses restored to him, his barrenness made fertile, and all the rooms of the house made full of life – the drawing-room; behind the drawing-room the kitchen; above the kitchen the bedrooms; and beyond them the nurseries; they must be furnished, they must be filled with life.   (p. 44)

and short, jabbing, thrusting phrases (the male, prodding, demanding): '. . . the beak of brass, the arid scimitar of the male, which smote mercilessly, again and again, demanding sympathy.' There is therefore a kind of mutual heightening of effect as meaning and rhythm come together. There is signification at the level of the sound of reading the text. And a further dimension is yet to be added. There is signification even at the level of the bodily 'performance' of the text, in the way in which it controls the breathing of the reader, his physical reception of its meanings. For example it is natural to end with a kind of sigh of expiration when one reads the following sentence:

Immediately, Mrs Ramsay seemed to fold herself together, one petal closed in another, and the whole fabric fell in exhaustion upon itself, so that she had only strength enough to move her finger, in exquisite abandonment to exhaustion, across the page of Grimm's fairy story, while there throbbed through her, like the pulse in a spring which has expanded to its full width and now gently ceases to beat, the rapture of successful creation. (p. 45)

The effect is achieved by the regular spacing between the commas (the petals folded in) leading to a doubling of this space in the penultimate phrase (it expands to its full width). There is a sense, at the level of one's breathing, of a completion of a process, of the waves beating a measure and then spreading out across the beach.

In the narration of this key episode traces laid down earlier now thicken out and new deposits are formed. A pattern begins to become clear, a unifying framework beneath the colour of the surface. I shall describe some of the shapes of the framework. Firstly the metaphors. To the knife blade is now added the bird. Mr Ramsay has become a metallic bird of prey. James hates 'the twang and twitter of his father's emotion, vibrating round them', and sees the curve of his father's movement as that of a beak of brass and an arid scimitar (metaphors which are repeated three times in the space of a page).

Secondly the male postures and gestures. To the earlier insistence on the stiff verticality of the male (much repeated in this present episode) is added a gesture. It is Mr Ramsay's threatening, aggressive prodding movement. It is aimed physically at his son's bare legs (repeated three times in quick succession) and figuratively at his wife's breast ('plunged and smote, demanding sympathy', repeated three times). This gesture, the knife blade and the target (James's bare legs) are held together in James's mind and add up no doubt to a threat calculated to stir his deepest anxieties. (By contrast with the verticality and the cutting gesture the female is sitting open-legged and is a fountain of spray and a rain of energy.)

Thirdly the phonetic pattern. The significance of the **st-** heard earlier is now confirmed and strengthened: **s**e**v**e**rity**/ **sterility**, **standing**, **stiff**, **smote**. (By contrast Mrs Ramsay is associated with the softer **spray**, and with **strength** in which the initial **st-** is neutralised and smoothed out by the **r** and the final **th**. The effect of Mrs Ramsay in calming her husband's fears and taming his aggression is to **soothe** him, so that his **senses** are **restored**, and again **restored**, **renewed**. Again the softer sounds combine with the harsh male sounds to neutralise them. The main female sound is the **f**, of which the insistence in these passages is extremely forceful, so that when the intercourse between the couple is over it is no surprise that Mr Ramsay should be described as **satisfied**, so that even at the phonetic level he is 'filled with life'.)

To this pattern of sounds is now added, however, an extra dimension with the appearance of a series of much-repeated combinations of **b**, **d**, **k** and **r** sounds (**beak** of **brass**, **barren** and **bare**, **drunk** and **quenched**). Later in the text these sounds will be found absorbed into the play of colour contrasts, most notably that between **black** and **blue**, the former, as by now we should confidently anticipate, being male, the latter female.

This framework, then, is that within which the clash between mother and father concerning the trip to the Lighthouse is set. The disappointment that Mr Ramsay causes his son is keen. As his mother knows, 'He will remember that all his life.' But the *form* of his memory of the incident, the aspects of it that are retained, is determined not by its literal, surface content but by the hidden framework of gesture, image and sound within which it has been captured in the narration on his behalf. And it will show itself in later years in the rhetoric of his perception and the organisation of his figuring imagination before it is consciously recalled as an incident from his childhood. This we shall see in the narration of part 3, which, as far as James is concerned, recounts an interlocking series of processes: the trip to the Lighthouse, a turning-point in his relationship with his father, the recall of his earlier experience, and an emerging sense of sureness about his own identity, the assumption of his manhood.

Ten years later it is a look on his sister's face which he suddenly recognises which triggers the slow, difficult process of recall. As Cam surrenders to her father's demands, 'he watched a look come upon her face, a look he remembered. They look down, he thought, at their knitting or something. Then suddenly they look up' (p. 191). Just that; a look, a movement, an indefinite 'they', capturing in his mind a moment of female surrender that had left him on his own.

There was a flash of blue, he remembered, and then somebody sitting with him laughed, surrendered, and he was very angry. It must have been his mother, he thought, sitting on a low chair, with his father standing over her. He began to search among the infinite series of impressions which time had laid down . . . (p. 192)

It was his mother, then, and a pattern of postures, a geometry of relationships, and a colour, a flash of blue.

With the memory of the childhood episode still incomplete but working in his mind, he watches his father turning the pages of a book and something about the gestures of his hand strikes him:

And James felt that each page was turned with *a peculiar gesture aimed at him*: now assertively, now commandingly; now with the intention of making people pity him; and all the time, as his father read and turned one after another of those little pages, James kept dreading the moment when he would look up and *speak sharply* to him . . . (p. 208)

166

The connection is made between this gesture and the earlier episode, not consciously but as an anxiety which finds its way into his inner speech ('sharply'). This quiet reminder of the blade is a hinge on which his thought turns, its curve taking him straight back to the central image: '. . . and if he does, James thought, then I shall take a knife and strike him to the heart.'

The threatening knife is an image in which James had always captured his ambivalent feelings for his father, fearing and hating him (his father the despot, 'making people do what they did not want, *cutting off* their right to speak'), yet also wishing to be like him. His ambivalence towards his father is also an ambivalence towards his own masculinity and towards the memory of his mother. He remembers that when his mother deserted him to turn towards his father he was left '*impotent*, ridiculous, *sitting* on the floor grasping a pair of *scissors*' (p. 212).

James remembers in his body that earlier experience, the psychic scar concretised in the form of a physical feeling, a trace, on his bare legs. The cutting movement of the beak is displaced, in his memory; the target is no longer his mother but himself, and the identity of the gesture with that aimed at his legs, implicit before, is now made manifest by this displacement and clearly indicates the real site of his anxiety. But the meaning of it has become generalised, not quite consciously, into a struggle against the oppressiveness of paternal law (narrated with a marvellous use of indeterminacy of attributive mode):

Only now, as he grew older, and *sat* staring at his father in an *impotent* rage, it was not him, that old man reading, whom he wanted to kill, but it was the thing that descended on him – without his knowing it perhaps: that fierce sudden **black**-winged harpy, with its talons and its **beak** all *cold* and *hard*, that **struck** and **struck** at you (he could feel the **beak** on his **bare** legs, where it had **struck** when he was a child) . . .   (p. 209)

The narration of the struggle to bring the memory to consciousness is interwoven with that of the approach to the Lighthouse. (The connection between the childhood

167

episode of the attack by his father and desertion by his mother and the disappointment about the promised trip to the Lighthouse suddenly comes back to James.) The inner drama is projected on to the objective event and shapes the narration of it. The Lighthouse, by virtue of this contingent episodic relation to the psychological drama, is invested with meaning. It is caught up in the network of contrasting images and sounds. As they approach the Lighthouse James sees that it is a '*tower, stark* and *straight*', '*barred* with *black* and white'; and again 'a *stark tower* on a *bare rock*'. A third time this pattern is repeated, this time with the addition of the waves breaking over the rocks which is so significant an object of descriptive variation throughout the text. 'Indeed they were very close to the Lighthouse now. There it *loomed up*, **stark** and **straight**, *glaring* white and **black**, and one could see the waves **brea**king in white *splinters* like *smashed glass upon the* **rocks**'[2] (p. 230). Apart from its patterns this passage is also interesting from the point of view of attribution. The nearest intra-fictional attribution is 'James thought' in the previous paragraph. It is separated from this passage by a fresh paragraph and by the non-attributive 'they were' of the first sentence. To this indeterminacy of scope is added an indeterminacy of subject, for when the attribution eventually arrives in this passage it is to 'one'. Although it is clearly *James*'s perception of the waves and the Lighthouse that is at stake (and this becomes even more clear when seen in contrast with other descriptions of the waves breaking on the rocks), it is very carefully withheld from clear attribution to him since it is the *narration* of his perception, and thereby the contrasts and patterns that are established between the narration of different subjectivities, that are the source of the play of narrational sounds. What *James* can hear is waves breaking on rocks; what *we* can hear is the valorisation of certain consonants in the description.

The tension of the contrasts, the polarity, the unresolved ambivalence is great; 'the strain became acute'. Suspended between past and future, mother and father, male and female, childhood and adulthood, he is powerless, impotent: '. . . powerless to flick off these grains of misery which settled on his mind one after another. A rope seemed to bind him there, and his father had knotted it and he could only escape by taking a knife and plunging it. . .' (p. 213). This is the form in which his body and mind have been marked by their past; grains of misery, a knot: little things, on the surface, the movement of a hand, colours, sounds, but so condensed that they add up to a contradiction that holds him paralysed in its grip.

Finally the knot is cut through. The Lighthouse focuses the puzzle for him, confirms 'some obscure feeling of his about his own character'. He rejects the facile sentimentality and optimism which he now associates, as does his father, with the female view of things. He is released from the infantile world of the yellow-eyed Lighthouse, and at last joins his father, to gaze unflinchingly, but rather happily, at the impersonality of nature and the certainty of death.

V

Throughout the fiction of *To the Lighthouse* waves break on rocks. Each time they do so the narration makes the same series of little moves. It goes from determinate attribution (' . . . James thought') to a new paragraph which starts with a non-attributed sentence with a plural subject ('They were . . .'); and then into a description indeterminately attributed to 'one'. This pattern of narrative movement (James thought → they were → one could see, in the example involving James discussed above) is repeated systematically. So we have a common fictional object of description (waves breaking) and a common pattern of narrative moves. But it is like a theme and variations in music, for each time the description varies depending on which intra-fictional subject is contributing his or her voice to it. The 'one' on which the narration settles each time characterises that indeterminate location, at the intersection of the narrative order and the fictional order, at which is effected a fusion between a fictional subject's selective and forming vision and the framework of steel which clamps it firmly in its place within the semantic space of the narrative order. The case of James has been discussed above. Let us examine a few of the other variants.

1 *Cam*

Cam's version of the scene comes very close to that of her brother (they are nearing the Lighthouse), and the contrast with it is all the greater because the two 'voices' with their characteristic marks have been alternating throughout many of the sections of part 3. The density of association of Cam's own voice and the contrast with that of James is therefore very striking.

But you've got it now, *Cam thought.*

They had tacked, and they were sailing swiftly, buoyantly on long rocking waves which handed them on from one to another with an extraordinary lilt and exhilaration beside the reef. On the left a row of rocks showed brown through the water which thinned and became greener and on one, a higher rock, a wave incessantly broke and spurted a little column of drops which fell down in a shower. *One could hear* the slap of the water and the patter of falling drops and a kind of hushing and hissing sound from the waves rolling and gambolling and slapping the rocks as if they were wild creatures who were perfectly free and tossed and tumbled and sported like this for ever. (p. 235)

While James is figuratively and phonetically associated with his father, Cam is equally so with their mother (*'fell* down in a *shower'*, '*falling drops'*, 'a *column* of drops', '*slap'*). Her vision is pastoral (brown, green, wild creatures). The 'rolling', 'gambolling' and 'slapping' of her waves contrasts strongly both figuratively and phonetically with those of James, which 'break' in 'white splinters like smashed glass'. The water has become a 'little column of drops which fell down in a shower'; it has been transformed into some mixed vision of a waterfall and a shower of rain. Any threat in the waves has been tamed by this selection of colour, sound and figure. The description is associated, as was that of James, with what one might take to be a semi-conscious recall of her mother and of a childhood scene.

Her hand cut a trail in the sea, as her mind made the green
swirls and streaks into patterns and, numbed and shrouded, wandered in imagination in that underworld of waters where the pearls
stuck in clusters to white sprays, where in the green light a change
came over one's entire mind and one's body shone half transparent
enveloped in a green cloak. (p. 207)

This is equivalent to James's way of thinking ('without his
knowing it perhaps') of his father as a black-winged harpy,
an imaginative vision formed in that 'underworld of waters'
in which traces of childhood are stored as coloured curves
('swirls and streaks'), and where Cam's mind fashions a
ghostly green figure in a cloak.

The source of this figure is to be found in that childhood
scene where Mrs Ramsay covered James's boar's skull with
her green shawl and soothed Cam to sleep with talk of animals
and country scenes (hence the 'hushing', in the sound of
the waves). The figure of her mother here is very complex,
for Cam's mind is playing both with the theme of death
(the transparent, ghostly quality of the figure, the words
'numbed' and 'shrouded', the boar's skull) and also with that
of identification with her mother ('a change came over one's
entire mind and one's body shone . . .', the 'one' here hiding
the identity of the figure and allowing it the ambiguity of
dead mother and imaginary Cam).

Thus the web of associations is so dense that there can
be contained in Cam's waterfall and James's broken glass
a whole world of difference – between the little girl whose
mother shielded her from the sight of death with stories
of pastoral bliss, and the little boy who would not have
the skull removed, and who hated his father so fiercely that
he longed to kill him with an axe.

2 *Mr and Mrs Ramsay*

With the Ramsay parents the waves breaking on the rocks
appear not in perception but as metaphor. There are two
versions, one a kind of inversion of the other. Mr Ramsay's
angry outburst at Mrs Ramsay is described as a downpour,
Mr Ramsay smashing down on his wife, who is left passive

and helpless. By contrast Mrs Ramsay's outpouring of sympathy for her husband is described as a fountain and a shower, the whole curve of the motion of the water thrown up by the rocks, with emphasis on the upward force of it; it sustains Mr Ramsay, fills him with life. Mr Ramsay's version comes as he dismisses any hopes for the trip to the Lighthouse; he yells 'Damn you!' at his wife: '. . . dazed and blinded, she bent her head as if to let the pelt of jagged hail, the drench of dirty water, bespatter her unrebuked. There was nothing to be said' (p. 38). The words 'pelt', 'jagged', 'drench', 'dirty' and 'bespatter' need no further comment.

Mrs Ramsay's version is very long and becomes extremely elaborate metaphorically and phonetically. It is probably, of all sections of the text, the one in which the general principles of narrative description which I have been discussing are most manifestly in evidence. Parts of this section have already received comment above.

Mrs Ramsay, who had been sitting loosely, folding her son in her arm, braced herself, and, half turning, seemed to raise herself with an effort, and at once to pour erect into the air a rain of energy, a column of spray, looking at the same time animated and alive as if all her energies were being fused into force, burning and illuminating (quietly though she sat, taking up her stocking again), and into this delicious fecundity, this fountain and spray of life, the fatal sterility of the male plunged itself, like a beak of brass, barren and bare . . . It was sympathy he wanted, to be assured of his genius, first of all, and then to be taken within the circle of life, warmed and soothed, to have his senses restored to him, his barrenness made fertile, and all the rooms of the house made full of life – the drawing-room; behind the drawing-room the kitchen; above the kitchen the bedrooms; and beyond them the nurseries; they must be furnished, they must be filled with life. (p. 44)

I have already commented above on some aspects of this and surrounding passages – on metre and rhythm; on the phonetic pattern in as much as it relates to the 'male' aspect of the polarity (the play of **b**/**k**/**d**/**t** sounds and the variations and combinations of the **s** sound; **s**/**d** and **s**/**t** contrasted with **s**/**th** and **s**/**f**); and on the 'male' metaphor series. I shall now point out some other aspects of these passages that are central in the functioning of the narration, in particular those which are associated with Mrs Ramsay.

Firstly the phonetics: it is worth adding to what I have said before one little detail, which illustrates a procedure of phonetic variation that I have not so far mentioned. It is a phonetic variation on the male phonetic themes. Compare, from the present passage, 'drunk and quenched', with the 'drench of dirty water' which appears in the inverted form of the passage (Mr Ramsay's version, quoted above). The former describes the male curving down to drink from the female, the latter describes the male downpour on to the submissive female rock. The sound elements **dr, ench, d**, and **w** occur in both. But the repeated **t** sound of Mr Ramsay's version has become now a repeated **k** sound in Mrs Ramsay's version. This change corresponds to the change of central metaphor from 'pelt' to 'beak'. Mr Ramsay has changed from a downpour to a metallic bird and as the metaphors change the sounds change with them. This is the music of Mr Ramsay and his variations. The equivalent for his wife is her transformation from oppressed and silent ('there was nothing to be said') to life-giving, a rain of energy. She is **'dazed'** in the former description, whereas in the latter her energies are **'fused'** into force, the substitution of **f** for **d** again strengthening the contrast of metaphor.

It is this **f**, of course, which is the most striking feature of these pages. Nowhere else in the text is a phonetic marker used in so concentrated a way. Its appearances are numerous: 'fecundity', 'fountain', 'heart of life', 'flaring up', 'full', 'filled', 'fold', 'flowered', 'fruit tree'. There are alliterations ('fused into force') and inversions ('filled with life'). There are repetitions ('life', repeated five times, 'flashing' three times, 'full' twice and 'filled' twice). And there are combinations with other significant sounds (**'force'**, **'circle of life'**, **'furnished'**, **'satisfied'**). And there are combinations which echo the struggle between the male and the female (**'fatal sterility'** → **'barrenness made fertile'**, the **f** neutralised by the dominant **t** and **st** in the former, but retaining its strength against the weaker male forces in the latter).

Secondly the metaphors: the metaphoric texture of these pages is extremely rich. This is because it is not only a matter of a *series* of metaphors coming rapidly one after the other. The metaphors are consolidated, interlocked, by metonymic transition words, words that have a place in more than one metaphor and therefore enable the text to slide smoothly from one to another. The interweaving is so thorough that the fabric is seamless. The main series of metaphors is as follows: first there is the fountain of spray, which is drunk, which is delicious, which leaves Mr Ramsay satisfied, filled like a child; these words then serve to shift the metaphor from that of the rain shower, the waves, the water, to that of a child at its mother's breast. This constitutes a displacement from James to his father and this is mirrored in Mrs Ramsay's movement: from folding her son in her arm she half turns to the father. The metaphor of maternal nourishment (interlocked with that of the prodding beak of the male at the breast) is enriched by the dimensions of warmth, comfort and protection ('warmed and soothed', 'surround and protect'), and by means of this expansion of the metaphor there is a consolidation with the theme of the house. The house is drawn into the net to become a kind of physical projection and expansion of the mother's body, which is 'the circle of life' and is 'furnished' and 'filled with life'.

The combination of erect, life-giving maternal breast and the emphasis on fertility, fecundity and life inevitably introduce a kind of background of associations with the sexual, orgasmic aspects of this coming together of man and wife. This sexual theme is present in the contrasting rhythms and metres already mentioned. It is also present in a series of words which function simultaneously in several of these strands of metaphor ('pulse', 'throb', 'erect', 'aglow', 'she bade him take his ease there, go in and out, enjoy himself'). There is a curious sexual reversal at work: the sterile male with his curved scimitar contrasts with the female, who is 'erect' and who fertilises the male with a 'rain of energy', a 'column of spray'. The boy meanwhile, from whom female attention has been diverted, remains unnoticed 'between her knees, very stiff'. The sexuality of the incident is emphasised again at the end when Mrs Ramsay 'seemed to fold herself together, one petal closed in another, and the whole fabric fell in exhaustion upon itself' while the throbbing pulse gently ceases to beat. This same combination of sterile male and pulsating female engaged in the labour of creation occurs again later (p. 96) when Mrs Ramsay notes again 'the sterility of men', and taking upon herself the task of creation feels 'that old familiar pulse' beating in her. Weaving in and out of the passage are a host of secondary metaphors, and some of the words which are associated with several of them act as a kind of cement which keeps the whole seething, figurating cauldron from shattering. Note especially the mechanical and physical metaphors – the heat engine, the piston, the spring, the machine – located in such words as 'burning', 'fuse', 'force', 'energy', 'spring', 'pulse'. They help to incorporate that mechanical, metallic beak into the fabric.

Enclosing all these metaphors, the unifying link of the whole assemblage, is 'the rapture of successful creation'. It is this figure which allows connections to be made with other incidents in Mrs Ramsay's day (notably the dinner party) and also with Lily Briscoe and her art. Above the level of the particular metaphors here and embracing them all is a set of abstract themes, themes which are also those in terms of which Lily thinks about the problem of artistic creation. There are the oppositions between life and death, presence and absence, sterility and fertility, fullness and emptiness, and the abstract process of creating unity out of disorder, harmony out of imbalance, permanence out of instability. Mrs Ramsay is figured as one who creates, in the fleeting order of interpersonal relationships, momentary harmonies; who fashions out of the material of the human gathering beautiful but temporary little works of art.

VI

Whereas the narrative order of *To the Lighthouse* is, then, coherent, unified, semantically saturated, the subjective fictional order is characterised rather by instability, ambiguity, confusion and contradiction. The fictional subjects live predominantly in an interrogative mood and suffer a sense of inadequacy of expression.

> And she wanted to say not one thing, but everything. Little words that broke up the thought and dismembered it said nothing. 'About life, about death; about Mrs Ramsay'—no, she thought, one could say nothing to nobody. The urgency of the moment always missed its mark. Words fluttered sideways and struck the object inches too low. Then one gave it up; then the idea sunk back again; then one became like most middle-aged people, cautious, furtive, with wrinkles between the eyes and a look of perpetual apprehension. For how could one express in words these emotions of the body? express that emptiness there?   (p. 202)

But although the narrative order organises the fictional subjectivities into a system of expression and therefore, in a sense, provides them with fullness of speech, it is important to note that it does this without providing any answers to the questions the fictional subjects are always asking.

In the fiction contradictions abound. Questions go unanswered. Judgements are uncertain. There is no extra-fictional resolution of the contradictions, reply to the questions, verification of the judgements. There is unity but it is not the unity of an external narrative identity, nor is it the unity of some doctrine or system of values or view of life. Fictional subjectivity is often, very often, represented in the interrogative mode. 'But what have I done with my life?' asks Mrs Ramsay. 'Will it last?' asks her husband. 'What about love?' asks Lily Briscoe. Is love the most barbaric of human passions or is it a fine and beautiful thing?

> Such was the complexity of things. For what happened to her, especially staying with the Ramsays, was to be made to feel violently two opposite things at the same time: that's what you feel, was one; that's what I feel was the other, and then they fought together in the mind, as now.   (p. 118)

But the fight is never finished. There is no coming down once for all on one side or the other. The narration does not step in to arbitrate, to pronounce, to choose. It narrates minds in movement, it attempts to catch the movement, to represent it, not to stop it. It concerns itself with recounting the tactics employed by those restless minds when faced with contradictions and with the insolubility of life's puzzles. But it never steers them into situations where answers can be given. On the contrary:

Well then, well then? she asked, somehow expecting the others to go on with the argument, as if in an argument like this one threw one's own little bolt which fell short obviously and left the others to carry it on. So she listened again to what they were saying in case they should throw any light upon the question of love.

'Then,' said Mr Bankes, 'there is that liquid the English call coffee.' (p. 119)

There is, within the fiction, an analogue of the narrative order. It is Lily Briscoe's painting. Lily's is certainly a mind on which the shadows of unanswerable questions fall. But her painting does not have the function for her of providing solutions in the form of answers to her questions. Her painting is unity, it is harmony, and it satisfies an almost physical need, a need to catch her vision. But it answers no questions.

. . . the old question which traversed the sky of the soul perpetually, the vast, the general question which was apt to particularise itself at such moments as these, when she released faculties that had been on the strain, stood over her, paused over her, darkened over her. What is the meaning of life? That was all – a simple question; one that tended to close in on one with years. The great revelation had never come. The great revelation perhaps never did come. (p. 183)

There is no settling on a solution. There is not, either in the fiction or in the narrative order, any pronouncement: Life is that! The narration does not have a truth as its *telos*; it registers in words the effects of desire. The narration announces no choices except the choice of art itself, in which the restless questioning of minds, wandering in places where their concepts have no power to order things, is represented in a fabric of figurative prose. If there is unity it is because 'a light here requires a shadow there' and not because a meaning has been found.

Art, then, can capture the pregnant experience, the experience which is intense but in which speech fails, in which the order that is somehow potentially there remains obscure, amorphous, fragmentary. The archetype in modern literature of the pregnant experience is that of Proust savouring the odour of his madeleine and *tilleul*. This one small experience, this odour, contains a whole world of meaning which makes itself felt but which remains mute. The experience is (as is James's recognition of a look on his sister's face) pregnant with memory. But as we have seen, this is not the literal memory of one scene but a memory of which the forms and shapes are expressive of the whole drama of a life. It contains in a dense and unreadable way the hidden outlines of his feelings, and of the figurative perceptions in which these outlines are projected on to the world; it contains the geometry of his relationships with others. Proust's experience of the odour does not simply trigger a photographic recall of some childhood scene. It releases all that was condensed in that scene, the secret forms of his life. Lily's groping attempt to paint her picture is also associated with a painful process of recall, which starts by being chaotic, tumultuous, uncontrolled, but which later settles and forms itself more steadily as she finds her way into her painting. The rush of memory is the occasion for the narration to reintroduce a familiar image: '. . . her mind kept throwing up from its depths, scenes, and names, and sayings, and memories and ideas, like a fountain spurting over that glaring, hideously difficult, white space, while she modelled it with greens and blues' (p. 181).

The other case in *To the Lighthouse* of the haunting memory associated with the power of art is that of Mrs Ramsay. She seems to live with the faintest outline of a memory always in the background of her thoughts. It is the memory of some loss about which rumours circulate. It is the memory of some terrible experience which she does not name to herself. It is a memory which she cannot or will not allow to fully form in her mind and yet which is active quietly in her feelings and perceptions. It finds its way into her mind when she is released from the rush of the day's activities and, shrinking to 'a wedge-shaped core of darkness' allows herself to listen to the sounds from the 'all spreading, unfathomably deep' layers of her mind. She conjures up the phantom of her lover, offers herself to him as a bride, experiences a moment of orgasmic ecstasy as the ghostly silver fingers of the Lighthouse caress some sealed vessel in her brain. The theme of Mrs Ramsay's day, scarcely known even to herself, has been her desire for her absent love.

Later in the evening art, in the form of poetry, provides her with a voice, 'her own voice, outside herself'. It speaks of time and death and love, and all the things she had had somehow in her mind, unsaid, during the day. She reads a Shakespeare sonnet. It is about an absent lover. It talks of the 'figures of delight' that are projected into the world in the absence of one's love (those silver fingers had produced for her a 'flood of delight', her ecstasy had been 'waves of pure delight'). The shadow of her memory, the shadow of her loss, had thrown itself upon the impressions of the day, and its outline now at last emerges. Its presence is at last acknowledged.

How satisfying! How restful! All the odds and ends of the day stuck to this magnet; her mind felt swept, felt clean. And then there it was, suddenly entire shaped in her hands, beautiful and reasonable, clear and complete, the essence sucked out of life and held rounded here – the sonnet.   (p. 139)

The shape of her day's experience is expressed. The fragments collected up. Their secret order revealed.

> Yet seem'd it winter still, and, you away,
> As with your shadow I with these did play.

VII

Our speech is inadequate to the density of our experience. But desire drives us to speak. Desire is a power which works on words; it creates figures, it invests sounds with meaning.

It strives to draw into the net the debris of the day. Art is one of its manifestations.

In *To the Lighthouse* this is dramatised in Lily's struggle to fill that empty white space, to concretise her vision. She is driven by the bodily emotions of love and loss. While she had known about Mrs Ramsay's death for many years she now comes to experience it. It becomes a concrete visual experience. 'She was dead. The step where she used to sit was empty. She was dead' (p. 170). The visual emptiness of that place triggers a torrent of memories, fantasies, questions, and an acute sense of physical distress at the inadequacy of speech, the poverty of expression.

For how could one express in words these emotions of the body? express that emptiness there? (She was looking at the drawing-room steps; they looked extraordinarily empty.) It was one's body feeling, not one's mind. The physical sensations that went with the bare look of the steps had become suddenly extremely unpleasant. To want and not to have, sent all up her body a hardness, a hollowness, a strain . . . Suddenly, the empty drawing-room steps, the frill of the chair inside, the puppy tumbling on the terrace, the whole wave and whisper of the garden became like curves and arabesques fourishing round a centre of complete emptiness. (p. 202)

The narration is preparing itself for its most intense effort, as if under the pressure of the narrated emotion the text itself must somehow form into an appropriate shape, must organise itself round an empty centre. We shall find in the strained fabric a narrative, even a graphic hole, a visual representation of this desolate moment of emptiness. Meanwhile the narration organises itself, marshals its figures, orders its rhythms, lays down patterns of sound in readiness for the instant at which it will leap into space.

The curves and arabesques of Lily's visual experience of the house and the garden transform the scene into a marine space, the world seen and heard as if under water ('the whole wave and whisper of the garden'). They also figure the narration itself, for its sentences have become curves and arabesques, turning back on themselves, repeating, curling round and round their theme: 'To want and not to have, sent all up her body a hardness, a hollowness, a strain. And then to want and not to have – to want and want – how that wrung the heart, and wrung it again and again' (p. 203). The narrative brings into a figurative relation, assembles into a consolidated metaphor, the visual spaces (Lily's view of the house and garden, her painting) and the text itself. To this it adds the metaphor of the surface, the surface of the sea and that of a strained fabric that tears.

'What does it mean? How do you explain it all?' she wanted to say, turning to Mr Carmichael again. For the whole world seemed to have dissolved in this early morning hour into a pool of thought, a deep basin of reality, and one could almost fancy that had Mr Carmichael spoken, a little tear would have rent the surface of the pool. And then? (p. 203)

And then? What does it all mean? What would happen in that brief moment when all attention is agonisingly focused on the empty centre, when desire is concentrated like a kind of suction on to a total void, an irreparable loss. How could it figure such vacuity, such hopelessness? 'And then? Something would emerge. A hand would be shoved up, a blade would be flashed. It was nonsense of course' (p. 203). Some awful, unintelligible, fearful thing emerges – a threat of everlasting pain, an announcement that life cannot be safe, that anxiety and pain can spring up on one at any moment, that desire cannot be guaranteed to cover itself over, to weave a secure surface which can stand the strain of loss. There is no safety. There is the gap in the surface. 'What was it then? What did it mean? Could things thrust their hands up and grip one; could the blade cut; the fist grasp? Was there no safety?' (p. 204). And, now, into the fabric of the narration, strained beyond breaking-point, there appears suddenly and dramatically a gaping hole, and in the hole a blade:

For one moment she felt that if they both got up, here, now on the lawn, and demanded an explanation, why was it so short, why was it so inexplicable, said it with violence, as two fully equipped human beings from whom nothing should be hid might speak, then, beauty would roll itself up; the space would fill; those empty flourishes would form into shape; if they shouted loud enough

Mrs Ramsay would return. 'Mrs Ramsay!' she said aloud. 'Mrs Ramsay!' The tears ran down her face.

6

[Macalister's boy took one of the fish and cut a square out of its side to bait his hook with. The mutilated body (it was alive still) was thrown back into the sea.]

7

'Mrs Ramsay!' Lily cried, 'Mrs Ramsay!' But nothing happened. The pain increased. That anguish could reduce one to such a pitch of imbecility, she thought! . . . No one had seen her step off her strip of board into the waters of annihilation. She remained a skimpy old maid, holding a paint-brush on the lawn.   (p. 205)

The time of the fiction and the time of the narration here diverge. For there is no passage of fictional time between the end of section 5 and the beginning of section 7. These two moments of the narration are the same moment of the fiction. But a gap has opened up, a gap with a particular shape (the square brackets/the square wound). The typographical arrangement of the text, even the graphical shape of the punctuation marks are brought into play – they *signify*. The brackets contain the narration of an incident apparently of utmost insignificance, of triviality. Of all the processes and journeys that are marshalled by the narration into fictional simultaneity in part 3, this one, the story of Macalister's boy fishing, which has been unobtrusively present throughout, is the one which has the least significant relationship to any of the other stories being told. It has no connection (no *fictional* connection, except as a matter of coincidence) with the dramas of Mr Ramsay and his son, or with that of Lily and her painting. There is no fictional reason for it to be there at all. It is there for a narrative reason. It is there so that it is available, when the moment comes, so that the narration can fly across space and find ready-prepared just what it needs – a mutilated body thrown into the sea.

The effect of this narrative device is, as usual, confirmed and strengthened by its contrast with other parts of the text: partly by contrast with the narrative use of brackets and methods of transition in parts 1 and 2, but also by contrast with the other use of this same device. It is used only once more. This second case occurs as James's recall of his mother and the misery which it causes are at their height. He sits in the boat powerless to move, absorbed in his misery and in the knot that binds him to the past. It seems release can come only if he takes a knife and cuts himself free. But then, just as the gap might open up and terror strike, the wind blows, the boat moves and James's attention is called back to the task of steering the boat.

The relief was extraordinary. They all seemed to fall away from each other again and to be at their ease and the fishing lines slanted taut across the side of the boat. But his father did not rouse himself. He only raised his right hand mysteriously high in the air, and let it fall upon his knee again as if he were conducting some secret symphony.

9

[The sea without a stain on it, thought Lily Briscoe, still standing and looking out over the bay. The sea is stretched like silk across the bay. Distance had an extraordinary power; they had been swallowed up in it, she felt, they were gone for ever, they had become part of the nature of things. It was so calm; it was so quiet. The steamer itself had vanished, but the great scroll of smoke still hung in the air and dropped like a flag mournfully in valediction.]

10

It was like that then, the island, thought Cam, once more drawing her fingers through the waves. She had never seen it from out at sea before.   (p. 213)

The two cases are symmetrical. One is the negative of the other. In the first case the person in pain is Lily on the island and the narration leaps to the boat to express her emptiness. In the second case the pain is in the boat. But it is relieved there. The gap is avoided; the knife disappears before it can do its damage. The fabric remains 'stretched like silk'. The relief is expressed by Lily's view of the calm surface of the sea. In the first case the strain causes a hole to appear which is not covered over in the fiction. It is filled in the narration. It is filled with a fictionally discontinuous but metaphorically related episode. In the second case the strain is relieved in the fiction itself. The narration fills the covered-over gap with a fictionally connected episode (connected by the usual mechanism of metonymy – the object of the narration, the sea, remaining constant while the point of view changes).

Within the narrative order there is, in such passages, a movement towards intense concentration on individual pain and grief, but at the same time a vivid reminder of the larger impersonal order within which these subjective feelings are so small and insignificant. The narration holds together a vision of individual desire and its context of space and sea, of impersonal time and natural process. The orderliness of art and its expressive power do not cancel out the impersonality of time. When the narration has done its work we are left with 'a globed compacted thing', a harmonious, orderly object, a fabrication of fullness replacing what in life is not full, of completeness replacing what in life is partial and fragmentary.

It was some such feeling of completeness perhaps which, ten years ago, standing almost where she stood now, had made her say that she must be in love with the place. Love had a thousand shapes. There might be lovers whose gift it was to choose out the elements of things and place them together and so, giving them a wholeness not theirs in life, make of some scene, or meeting of people (all now gone and separate), one of those globed compacted things over which thought lingers, and love plays.   (p. 219)

The text registers the play of desire, the power of desire to fill the blank white space with figures. The space is that of an absence, of an utterly irreversible loss. Expression can

184

help us to come to terms with this loss but it cannot change the fact that it is a basic force which shapes our experience.

1 Virginia Woolf, *To the Lighthouse* (Harmondsworth, 1964); page numbers in brackets refer to this edition
2 Charlotte Brontë, *Shirley* (Harmondsworth, 1974), 501
3 ibid., 542
4 Throughout this chapter italics in quoted passages are my own, not the author's

9 The innocence of P.G. Wodehouse

Stephen Medcalf

C.S. Lewis, in his autobiography *Surprised by Joy*, describes as one of the crucial events in his mental life the discovery of C.F. Alexander's distinction between Enjoyment and Contemplation. They compose an analysis of consciousness. As I read this book, I contemplate it: I enjoy my act of contemplation. If I turn to examining my consciousness of this book, then I cease to contemplate the book, and cease to enjoy that contemplation: I contemplate my consciousness and enjoy a certain second-order consciousness of that contemplation. In fact, I have stopped reading.

Lewis drew from this distinction the doctrine that to examine one's own consciousness is a necessarily falsifying act. 'The enjoyment and the contemplation of our inner activities are incompatible.'[1] He would admit no activity between the two aspects of consciousness, no looking, as he would regard it, out of the corner of one's eye to see what seeing is like. Introspection finds only 'mental images and physical sensations', left behind by 'the thought or the appreciation, when interrupted . . . like the swell at sea, working after the wind has dropped'.[2] The only kind of introspection Lewis would allow was self-examination before God in terms of clearly defined concepts of good and evil – the tradition, the way, the Tao. The Tao is like a Copernican system by which you can stand outside yourself and see your own world moving in relation to God.

The fact that Lewis disliked most 'modern' authors – Kierkegaard, Freud, James Joyce, D.H. Lawrence, T.S. Eliot, Sartre – is to be ascribed, I think, not to something automatically reactionary in him, but to the perfectly correct perception that such literature is necessarily involved with the

186

attempt to catch consciousness in the act. He sets up, for example, a distinction between lovers of Milton and lovers of James Joyce. Miltonists believe that the essence of consciousness is choice, preference, so that it and its expression have necessarily a certain buildedness about them. Joycians desire to investigate consciousness as it exists prior to any deliberate direction of attention. But the Joycians are deceiving themselves. 'The poet who finds by introspection that the soul is mere chaos is like a policeman who, having himself stopped all the traffic in a certain street, should then solemnly write down in his notebook "The stillness in this street is highly suspicious."'3

These doctrines necessarily affect the way Lewis used words. His language cannot appear to be altering itself as he writes: it can only be corrected afterwards. 'As I write this book' is subject to the same laws as 'As I read this book'. We find therefore:

You asked for a loving God: you have one. The great spirit you so lightly invoked, the 'lord of terrible aspect', is present: not a senile benevolence that drowsily wishes you to be happy in your own way, not the cold philanthropy of a conscientious magistrate, nor the care of a host who feels responsible for the comfort of his guests, but the consuming fire, Himself, the love that made the worlds, persistent as the artist's love for his work and despotic as a man's love for a dog, provident and venerable as a father's love for a child, jealous, inexorable, exacting as love between the sexes.4

That is tremendous, yet it is a rhetoric based on an absolute assurance that the meaning of certain words can be found with certainty in their past uses in a particular tradition of Christian and English writing. Compare what Lewis says here with a sentence from Charles Williams, whom he admired, equally working within the tradition to reform our ordinary conception of love: 'The famous saying "God is love", it is generally assumed, means that God is like our immediate emotional indulgence, and not that our meaning of love ought to have something of the "otherness" and terror of God.'5

Lewis would not have quarrelled with this thought about love (he copies it in *The Weight of Glory*). But except in his last books, in *Till we have Faces* and *A Grief Observed*, when he changed his style markedly, he would have eschewed its interactive form – Williams's awareness that if you intend to enlarge the meaning of 'love' or any other word you must not confine yourself to multiplying existing models for its use, but show how those models are themselves modified in the process.

Lewis aggressively proclaims his faith in 'stock responses'; he is a master of integrating scraps of language into his writing from writers he loved, neither losing anything of their power, nor changing it, nor increasing it. His style rests in a certain assumed or chosen security about the relation of consciousness to the world and of language to the objects it describes. It has expressed, perhaps, a similar security in English culture. You can find the same style, for example, in Winston Churchill's books of speeches, and in Harold Nicolson: it is very instructive to compare *A la recherche du temps perdu* with *Helen's Tower* and *The Desire to Please*, the first two volumes of Nicolson's projected *In Search of the Past*, in the light of Nicolson's ambition to be remembered as 'the Proust of England'. Somehow Nicolson never properly developed the ironic edge of his early *Some People*: perhaps because he was a part of, therefore secure in, the aristocratic tradition which Proust looked on from outside.

Plenty of lords of English culture have chosen modernism – Yeats deliberately, Eliot through an infinite need of introspection, Golding for his canon of 'intransigence', and so on. I want to consider in this essay, however, one of a group of writers who might at first sight seem to have chosen very deliberately to remain with security, tradition in the sense of what has been done, and attention to the given external world, but who nevertheless provide paths through insecurity which show an intuitive knowledge of its nature, extend awareness and create new inner worlds. I think of G.K. Chesterton, P.G. Wodehouse, Evelyn Waugh and John Betjeman.

There is in ordinary language, in the coverage of meaning

of words, a latent store of experience, therefore of wisdom, derived from the way in which words have been used, and their meaning extended, by diverse people in indefinitely diverse situations. Each of the four writers I mention, using a standard and traditional vocabulary and syntax which he has no wish to disturb, has his own method for tapping this wisdom and displaying it as fresh. Chesterton has especially his paradox, Wodehouse his simile, Waugh one kind of irony (a classic, suave, even creamy surface covering accidie and terror) and Betjeman another (a beautiful double-take which doubles itself again, so that the very choice of metre and word declares, 'I like directly what I like ironically to parody'). Of these four I want to look at the greatest and most original as a writer, and, except as a writer, the least deliberate – P.G. Wodehouse.

Wodehouse is as secure in the matrix of the traditionally English and ethically Christian as C.S. Lewis himself – the more so in that, unlike Lewis, his ethics have no basis in religion, in which he disclaimed all interest. His subject-matter is English society as it existed before the First World War or survived unharmed by it. The one notable public incident of his life, the broadcasts from Berlin in 1940, shows a notable innocence, but a complete unawareness that anyone could be as ungentlemanly as the Nazis actually were. Of his ethics, W.H. Auden says that Bertie Wooster could be thought of as a suitable object of attention only in a Christian, never in a Classical or a Marxist society:

The Communist would probably say: 'It is incredible that anybody should *like* people so silly and useless as Mr Pickwick, Miss Prism, Madame Wetme and Bertie Wooster.' The Greek would probably have said 'It is incredible that such people, so plain, middle-aged and untalented, should be *happy*.'[6]

Bertie belongs in a society which places absolute value on any and every individual. More: he belongs in a society that could produce fairy stories of the idiot and innocent younger son who succeeds where his clever elder brothers fail, where Don Quixote, Parson Adams and Mr Pickwick can be regarded as paradigms of virtue.

Wodehouse is also, it might seem, a very trivial writer. He has neither the irony nor the undercurrent of *Angst* which make Evelyn Waugh a candidate for high seriousness.

But look at his language. It lies very much in one tradition of English writing, perhaps the most enduring and specifically English – humour.

Chaucer (quite probably the father of it all) enjoys producing opposite effects with the same line by exploiting the determination of meaning by context – effects with infinite reverberations. Arcite cries out in 'The Knight's Tale':

> What is this world? What asketh men to have?
> Now with his love, now in his colde grave
> Allone, withouten any companye.[7]

A few lines later, at the beginning of the next tale, the Miller says of Nicholas the Oxford clerk:

> A chambre hadde he in that hostelrye
> Allone, withouten any companye.[8]

The passion of Arcite and the flatness of the Miller both ring true, but when you put them side by side, you begin to wonder about the power of self-recognition and creation which humanity has, that it can stand back from and create both lines. Already in Chaucer we find that contemplation of his own creativity in the act of creation which C.S. Lewis rebuts.

One might guess that Chaucer is exploiting an existing literary cliché; and that his gentle, his traditionally noble knight, his C.S. Lewis figure, is using unself-consciously and with its full original meaning a tag of noble literature which the Miller converts into mock-heroic with flat-footed unawareness – or perhaps with a leering debasement of the overtone 'love-company' in 'companye'. This is probably true – it goes back at least to Dante's

> Taciti, soli, sanza compagnia

of himself and Virgil in hell.[9]

Wodehouse's art likewise centres on his ability to bring a cliché just enough to life to kill it. Gussie Fink-Nottle, a teetotaller from youth, is about to distribute the prizes at Market Snodsbury Grammar School 'before an audience of all that is fairest and most refined in the county' while liberally primed with whisky and gin. Bertie begins a conversation:

'It seems to me, Jeeves, that the ceremony may be one fraught with considerable interest.'
'Yes, sir.'
'What, in your opinion, will the harvest be?'
'One finds it difficult to hazard a conjecture, sir.'
'You mean imagination boggles?'
'Yes, sir.'
I inspected my imagination. He was right. It boggled.[10]

Both halves of the process are important. Wodehouse enjoys the cliché he kills, and enjoys killing it. His use of words is not unlike that of the philosopher Austin, who says that existing 'does not describe something that things do all the time, like breathing, only quieter . . .'[11] There is a lively sense in that sentence of what the meaning of 'exist' which Austin wants to discredit actually is, and the metaphor of breathing succinctly revives it in a way designed for ridicule.

Wodehouse intuitively hits on just such a philosophic appeal to common sense as Austin or Gilbert Ryle love. If you put self-consciousness through the kind of slow motion which Bertie applies to it here, you realise that it is a category mistake to think you can so isolate and inspect imagination as to see it boggling.

But Wodehouse is not out to discredit 'boggle', like Ryle and Austin. He continues to enjoy the fustian use of 'imagination boggles'; and he uses it to convey his meaning. In a sense what he does is to use the cliché more seriously than most people do. 'He shook like a jelly' is nothing. But 'He shook like a jelly in a high wind' at once destroys the simile by exaggerating it beyond all credence and makes it vivid with physical exactness.

Again, Wodehouse shares with C.S. Lewis and Chaucer a love for using noble quotations that are a little hackneyed. But he uses them not, like C.S. Lewis, simply to draw on their power without changing it, but in Chaucer's way, seeing them in the new context he puts them into even while he puts them into it, as when he quotes from Byron's *Destruction of Sennacherib*: 'His demeanour was that of an Assyrian who, having come down like a wolf on the fold, had found in residence not lambs but wildcats.' There is in that sentence an awareness of Byron's real power and an awareness that it is a power which even in the original has loosened itself from contact with the objective reality it professes to describe. The strength and weakness of Byron's line is connected with a slight dislocation of metaphor and reality, so that one reads 'The Assyrian came down like a wolf', feels that the simile is over, and sees, for the fraction of the blink of an eye, the Assyrian attacking a real walled sheepfold. Almost immediately one transfers not only the wrath of the wolf to the Assyrian, but the protective walls and the innocence to Jerusalem. But there was a moment when one could have taken another path, and made a quite complicated fool of the Assyrian for attacking the wrong thing. Wodehouse slips in smartly at that point, puts wildcats into the fold and draws the actual power – Byron's power – off to his own uses. It is not surprising that T.S. Eliot admired Wodehouse. For Wodehouse does for other purposes, but with the same kind of Protean consciousness of language, and indeed more deftly, what Eliot himself does when he describes London in the rush hour with a literal translation of Dante's lines about the vagrant dead in the antechamber of hell:

> A crowd flowed over London Bridge, so many
> I had not thought death had undone so many.[12]

It cannot be too much stressed that Wodehouse delights in his original quotations and clichés and does not discredit them. This is the case, to return to my first example, even with: 'I inspected my imagination. He was right. It boggled.' Drive that too far, and it is nonsense. But in fact use the phrase gently, and you find exactly the process which I am describing as characteristic of Wodehouse, Chaucer and Eliot. They inspect their imaginations in the act and moment of boggling, and write out of that narrow point. Nevertheless, what it seems to Bertie comically impossible to do, not only is he doing, but his creator is doing as he creates him, and the reader as he reads the result.

Wodehouse's wit is often intuitively metaphysical. Any humour is apt to be. There is the example of man's affinity and unlikeness with the animals, which has been a joke certainly since Egyptian days, and perhaps from the cave painters, if the Spanish drawing of a stag sticking out its tongue at a man trying to shoot it means the mockery it might mean. Wodehouse compares man to dog: 'Bingo uttered a stricken woofle, like a bulldog that has been refused cake',[13] or, submerging the reference, 'Sir Roderick sort of just waggled an eyebrow in my direction, and I saw that it was back to the basket for Bertram',[14] and dog to man:

Nothing can ever render the experience of being treed on top of a chest of drawers by an Aberdeen terrier pleasant, but it seemed to me that the least you can expect on such an occasion is that the animal will meet you halfway, and not drop salt into the wound by looking at you as if he were asking if you were saved.[15]

But he goes further. Chesterton once observed that a great part of theology could be deduced from the fact which is the heart of the animal joke, that we find our existence as mind and body funny. Pascal made a heroic affirmation from it when he said that it does not need the whole universe in arms to kill a man. A drop of water will do it. But if the whole universe combined in arms to kill a man, the man would still be the greater. For he knows what is happening, and the universe knows nothing.[16] Andrew Marvell concentrated this heroic affirmation in a metaphysical pun about Charles I's execution:

> But with his keener eye
> The axe's edge did try

'Keen' applied to eyes means something greater than 'keen' applied to axes.

Wodehouse uses almost the same thought in what is at first sight a joke conveying a vivid physical perception, but turns out in the whole context of *The Code of the Woosters* to be carrying on a process of deflation of the evil hero-figure of the twentieth century – the dictator: 'Big chap with a small moustache and the sort of eye that can open an oyster at sixty paces.'[17] It is an accurate description of most would-be, real or fictitious, dictators. And with the Wode-housian flight between hyperbole and emperor's clothes literalness it puts them in their place even more neatly than the more extended bathos of an earlier description of Roderick Spode: 'I don't know if you have ever seen those pictures in the papers of Dictators with tilted chins and blazing eyes, inflaming the populace with fiery words on the occasion of the opening of a new skittle alley, but that was what he reminded me of.'[18]

Wodehouse's language, his characters' modes of thought, and their natures, are all three pervaded by this duality of acceptance and sharp criticism. It is a dual innocence: an innocent wisdom which goes straight to the point, and a preternaturally innocent gullibility. Either side can be upper-most, and we flash from one to the other with a rapidity which is a great part of the humour. The language depends on exploiting the gap between what words mean and what they might mean – the characters are like Tony Hancock, mugs, but shrewd, hard-thinking mugs, and, as Chesterton said of Mr Pickwick, they are eternally taken in by life, while the sceptic and the cynic are cast out.[19] Consider how the Honourable Galahad Threepwood's mind works:

'Did I ever tell you about poor Buffy Struggles back in 'ninety-three? Some misguided person lured poor old Buffy into one of those temperance lectures illustrated with coloured slides, and he called on me next day ashen, poor old chap – ashen. "Gally", he said, "what would you say the procedure was when a fellow wants to buy tea? How would a fellow set about it?" "Tea?" I said "what do you want tea for?" "To drink," said Buffy. "Pull yourself together, dear boy," I said. "You're talking wildly. You can't drink tea. Have a brandy and soda." "No more alcohol for me," said Buffy. "Look what it does to the common earthworm." "But you're not a common earthworm," I said, putting my finger on the flaw in his argument right away. "I dashed soon shall be if I go on drinking alcohol'', said Buffy. Well, I begged him with tears in my eyes not to do anything rash, but I couldn't move him. He ordered in ten pounds of the muck and was dead inside the year.'

'Good heavens! Really?'

The Hon. Galahad nodded impressively.

'Dead as a doornail. Got run over by a hansom cab, poor dear old chap, as he was crossing Piccadilly.'[20]

The two high moments of comedy in this rest on the distinction between what the words might mean and what they do mean. First: 'No more alcohol for me. Look what it does to the common earthworm . . .' – that is, it is generally harmful. But there is an undistributed middle here: Buffy is not a common earthworm, and Gally knows it. And then: 'He ordered ten pounds of the muck and was dead inside the year.' It is less Gally's conviction of *post hoc ergo propter hoc* that is funny here than the fact of our being ourselves temporarily duped by a trick of language which suggests his conviction without his having to state it.

Galahad in action works like Galahad in language: full of ingenuity, easily mistaken (an early experience misapplied, perhaps, as in his unremitting belief in Sir Gregory Parsloe-Parsloe's criminality) and good-hearted. He is on the side of those girls in Wodehouse who love without difficulty. 'The Honourable Galahad Threepwood was himself an Old Etonian and in his time had frequently had occasion to employ the Eton manner to the undoing of his fellow men.'[21] But when Ronald Fish turns the same manner on to Sue Brown, Gally responds straight away, and is furious.

But the fullest objective correlative of this dual innocence and shrewdness is, of course, Bertie Wooster: 'mentally negligible', as Jeeves said, but 'capable of acting very shrewdly on occasion', and wholly obedient to the Code of the Woosters. In his creation there is again an immense awareness of what is happening, both on the language level and on the level of morality. It is so from the first question ever asked of him, in 1917, by his Aunt Agatha.

'What are your immediate plans, Bertie?'

'Well, I rather thought of tottering out for a bite of lunch later on, and then possibly staggering round to the club, and after that, if I felt strong enough, I might trickle off to Walton Heath for a round of golf.'

'I am not interested in your totterings and tricklings.'[22]

For an infinitesimal moment we see through Aunt Agatha's disdain the possibility of taking Bertie's tricklings and totterings literally. They were created as a kind of metaphor: for a moment we experience the flash of imagination which created them, which saw the point of contact between what Bertie actually does and these other actions, 'stagger', 'totter', 'trickle', which connote weakness and even inanimate action. But Aunt Agatha forces the metaphorical leap to go backwards: instead of seeing how aptly Bertie's acts might be imagined in this way if the meaning of the words were a little extended, we see how stupid Bertie's acts must be if the meaning of the words is extended as little as possible. Bertie totters. The whole style depends on an awareness of the point from which language is created, of that in man which perceives metaphor. It has therefore that awareness of the interactive nature of metaphor which puts Wodehouse as an artist with Charles Williams and James Joyce, rather than with C.S. Lewis and Harold Nicolson, puts him among those who not only enjoy their own creativity but contemplate it and modify it in the light of that contemplation.

But there is more. The play of consciousness in language in this passage reflects a play of consciousness in ethics. Under the game of language, a complicated game of evaluation is going on. The point of Bertie's language, here as very often, is self-deprecation, a self-deprecation which is, alas, fairly just. Bertie senses, even before Aunt Agatha does her hatchet job, the irredeemable futility all his actions must have in her eyes; and gently, humbly – but to all appearances cheerfully – puts his head firmly on the block. In that Bertie can sense such things we have a counterweight to his objective and real limitations. Do we then praise Bertie's sweetness of character – it is humility after all – and think that Aunt Agatha takes unfair advantage of him? Surely in the book we do. But that decision is given edge by the realisation that we might not: that in a way Bertie is a weak tottering creature who disguises his weakness by flourishing it rhetorically. The complicated to and fro here does depend on the point Auden makes, which I have already quoted: that the ethics of finding Bertie a sufficiently interesting hero are Christian ethics, ethics of humility with their complicated to and fro of self-realisation and avoidance of self-realisation (you can never say, 'I am humble'), ethics of forgiveness with their simultaneous awareness and abolition of awareness as if it had never been. 'No cause, no cause,' said Cordelia to Lear.

To analyse Wodehouse's language should involve going far beyond looking at his general habits of thought into minute descriptions of the utter, poet's rightness of every word. But all the time one would have to bear in mind the perfect aptness of his language to his peculiar way of describing character, his particular ethics and his whole individual world of fiction. The best criticism I have found of Wodehouse comes from Basil Boothroyd's essay in *Homage to P.G. Wodehouse*;[23] he analyses the sentence in which Bertie, arriving on a yacht, says he 'handed the hat and light overcoat to a passing salt'.[24] Bertie's characteristic self-deprecation is apparent in his saying not 'my', but 'the', and in his attempts to accommodate himself to the world of the tailor and his jargon – 'the light overcoat' – and the nautical world as he understands it – 'a passing salt'. With those proprieties goes the duality of meaning in 'light' – colour and weight, both proper to the season, as it was summer – and the rightness of sound, the crisp consonants at the close of the sentence, of 'salt'. And that last is supported by the echo of a perfectly irrelevant common phrase – 'Please pass the salt.'

Much the same applies to Madeline Bassett's telegram: 'Please come here if you wish but, Oh Bertie, is this wise? Will not it cause you needless pain seeing me? Surely merely twisting knife wound. Madeline.'[25] The main humour lies in the idiocy of omitting 'in the', after putting in 'Oh Bertie'. This is an idiocy exactly appropriate for the girl who thought the rabbits were gnomes in attendance on the Fairy Queen ('Perfect rot, of course. They're nothing of the kind') and that every time a fairy hiccoughs a wee baby is born. But it also makes the cliché 'twisting the knife in the wound' effective by reducing it to its mere skeleton. And there is a rightness of sound about ending with the clean monosyllables of 'knife wound' – again supported by the existence of an irrelevant hyphenated compound: knife-wound.

Wodehouse has, very much in conformity with this general picture, a combination of freedom and inwardness when he handles the meanings of words. I doubt if he has contributed many new meanings of specific words to the language: his world is too specific to extract single words from it. But he has contributed a whole idiom with this freedom, as when he makes a back-formation not previously used: 'He spoke with a certain what-is-it in his voice, and I could see that, if not actually disgruntled, he was far from being gruntled, so I tactfully changed the subject.'[26]

John Bayley observes, rightly I think, that the Shakespearean joy in language, the love of the creator rather than the engineer, is better to be found in the experiments of Wodehouse than in the experiments of Joyce. Wodehouse follows the prescription that C.S. Lewis, in *The Abolition of Man*,[27] quotes from Confucius: 'It is upon the trunk, it is from within the tradition, that a gentleman works.' In this sense his style is within the Lewis–Nicolson canons. It is his freedom that puts him within tradition in T.S. Eliot's sense (*Tradition and the Individual Talent*),[28] the tradition which necessarily changes in carrying on rather than fossilising. His freedom goes with inwardness in ways which both Lewis's tendency to fossilise and Joyce's stony Irish intellectuality deny them.

Bayley goes on: 'In Wodehouse as in Shakespeare we feel that the source of lightness and joy is ultimately, and quite simply, the virtue of the writer.'[29] The loving disinterestedness of the creator pervades his world as well as his language. The language works perfectly with the emergence of character in plot. Once you have looked closely at Bertie's language it is no surprise that he evolves schemes fully as ingenious as those of Jeeves, but that, to some readers' recurring regret, his schemes must fail where Jeeves's succeed. It is again the combination of shrewdness and innocence: but alas, Bertie represents the gullible side of Wodehousian man, Jeeves the shrewdness. Again, once you have noticed exactly how Bertie responds to Spode in the quotations I have given, you find natural enough the discovery that Spode's bluster and fascism are flawed by the way he finances his movement – his considerable talent for designing women's underclothing. Everything emerges inevitably, with the utmost consistency. And it is the combination of plot and language that makes a good many readers of Wodehouse remember gratefully moments when they rolled about with a laughter that they wanted to continue though in all literalness it hurt their ribs.

It seems that in the writing of individual books it was the plot that had to be contrived first, and the language then flowed. Wodehouse says in a letter, wondering if Trollope really did write fifteen hundred words a day:

Of course, if he did plan the whole thing out first, there is nothing so very bizarre in the idea of writing so many hundred words of it each day. After all, it is more or less what one does oneself. One sits down to work each morning, no matter whether one feels bright or lethargic, and before one gets up a certain amount of stuff, generally about fifteen hundred words, has emerged.[30]

But over the whole course of his writing it looks as if the language came first, and the world was created from it. His style seems to come directly out of his first school stories (compare those of Frank Richards), out of the self-consciousness of the sixth-former who is just becoming aware of the richness of English literature and language, and beneath a sophisticated carapace is too insecure to use it straightforwardly. The Hindu babu would have provided a similar starting-point, but in fact the first authentic Wodehouse man is Psmith, who preserves all his life the way of speaking he learnt at Eton:

'Oh, it's you?' [Baxter] said morosely.

'I in person,' said Psmith genially. 'Awake, beloved! Awake, for morning in the bowl of night has flung the stone that puts the stars to flight; and lo! the hunter of the East has caught the Sultan's turret in a noose of light. The Sultan himself,' he added, 'you will find behind yonder window, speculating idly on your motives for bunging flower-pots at him.'[31]

Psmith talks like this from *Mike* (1909) onwards, but this quotation comes from *Leave it to Psmith* (1923), when he attained his apotheosis by being grafted into the world of Blandings Castle, which had already been created (but by no means perfected) in *Something Fresh* (1915). Wodehouse's external life seems to have helped here, through his move to the United States. American English is after all a thing of different spirit and pattern from English English, with different overtones, intensities and relaxations. The handling of the two languages perhaps contributed to Wodehouse's intuitive self-consciousness about meaning. And the difference in cultures undoubtedly helped to create his own special world, as he introduced Psmith to New York in *Psmith, Journalist* (1915) and wrote about Blandings Castle for the *Saturday Evening Post*. The development is something like standing Henry James on his head.

When one adds the self-deprecating idiom of Bertie Wooster (the exchange with Aunt Agatha I quoted is also from this developing period, from 1917), the conditions for forming the worlds of P.G. Wodehouse are present. Of course there are worlds which I have not mentioned – those of Ukridge, Mulliner, Hollywood, golf, and others which never developed beyond a single book. But they have all of them the same kinds of co-inhering exaggeration and realisation, formalising and life. And they all have the pervasive innocence into which Wodehouse, strangely enough, develops, out of the confused motives and debased mingling of realism and wish-fulfilment of ordinary school stories and light romances.

'The gardens of Blandings Castle', says Evelyn Waugh, 'are that original garden from which we are all exiled.'[32] It will be clear that I take this statement fairly seriously – by virtue perhaps of a displacement of concepts from myth to comedy such as Northrop Frye speaks of. But, having in particular consideration the degree to which the perfection of the Wodehouse world is a creation of art, I should also

200

offer a comparison with the Arcadia of Virgil's *Eclogues* – a golden world, largely created by a perfection of style and a living observant humour, which has two connections with the world outside. *First*, that by its innocence it reproaches it. Even the villains in Wodehouse have the whole-heartedness and innocence of Falstaff, the qualities which enable Auden to declare that Falstaff is a parable of divine charity.[33] *Second*, in that the pressure of external events is always present in it, seen dimly in a golden shadow; Wodehouse, of course, had tremendous capacity as an observer. His encounter with Hugh Walpole at Magdalen College, Oxford, could not be bettered if it had been Bertie himself meeting someone like Florence Craye (the author of *Spindrift*):

It was just after Hilaire Belloc had said that I was the best living English writer. It was just a gag, of course, but it worried Hugh terribly. He said to me, 'Did you see what Belloc said about you?' I said I had. 'I wonder why he said that.' 'I wonder,' I said. Long silence. 'I can't imagine why he said that,' said Hugh. I said I couldn't either. Another long silence. 'It seems such an extraordinary thing to say!' 'Most extraordinary.' Long silence again. 'Ah well,' said Hugh, having apparently found the solution, 'the old man's getting very old.'[34]

But I should be inclined to say that there was some rigidity after *Money in the Bank* (1946), which Wodehouse wrote in his internment camp and in which the principal source of freshness, Lord Uffenham, was actually 'drawn from a man in my dormitory'. The language after the war tends to become a little like epic diction, a mechanism for digesting experience which is a little too successful to be alive. And external conditions like the welfare state sit very unhappily in some of the books, lacking the naturalness with which the Great Dictator takes his place among Wodehouse's earlier efficient villains. Yet I'm not sure. In his very last novel, *Aunts Aren't Gentlemen* (1974), Wodehouse showed signs of being capable of absorbing protest marches. The book is very lacking in the great sign of Wodehouse life, the simile, but what else would Jeeves say when asked why a protest march was taking place, than this:

201

'I could not say, sir. It might be one thing or it might be another. Men are suspicious, prone to discontent. Subjects still loathe the present Government.'

'The poet Nash?'

'No, sir. The poet Herrick.'[35]

(The poet Nash is, of course, Ogden Nash.)

However that may be, in the thirties Wodehouse undoubtedly had the root of the matter in him. An article by Philip Thody professes to be mock-solemn in comparing Jeeves's relation with Bertie with the principles of Dostoevsky's Grand Inquisitor.[36] The trouble is, it cannot be wholly mock-solemn, because it is true, and most readers have some trouble deciding how serious Thody was in his unseriousness. That the moral problem of authority and acceptance is really at work in Wodehouse is shown by the way in which Jeeves, the Efficient Baxter and Roderick Spode set one another off. The terrible analysis of power and subjection and the urge to be without responsibility even at the cost of the servile state are undeniably reflected in Jeeves and Bertie. It has been said that the only difference between tragedy and comedy is timing; tragedy looks slowly at what comedy plays quickly. But I would add that comedy has something to do with love. Again, it is not quite nonsense to say that the silence of Christ in the fable of the Grand Inquisitor, the answer of grace and the morality of the spirit to the Inquisitor's remorseless conviction are reflected in the helpless innocence of Sue Brown or Bertie Wooster. What Bertie's innocence called out is the benevolence of Jeeves. Admittedly, Jeeves's benevolence is that of the dictator who controls his subjects, as we see in the one story he tells himself, the uncomfortable 'Bertie changes his mind'.[37] Yet there is an acceptable moral paradox in the fact that it is the dictator, Jeeves, who is the servant. There is, after all, real non-puritan morality, morality of the spirit, in Wodehouse's world.

From this intuitive grasp of principle follows an equally fine grasp of particular facts. To the remarks about the Dictator Spode which I have already quoted I would add Gussie Fink-Nottle's description:

'Roderick Spode is founder and head of the Saviours of Britain, a Fascist organisation better known as the Black Shorts . . .'

'By the way, when you say "shorts", you mean "shirts", of course.'

'No. By the time Spode formed his association, there were no shirts left. He and his adherents wear black shorts.'

'Footer bags, you mean?'

'Yes.'

'How perfectly foul.'[38]

That is both cheerfully funny, and a comment on British attitudes to fascism which tells one more than whole books might. Nigel Nicolson writes in the introduction to Harold Nicolson's *Diaries and Letters 1930–39*:

'There is one passage in his diary which is so typical of him that I laughed aloud with remembered affection when I first read it. He was talking to Sir Oswald Mosley in 1931 about the new 'trained and disciplined force' by which Mosley intended to bolster up his crumbling New Party. 'We discuss their uniforms', the diary records. 'I suggest grey flannel trousers and shirts.'[39]

Wodehouse cannot have known of that conversation: but he knew, not self-consciously but because he shared it, of the traditional and decent Englishman's total incomprehension of what fascism was really like. In this joke you can readily see why there was appeasement, why there was no successful fascist movement in Britain, and why Wodehouse himself broadcast a cheerful talk from Berlin in 1940 about what it had been like in his concentration camp. But Wodehouse substitutes for incomprehension of the cult of fascism today an awareness of its absurdity *sub specie aeternitatis*. If you put Wodehouse on Spode alongside such cartoons as Pont's man with a walrus moustache and a bucket observing: 'Suppose we hear a little less about him being *only* a paperhanger', you can see too why the British never really thought Hitler could be victorious. It is possible that the straightforward revival of traditional values by a C.S. Lewis or a Churchill was no more important in confronting Hitler than the humorous half-awareness of the new thing in the world of P.G. Wodehouse, Pont and Tommy Handley.

Kierkegaard says somewhere that wit arises at the frontier

of the aesthetic and the ethical, humour between the ethical and the religious. As I understand it, then, wit, or satire, is the product of a man accustomed to live by satisfying his immediate and momentary impulses and responses (aesthetic) who is nevertheless aware of the demand of moral norms which he will not quite accept for himself, but will accept to scald the world. There are qualities in Joyce like that, particularly in Stephen Dedalus, and in the early Evelyn Waugh.

But humour arises in a man who has thoroughly assimilated the ethical universals and norms of his society and made his world of them. A very good man, a patient, humble man – the sort of man whose comment after nineteen hours in one of 'those *Quarante Hommes, Huit Chevaux* things . . . in other words, cattle trucks' is that he'd often wondered what it would be like to be one of the *quarante hommes*. 'The answer is, as I had rather suspected, is that it is not so good . . . Forty men are cramped, especially if they are fifty men, as we were.'[40] Humour in Kierkegaard's sense arises in such a man when he is aware at the back of his mind, and perhaps in practice, that all genuine and moral decisions are unique, that we stand alone before God, and that human nature includes the martyr, the monster and the ambiguous state, impossible for an external observer to judge, of Abraham commanded to sacrifice Isaac. The response of such a man, not fully conscious of this, of which he feels the pressure, seems to me to be the ideal world of Wodehouse's fictions, its language and the triumphant innocence which runs through it. There is still truth in the fact that 'silly' originally meant 'blessed', innocent and blessed.

In writing this essay I have made use of R.D.B. French, *P.G. Wodehouse* (London and Edinburgh, 1966) and R.A. Hall, *The Comic Style of P.G. Wodehouse* (Hamden, Conn., 1974).

1 C.S. Lewis, *Surprised by Joy* (London, 1955), 206
2 ibid., 207
3 Lewis, *A Preface to Paradise Lost* (London, 1942), 131
4 Lewis, *The Problem of Pain* (London, 1940), 35

5   Charles Williams, *He Came Down from Heaven* (London, 1950), 15

6   W.H. Auden, *The Dyer's Hand* (London, 1963), 412

7   Geoffrey Chaucer, 'The Knight's Tale', lines 1919–21

8   Chaucer, 'The Miller's Tale', line 17

9   Dante, *Divine Comedy, Inferno*, canto 23, line 1

10 P.G. Wodehouse, *Right Ho, Jeeves* (London, 1934), 207

11 J.L. Austin, *Sense and Sensibilia* (Oxford, 1962), 68

12 T.S. Eliot, *The Waste Land*, lines 62–3

13 Wodehouse, 'Jeeves and the Impending Doom', *Very Good, Jeeves* (London, 1930)

14 Wodehouse, 'The Rummy Affair of Old Biffy', *Carry on, Jeeves* (London, 1925)

15 Wodehouse, *The Code of the Woosters* (London, 1938), 180

16 *Pensées*, ed. L. Lafuma (Paris, 1952), no 200

17 ibid., 45

18 ibid., 21

19 G.K. Chesterton, *Charles Dickens* (London, 1906), chapter 4

20 Wodehouse, *Summer Lightning* (London, 1929), 28

21 Wodehouse, *Heavy Weather* (London, 1933), 194

22 Wodehouse, 'Extricating Young Gussie', *The Man with Two Left Feet* (London, 1917), 13

23 Thelma Cazalet-Keir (ed.), *Homage to P.G. Wodehouse* (London, 1973), 58–76

24 Wodehouse, *Thank you, Jeeves* (London, 1934), 155

25 Wodehouse, *The Code of the Woosters*, 32

26 ibid., 9

27 Lewis, *The Abolition of Man* (London, 1946), 58

28 In *Selected Essays* (London, 1951), 13–22

29 John Bayley, *The Characters of Love* (London, 1960), 285

30 Wodehouse, *Performing Flea* (London, 1953), 126–7

31 Wodehouse, *Leave it to Psmith* (London, 1923), 262

32 Evelyn Waugh, 'An act of Homage and Reparation to P.G. Wodehouse', *Sunday Times* (16 July 1961)

33 Auden, 'The Prince's Dog', *The Dyer's Hand*, 198–208

34 Wodehouse, *Performing Flea*, 128

35 Wodehouse, *Aunts Aren't Gentlemen* (London, 1974), 7

36 'Jeeves, Dostoievski and the Double Paradox', *University of Leeds Review*, 14: 2, 319–31

37 In *Carry On, Jeeves* (London, 1925)

38 Wodehouse, *The Code of the Woosters*, 71–2

39 Harold Nicolson, *Diaries and Letters 1930–39*, ed. Nigel Nicolson (London, 1969), 25

40 *Encounter* (November 1954), 29

10 The fictional topography of Samuel Beckett
Robin Lee

. . . what he called his mind functioned not as an instrument but as a place . . . (*Murphy*)

. . . that's where you should be, where you are, far from here, far from everything, if only I could go there, if only I could describe it, I who am so good at topography . . . (*The Unnamable*)

'The facts in a highly organized novel . . . are often in the nature of cross-correspondences and the ideal spectator cannot expect to view them properly until he is sitting up on a hill at the end.'[1] This observation from E.M. Forster's useful storehouse of assumptions, *Aspects of the Novel*, offers an account of fiction's spatial dimension. We can say that language is linear, and that a book is written word by word, read phrase by phrase. Meaning, however, suggests a spatial analogy. The linear movements of time and language seem to pass over it, modifying, adjusting, damaging or defining. The meaning itself is not bound to their forward momentum. But this analogy is vulnerable to the probing of logic, for it is based not so much on particular characteristics of the novel, as on a series of assumptions about what it is and how it is read. What lies behind Forster's analogy is the assumption that the novel is like a narrow path across a broad landscape, and that the view of the landscape from the path becomes progressively more coherent. Implicitly, this view likens the path to the linear sequence of the words, phrases and periods, and the landscape to the imaginative construct by means of which the reader extends the words, phrases and periods into a sense of some overall meaning. This assumes that the novel is devoted to sustaining the illusion that a reality underlies the words on the page, and commits it to the use of language as a wholly transparent medium. At this level we can describe the novel as a linear phenomenon which attempts to foster the illusion of spatial extension. This essay will be concerned with the question: what are the mechanics of the creation of fictional space?

If we glance at the opening of Scott's *Waverley* we read:

It is, then, sixty years since Edward Waverley, the hero of the following pages, took leave of his family, to join the regiment of dragoons in which he had lately obtained a commission. It was a melancholy day at Waverley-Honour when the young officer parted with Sir Everard, the affectionate old uncle to whose title and estate he was presumptive heir.[2]

The first sentence is concerned exclusively with the sequence of years and pages, and with Waverley's movement as the effect of a given cause. The second sentence establishes Waverley-Honour as the place from which Waverley took his leave, and also as the place to which, as the heir, his future will direct him. Waverley-Honour is Waverley's and the novel's point of departure; now the reader 'knows where he is'. Moreover in a novel the place which the narrative gives as the location of the action attracts to itself the process of narration itself. Thus we say that Waverley-Honour is where the chapter is set, rather than saying that the chapter is where Waverley-Honour is set. The setting of a novel is like its meaning in that both are, so to speak, 'off the path'. In Scott's novel there is no description of Waverley-Honour until midway through the next chapter, when the library is briefly described. Nevertheless the reader takes the place as his essential reference-point from the outset, and the novel ends with a return to Waverley-Honour like a piece of music returning to its home key. In the same way the novel's final meaning is presumed to underlie its development, so that the view from the final pinnacle of comprehension is thought of as having been latent throughout the reading. The sense of meaning is reducible to a comforting assumption about meaning, just as the sense of place is reducible to a comfortable assumption about place.

But when a novel chooses to abandon a scheme which

207

involves passing from a latent to an overt meaning, with the author coaxing his reader into a prearranged pattern of comprehension, the linearity both of language and of the act of reading begins to reassert itself, while the landscape of the novel becomes increasingly problematic. In the novels of Samuel Beckett the reader is confronted by some very basic problems of topography and must struggle increasingly to achieve any sense of orientation.

The term 'fictional topography' is conveniently ambiguous, and will be used to mean both the concept of place in Beckett's fiction and the fictiveness of the places. In addition the term 'locus' will be used to refer to the points where Beckett constructs something related (if obliquely) to the spatial extension upon which illusionist fiction bases its effects. There are two kinds: the anecdotal and the verbal. The anecdotal loci are the stories from which the narrator of *The Unnamable* struggles to free his monologue, while the verbal loci, a characteristic feature of *Watt*, are the exhaustive accounts of logical possibilities listed as a series of permutations of words within a particular syntactical framework, and other similar verbal devices. The most sustained example of the verbal locus is the account of the attempt made by the members of the Grants Committee to look at one another during the exhibition of Mr Nackybal in the third part of *Watt*, the story of which can be classed as an anecdotal locus.

It is in the chapter entitled 'Ding-Dong' of the fragmentary *More Pricks Than Kicks* that the idea of place first takes on its characteristically Beckettian significance. The chapter opens with the narrator's account of his 'sometime friend Belacqua' who:

... enlivened the last phase of his solipsism ... with the belief that the best thing he had to do was to move constantly from place to place ... it was not thanks to his preferring one place to another he felt sure. He was pleased to think that he could give what he called the Furies the slip by merely setting himself in motion. But as for sites, one was as good as another, because they all disappeared as soon as he came to rest in them. (p. 39)

Movement in space is commonly used in fiction to represent the movement towards a fuller understanding. The narrative moves from *a* to *b* as a piece of music moves from the dominant to the tonic, and there follows a corresponding resolution of tension. Waverley returns home to Waverley-Honour a sadder and wiser man. But Belacqua is depicted in a context which offers only a series of dominants, each leading to another but none offering any final resolution. No place is *the* place, the final place. So in *Murphy*, the impulse expressed in Wylie's dictum: 'The horse leech's daughter is a closed system. Her quantum of wantum cannot vary' (p. 43), drives Neary out of Miss Dwyer's frying-pan into Miss Counihan's fire, and from the pillar of Murphy to the post of Celia.

Like Joyce's *Ulysses*, *More Pricks Than Kicks* and *Murphy* make use of a 'factual' topography. But the topography of *Murphy* is ironic in a quite un-Joycean way. Consider, for example, the account of Celia's first sight of Murphy:

She had turned out of Edith Grove into Cremorne Road, intending to refresh herself with a smell of the Reach and then return to Lot's Road, when chancing to glance to her right she saw, motionless in the mouth of Stadium Street, considering alternately the sky and a sheet of paper, a man. Murphy. (p. 13)

In this novel of empty sexual *teloi*, places are significant only for as long as they carry an erotic charge, such as Wynn's Hotel carries for Neary, Brewery Road for Murphy:

From the practical point of view he could see no difference between hanging about in Brewery Road and hanging about in Lombard Street . . . But from the sentimental point of view the difference was most marked. Brewery Road was her forecourt, in certain moods almost her ruelle. (p. 51)

But sexuality cannot impose a stable ordering of significance, and Murphy attempts to escape from the 'big world' of topography, work and sexual music into the 'little world' of his mind, which functioned, we are told, 'not as an instrument but as a place' (p. 123). The Magdalen Mental Mercyseat suggests itself to him as a possible point of egress from the big world. But here the novel gets out of its depth and Murphy is, very suitably, 'exploded' with the help of a naked flame and an erratic gas supply. Murphy's mind, as described in section 6, is simply not a workable feature of the novel. The difficulty becomes immediately clear if we try to imagine a version of *How It Is* set in the mind of a character whose bodily movements can be traced in a street atlas of Dublin or London.[3] Beckett is able to devote no more than three paragraphs to his account of Murphy's mind, for this figurative topography is obliged to co-exist with Hyde Park and the Caledonian meat market. The move from the big world to the little world would seem to involve a move out of language, a move which the novel obviously cannot make. That it should seem to wish to do so reflects on the use of language in *Murphy*. It is a work of ironic virtuosity, with the virtuoso element still sufficiently strong to prevent its use of language from developing in the direction of serious self-reflection.

In *Watt* the issues raised in *Murphy* undergo a radical reformulation. Mr Knott's house, where Watt undertakes an eccentric kind of domestic service, is both more and less substantial than Murphy's mind. Ultimately it too must be thought to have its existence outside language, but this is not as a result of any difficulty inherent in talking about houses.

The relation of the place to the journey is central to the book. Although Mr Knott's house might seem to be *the* place – 'all the old ways lead to this' – it cannot function as a resolving tonic chord because the position it occupies in the novel is that which is appropriate to the dominant, suggesting that it is not the Waverley-Honour, but the Glennaquoich of *Watt*. Yet Mr Knott's establishment cannot function as a dominant either, for its final significance is a negative one. What confuses the issue is that: '. . . the only way one can speak of nothing is to speak of it as though it were something . . .' (p. 74). Arsene, in his monologue at the close of part I, asks: '. . . what is this shadow of the going in which we come, this shadow of the coming in which we go, this shadow of the coming and the going in which we wait, if not the shadow of purpose . . .?' (p. 56). If, as Nietzsche asserts, 'man would rather have the void for his purpose than be void of purpose'[4] he will thereby invest the void with 'the shadow of purpose'. And if language is to silence what something is to nothing, then clearly speech is no more appropriate to this subject than is purpose or its shadow. *Watt* makes a serious move towards 'the expression that there is nothing to express, nothing with which to express, no power to express, together with the obligation to express' of which Beckett speaks in the *Three Dialogues* with Georges Duthuit (p. 103).

The shadow of purpose hangs over the journey because of the destination, and over the destination because of the journey. But Mr Knott's establishment functions both as journey and as destination. Watt goes, as it were, *through* the concept of destination. For if Mr Knott's establishment seems the epitome of order and stasis, yet: '. . . nothing changed in Mr Knott's establishment, because nothing remained, and nothing came or went, because all was a coming and a going' (p. 130). Mr Knott himself 'moved about the house . . . as one unfamiliar with the premises', and his own stable characteristic is indeterminacy. The disruption of the novelistic use of place amounts, in practice, to a disruption of the novelistic presentation of meaning, and it is this formalised indeterminacy of everything to do with Mr Knott which is used to undermine it. The use of series achieves a similar effect by diffusing the significance of the particular members of the series.

The other important place in *Watt* is the asylum (a term which can certainly be used in the broad sense, and presumably in the narrow sense) where Watt tells his story to the narrator, Sam. The asylum, which figures in *Murphy*, *Watt* and *Malone Dies*, is used by Beckett as 'the ironic place'. It is not a destination; it is where one 'ends up', where one's journey takes one after its rational momentum has 'broken down'. The asylum, in Beckett's novels, is entirely free from the 'shadow of purpose' which falls even on Mr Knott's establishment. In the asylum both Watt's movement and his speech are found to be distorted as he attempts to talk his way into the meaning of his time with Mr Knott. His account, like his journey, passes *through* his stay and comes out the other end, having added to itself no more than the implication that, in this context, the linear and the spatial are finally irreconcilable because they are not properly distinct. The movement appropriate to the house is Mr Knott's circular rotation in his bed. Journeys like Watt's with their forward (or backward) momentum cast a shadow of purpose between the traveller and his destination in a way which cuts him off from its extra-purposive existence.

If the asylum in *Watt* is free from the metaphorical purposiveness which attaches to places in conventional fiction, its garden fencing suggests a metaphor of selfhood. The bridge (which breaks under Watt) conveys an optimistic view of interpersonal communication. The strip of no man's land between the two gardens, each surrounded with its own barbed-wire fence, suggests a more tenuous situation. The fact of the two facing holes in the fences is made to seem wildly improbable as a result of the long rigmarole of speculation about its possible, and impossible, causes. The eccentricities of Watt's speech and the narrator's diffidence about the accuracy of the text increase the sense of uncertainty, until finally it becomes convenient to see Watt's relation to Sam as not very different from that between Malone and Macmann. However, not only the fact but the possibility of an incidental metaphor, like that of the fences, is a measure of how far *Watt* is from the trilogy in its treatment of place. In *Watt*, *a* can be read as a metaphor for *b*; in Beckett's subsequent novels, place is presented in such a way that *a*'s existence as itself is as problematic as the nominal identity of the pots in Mr Knott's kitchen.

The development of the narrative in *Watt* shows a gradual breakdown of the central anecdote, and the increased use of what we have agreed to call verbal loci. These are worth some detailed consideration. What happens is that the forward movement of the narrative is taken over by a process which continues it without providing any genuine forward thrust. An early example is Arsene's account of the hypothetical housemaid, Mary. She is described as 'eating onions and peppermints turn and turn about': '. . . I mean first an onion, then a peppermint, then another onion, then another peppermint, then another onion, then another peppermint, then another onion, then another peppermint . . .' (p. 50). In all, the phrase 'then another onion, then another peppermint' is repeated eight times. The sequence mimes the meaning of the phrase 'turn and turn about', treating it with an absurd literalness. Thus the impression is of words describing other words, not of words describing the behaviour of the increasingly hypothetical Mary. The device is a purely mechanical one, and can be said both to continue and to undermine the movement of the narrative. It is a form of 'keeping going at all costs', an idea which becomes increasingly important in the trilogy. The account of Mary parodies the movement of language, and the more it is developed the greater emphasis is given to the need for it to end.

A later example of the verbal locus, the account of Mr Knott's footwear, is formally very similar:

As for his feet, sometimes he wore on each a sock, or on the one a sock and on the other a stocking, or a boot, or a shoe, or a slipper, or a sock and boot, or a sock and shoe, or a sock and slipper, or a stocking and boot, or a stocking and shoe, or a stocking and slipper, or nothing at all . . . (p. 200)

And so on for over a page. The difference between Mr Knott's footwear and Mary's eating habits is not only that the former involves a number of variables, but that information about Mr Knott has an altogether different status in the novel. Mr Knott becomes the focus of the reader's curiosity, but there is precisely nothing to be said about Mr Knott. The choices open to the narrative are to make no mention of him at all, or to give the kind of negative account we find in the samples of Watt's distorted speech: 'Ton taw, ton tonk. Ton dob, ton trips. Ton vila, ton deda. Ton kawa, ton pelsa. Ton das, don yag. (Not Watt, not Knott. Not body, not spirit. Not alive, not dead. Not awake, not asleep. Not sad, not gay.)' (p. 165). The final option is to keep going at all costs, as in the account of Mr Knott's footwear.

The negative approach of 'Ton dob, ton trips' and so on is stood on its head, so that all possible combinations of footwear are ascribed to Mr Knott, just as later all possible combinations of various physical characteristics are ascribed to him. The effect is to spread the forward impulse of the narrative into a kind of non-meaning. As with the spatial extension of the conventional narrative into meaning, the reader 'knows where he is', but he is aware that his being there relates negatively to his desire to achieve a final understanding from the vantage-point of some Forsterian pinnacle. The device is rather like the stopping of a clock on the grounds that it will then inevitably be right twice in every twenty-four hours. It will, indeed, be right twice in every twenty-four hours, but there will be no telling *when* it will be right.

The other device used to effect the breakdown of forward narrative movement in *Watt* is the superimposition of anecdotal loci one upon another in the manner of *Tristram Shandy*. Thus the story of Mary grows out of Arsene's address to Watt, the story of the Lynches' millennium out of the account of Mr Knott's meals, and the story of Mr Nackybal and the Grants Committee out of Arthur's attempt to recommend the aphrodisiac, Bando, to Mr Graves the gardener, itself an account of doubtful relevance. Each of these episodes creates more and more space in the novel, while the account of Watt's service with Mr Knott creates less and less. This has the effect of distorting the overall space of the novel, rather as Watt's verbal inversions and convolutions can be thought to distort the linear aspect of his narrative. The most significant aspect of the digressions is that the reader is initially concerned that they should end, so that the book can return to its principal subject. A measure of the degree to which forward momentum in *Watt* becomes dislocated is the fact that only the digressions show any development. And this amounts, in practice, to a negative development.

If we add together all these evasive devices, plus the equally digressive accounts of Mr Hackett and the Nixons, Mr Spiro, Lady McCann, Watt's mixed choir, the Galls father and son, and Mr Gorman's plans for reducing the number of station keys, all that remains is the series which determines the running of Mr Knott's establishment. This, too, has the effect of diffusing meaning, rather than concentrating it upon the claim to significance of any individual person, act or object.

Watt exists as a series of empty spaces which contrive to overwhelm the linear movement of a story which the novel finds itself unable to tell. The attempt to tell, and the failure to tell, are more central to the book than anything that is actually told. The text itself has taken over what was, in the previous novel, the function of Murphy's mind. It evades its narrative function, and provides instead the setting for Beckett's first serious approach to what in the *Three Dialogues* he calls 'the ultimate penury' (p. 121).

For all that, *Watt* is set in Ireland. *Molloy*, the first of the full-length novels to be written in French, is set in Ballyba and Turdyba. Whether or not the landscape of *Molloy* is recognisably that of Dublin and its environs, the laws which apply to it are radically different from those of a naturalistic topography. As Molloy's voices tell him:

... Molloy, your region is vast, you have never left it and you never shall. And wheresoever you wander, within its distant limits, things will always be the same, precisely ... And the confines of my room, of my bed, of my body, are as remote from me as were those of my region, in the days of splendour.   (pp. 65–6)

Ballyba is essentially what Moran calls it, 'the Molloy country' (p. 132). There is no question of a journey of the kind that Watt undertook, because it is Molloy himself who provides the wide criterion of definition for the space he occupies. The police station and Lousse's house are no more than contingent features. By the end of his narrative physical topography itself is found to be insignificant: 'Molloy could stay where he happened to be' (p. 91).

Throughout Beckett's trilogy the idea of space becomes more and more bound up with the structure of the novels themselves. *Molloy* can be described as comprising two spaces, Molloy's narrative and Moran's narrative, which are linked by a series of detailed correspondences, although these correspondences are unable to establish a perfect continuity between the two. The basis for such a continuity would be the assignation of a common identity to Molloy and Moran. But such an identification cannot finally be made. First, the connections are made as from one *space* to another, rather than from points along a single line of development. For example a knife rest is stolen by Molloy from Lousse, and a knife rest turns up on Moran's dinner table.[5] Molloy's knife rest can be identified with Moran's only if Molloy's narrative is allowed a temporal precedence over Moran's. But identification requires that Moran's narrative should be prior to Molloy's. This is a small point; a more substantial one is the importance of Molloy as Moran's destination. As Moran follows Molloy and yet must remain for ever divided from him, so Moran's narrative 'follows' Molloy's and must remain for ever divided from it. It is because the two narratives cannot be reduced to a single one that a sense of space is created by what would otherwise be a predominantly linear novel.

Both narratives begin at the end of a journey and at the beginning of the narration of that journey. Moran comments on the beginning of his journey: 'I had a methodical mind and never set out on a mission without prolonged reflection as to the best way of setting out' (p. 98). Molloy comments on the beginning of his narrative: 'I began at the beginning, like any old ballocks, can you imagine that?' (p. 8). The journey and the narrative are analogues one of the other, and to begin either is viewed as a necessary *faux pas*. To journey is to journey to the end, not of the journey, but of journeying. What happens to Molloy is what begins to happen to Moran: he experiences a deterioration of the means of locomotion, losing his bicycle and losing the use of his legs. Molloy's movement through space is an attempt to travel in a more or less straight line by going round in circles. And at the end of travelling is the telling, which also involves the gambit of going round in circles in the hope of getting somewhere. Bodily movement is as laborious and painful as, later in the trilogy, narrative movement is to become.

Like *Molloy*, the whole trilogy is a journey simultaneously forwards from one page to the next, and backward towards its own origins. Later the backwards aspect of the journey suggests the attempt of a space to contract inwards to a single point, but *Molloy*, which is concerned with the end of travel and the beginning of telling (which is a telling about the end of travel) suggests a line which marks a movement simultaneously forwards and back. Moran's putative goal is Molloy, and Molloy's putative goal is his mother: '. . . all my life, I had been going back to my mother . . .' (p. 87). His destination proves to be, not his mother, but his mother's room, the confined and confining space in which he sits writing. Birth exposes one to phenomena, of which Moran says: '. . . it is thanks to them I find myself a meaning' (p. 111). But the world of phenomena is only an infinite contingency, from which it is necessary to withdraw in order to consider the question of meaning itself. The only legitimate object of inquiry is the question of the source of that inquiry. In 'Molloy's country' the source is Molloy. But this inevitably involves the inquiry in a process of self-division. Moran goes in search of Molloy, but is divided from him by the logical barrier which divides one narrative from another, one narrating voice from another. The only way into Molloy's narrative is from inside through the narration, and there is only one object of narration, the narrator himself. As, then, the narrator is both subject and object, the inquiry finds itself involved in the quandry illustrated by Kierkegaard's famous account of the self: 'The self is a relation which relates itself to its own self, or it is that in the relation that the relation relates itself to its own self.'[6] This central importance of the subject-as-object-as-subject would indicate that to identify Molloy and Moran would be to reverse the overall trend, which is towards the breakdown of single units of identity. Moran is a candidate for the role of subject, with Molloy as the intended object of his search. But Molloy is his own subject, while Moran gradually deteriorates into being his own object. The novel's task is to 'get out of itself' by moving towards a single point of departure for the second novel of the trilogy. It does so as follows: the movement of Molloy's narrative is not towards a conclusion, but back to its beginning (Molloy writing his narrative), it moves in a circle. Moran's narrative also describes a circle, but its gesture, as soon as it has come full circle, is one of self-refutation: 'Then I went back into the house and wrote, It is midnight. The rain is beating on the windows. It was not midnight. It was not raining' (p. 176). The function of Moran's narrative is finally to demonstrate that the novel's *ne plus ultra* is the ending of Molloy's narrative. The novel's second part, with its paragraphs and its shadow of purpose and meaning, is there precisely to discredit the pursuit of purpose and meaning. The quasi-spatial organisation of *Molloy* defines an *impasse* beyond which no further development is possible. It is this *impasse* which gives rise to the form of *Malone Dies*.

The verbal loci of *Watt* are conspicuously absent from *Molloy*. The account of Molloy's disposition of his sucking-stones, which would lend itself to this kind of handling, is developed anecdotally and then abandoned. The loci of *Molloy* are the two narratives themselves. They make up the two halves of the work, they would seem to compete together for precedence one over the other. But if the final emphasis is thrown upon the first part, both parts turn out to function in terms of something beyond and outside them.

Yet perhaps, in order to formulate a quasi-spatial description of the trilogy, it is more helpful to think of *Malone Dies* and *The Unnamable* as underlying (that is, as something *in*side) Molloy. *Malone Dies* and *The Unnamable* are very closely bound up one with the other, so that it is convenient to give an account of the two together, working, as it were, from the inside out. At the centre is the Unnamable himself; he is the self, the unnamable namer, to whom 'all these Murphys, Molloys, and Malones' are 'other'. For whatever the subject names becomes *de facto* an object, while the subject himself is: 'The one outside of life we always were in the end, all our long vain life long. Who is not spared by the need to speak . . . ?' (p. 349). Towards the end of his monologue the Unnamable says: '. . . here all is strange, all is strange when you come to think of it, no it's coming to think of it that is strange, am I to suppose I am inhabited,

I can't suppose anything, I have to go on . . .' (p. 406). He has to go on, but to go on is not necessarily to progress. All is strange because he inhabits a space of which he is the a-spatial centre, yet he is also the space itself, 'inhabited' by the Murphys, Molloys and Malones. At an early stage he describes it as a dim solar system with himself at the centre and Malone (or is it Molloy?) and 'the pseudocouple Mercier-Camier' revolving round him. No account of this space can be taken as finally authentic, as the determining criterion, the Unnamable himself, can never be included satisfactorily as a stable element in the account.

The two 'namables' of the novel are Mahood, who is both teller and object-hero of the story of a limbless head and trunk living in a jar outside a public eating-house, and Worm, of whom the Unnamable says: 'Feeling nothing, knowing nothing, he exists nevertheless . . . others conceive him and say, Worm is, since we conceive him . . .' (p. 349). Mahood and Worm are both aspects of the Unnamable, yet because they are named by him, they are beings entirely 'other' from him, projections away from the centre.

The unnamable underlies Malone, just as Malone underlies Molloy. The difference between the Unnamable's relationship to Malone and his relationship to Mahood is that while Mahood is presented from the first in terms of 'story', the anecdotal status of Malone himself is evident only outside the confines of his narration. It is from the viewpoint of the Unnamable that Malone, who tells his story of the life of an imaginary Macmann, is himself the subject of a story about the death of Malone. Each of these stories demands an increasing degree of effort on the part of the teller, and both finally break down.

It is into these two elements, the death of Malone and the life of Macmann, that *Malone Dies* subdivides. The one purports to be truth, the other fiction. *The Unnamable* can also be divided into stories and not-stories. But while Malone's account of himself is allowed to pass as the truth about him, all the Unnamable can say which is not immediately classified as 'story' is given a form of equivalent to Moran's final self-contradiction in *Molloy*. The Unnamable is a voice whose task is to refute everything it utters, thereby satisfying the claims of an extra-verbal criterion of truth.

Death, the anecdotal element which divides Malone from the Unnamable, can have no place in a first-person narrative. While Lady Pedal can be killed off with a sinister ease (she is 'written off'), the narrator can only fall silent. Death exists only as a possibility within silence, so that it is doubly beyond the reach of language. *The Unnamable*'s quasi-posthumous eternity of language and imagination is, in fact, the condition which underlies all the novels. But the novels that precede it, which cling to the anecdotes of a less than 'ultimate penury', pretend that it isn't.

Let us now consider how the pretence of space, the fictional topography of these two novels, is organised. Malone is confined to his bed in much the same way as Molloy was. What is new is that Malone's account is not of how he got there, but of his being there. While Molloy begins confidently, 'I am in my mother's room', Malone observes more tentatively, 'This room seems to be mine' (pp. 7, 83). Retrospectively, we can see that the room is anecdotal, only less blatantly so than the story of Macmann. 'Sometimes', says Malone, '. . . it seems to me that I am in a head . . . But thence to conclude the head is mine, no, never' (p. 222). His accounts of the room, which, like 'the Molloy country' is defined by his presence in it, begin increasingly to suggest that it must finally take its place as no more than an extension of '. . . the long familiar galleries, with my little suns and moons that I hang aloft . . .' (p. 237). Malone's loss of his stick robs him not only of the ability to reach his possessions, but of a means of measuring space. Thereafter essential space can be thought to have contracted to within the limits of the bed, and later to the still-sentient parts of Malone's body. In Beckett's ironic Cartesian universe, the separation of 'trips' from 'dob' is seen, if not exactly as a release, at least as something of a clarification.

Macmann, Malone's fiction, explores the fictional space which he inhabits by rolling in a huge circle round the plateau in falling rain, indicating its emptiness and freedom from the purposive shadow of direction. This contrasts with the

'great polygon' which is intended to take Molloy 'in a straight
line, in spite of everything, day and night towards [his]
mother' (p. 90). Macmann ends up in the ironic place, the
asylum, but towards the end of his story (or what is told
of it) he is taken on an excursion to 'the island', a place
defined in terms of its limits. The idea of 'the island' reappears in *The Unnamable*: 'The island, I'm on the island,
I've never left the island' (p. 329). The final problem of
the Unnamable's journey involves the reconciling of self to
self, and is expressed in spatial terms: '. . . how to get back
to me, back to where I am waiting for me . . .' (p. 324).
Under the solipsistic conditions which prevail in a work of
fiction, space (unlike time) cannot conveniently be transformed
into a feature of the individual's psychology. Space will not
forgo the claim that it is 'out there', even when it is invoked
as a measure of the 'little world' of consciousness.

In fiction the question of consciousness is reducible to
the use of language. Fictional space is the product of a moving
line of language, and the path /landscape distinction will not
hold up once language begins to project mutually contradictory
ideas of space. In *The Unnamable* the contradictory treatment
of identity results in a breakdown in the coherence of the
novel's presentation of the spatial dimension: '. . . I am afraid,
as always, of going on. For to go on means going from
here . . . and beginning again . . . in another place, where
I shall say I have always been' (p. 304). The Unnamable
is obliged to function as the place that he himself is in,
so that his inability to place himself is an extension of his
inability to name himself. In the same way his voice, rather
than the sum total of the words which it utters, is the context
within which the words are to be understood. It is the speaking
voice which provokes the assumption of a spatial context
out of which it speaks. And the meaning of what it says
attaches itself to the idea of an underlying spatial coherence.

A non-fictional text, like a shopping list or a government
white paper, yields its meaning without raising the question
of where the meaning comes from. The meaning, it is assumed,
comes from the words on the page. But in fiction there is
always the presumption of a speaking voice and a space in

which to locate it. Space is implied as a condition of the voice. So at the beginning of *Waverley* the speaking voice becomes attached to the idea of Waverley-Honour by virtue of the topographical dimension which it generates. The most fundamental response to a novel is for the reader to locate it off the page, somewhere *within itself*. We can see just how irresistible the process of place-making is if we consider the Unnamable struggling to place himself:

Help, help, if I could only describe this place, I who am so good at describing places, walls, ceilings, floors, they are my speciality, doors, windows, what haven't I managed in the way of windows in the course of my career, some opened on the sea, all you could see was sea and sky, if I could put myself in a room, that would be the end of the wordy-gurdy, even doorless, even windowless . . . (p. 403)

For the reader of *The Unnamable* this failure to describe functions as a description. A few words are all that is needed to provoke the sense of an adequate spatial context. The room that is negated is taken as being negated in the room that is negated. If, as Sartre suggests, the things of the imagination are jerry-built and partake of an 'essential poverty', they can be erected with an immeasurable speed out of less than nothing. The demand of the understanding for a spatial context is enough to guarantee a spatial context. At the beginning of *Waverley*, all we have is the bare place name, Waverley-Honour.

Beckett's recent short text, 'Lessness', can be seen as a final exposition of the issue of fictional topography. This work consists of a series of paragraphs, only a minority of the sentences having a main verb. A number of words and phrases, suggesting a simple landscape involving a human figure, ruins, earth, sand and sky, are combined and recombined. Four colour adjectives are used: black, white, blue and (ash-)grey. These descriptive clues combine with a series of commenting words and phrases ('refuge', 'issueless', 'he will live again', 'he will curse God again') to offer the reader a scene, and an anecdote, both for ever on the brink of realisation, but always held back by the fragmentary nature of their contradictory formulations, and the lack of forward movement indicated by the dearth of verbs. The voice, detached and unobtrusive, is in marked contrast to the despairing struggle of *The Unnamable*'s first-person narration. With the shadow of purpose departs the need to rationalise the topography, for the landscape is no longer the predicament of the voice which tells of it, although the problem of space as a 'wild imagining' is retained:

Face to calm eye touch close all calm all white all gone from mind. Never but imagined the blue celeste of poesy. Little void mighty light four square all white blank panes all gone from mind. (p. 13)

. . . Never was but grey air timeless no sound figment the passing light. (p. 16)

Beckett's novels are much more than an exploration of the problem of fictional space. But whereas many aspects of the novels become distorted in discussion, so that the all-important experience of reading them is left out of account, the insight they provide into the way the fictional voice creates a fictional topography is one of their more accessible features. If there remains anything further to be said, it is that if one casts one's mind back from the ethos of the novelist to that of the story-teller, this insight becomes self-evident truth. The naturalistic novel incorporates the voice of the (once visible) story-teller into the fiction itself, so that the voice becomes a subordinate feature of the illusion.

Page references are to the following editions of Beckett's works:
  More Pricks Than Kicks (London, 1970)
  Murphy (London, 1963)
  Watt (London, 1963)
  The Trilogy (Calder, 1959)
  Three Dialogues (with Georges Duthuit) (London, 1965)
  'Lessness' in *No's Knife* (London, 1970)

  1   E.M. Forster, *Aspects of the Novel* (Harmondsworth, 1962), 95
  2   W. Scott, *Waverley*, ed. Andrew Hook (Harmondsworth, 1972), 37

3   The reason why *How It Is* is not discussed in this paper is that as an illustration of the argument advanced here it is sufficiently straightforward not to require special consideration
4   Friedrich Nietzsche, *The Genealogy of Morals* (New York, 1963), 277
5   Molloy does not know what it is; see pp. 63, 116
6   S. Kierkegaard, *The Sickness Unto Death*, transl. Walter Lowrie (Princeton, 1968), 146

11 Muriel Spark and Jane Austen

Bernard Harrison

I

Here are some reasons for disliking the novels of Muriel Spark. First, that she is, as the mother of a friend of mine put it, a girl of slender means. Her books are too spun-out. They seem all surface, and a rather dry, sparsely furnished, though elegant and mannered surface at that. The one exception is *The Mandelbaum Gate*, which offers us, as the blurb-writers say, a vivid panorama of contemporary Israel. But *there*, if you like, is a book which lacks moral profundity. A serious young man once told me that he could find nothing but distaste for a writer who, confronted by the Arab–Israeli conflict with all its tragic moral and political dilemmas, chose to treat it all, as he put it, merely as the background for a trivial love story.

'Trivial.' The word is out. Yet Muriel Spark's novels seem, while one is reading them, to be profoundly, if obscurely, preoccupied with morality, not to say moral theology. Indeed they seem to be about nothing else. But there is no denying the obscurity. One is reminded of F.R. Leavis's remark about Henry James:

We have, characteristically, in reading him, a sense that important choices are in question, and that our finest discrimination is being challenged, while at the same time we can't easily produce for discussion any issues that have moral substance to correspond.'[1]

The trouble with James, however, is presumably that the nerve of morality often seems finally to be obscured by the very detail of the dissection through which James tries to expose it. In Muriel Spark obscurity has an exactly opposite

225

source, in what is felt by many readers as a kind of studied inconsequentiality which pervades her work, and which is also a prime source of the felt 'thinness' of the novels.

Partly the air of inconsequentiality stems from Miss Spark's authorial tone of voice, which is characteristically cool, level and uninvolved, and occasionally enigmatically flippant. Listen to the transition between the murder of Merle Coverdale by Mr Druce in *The Ballad of Peckham Rye*, and the next section of the chapter:

> He came towards her with the corkscrew and stabbed it into her long neck nine times, and killed her. Then he took his hat and went home to his wife.
>
> *
>
> 'Doug dear,' said Miss Maria Cheeseman. (p. 136)

This is very elegant: but is the blood real? And what of the enigmatic Dougal Douglas, whose unfathomable machinations have led to this death?

> Much could be told of Dougal's subsequent life. He returned from Africa and became a novice in a Franciscan monastery. Before he was asked to leave, the Prior had endured a nervous breakdown and several of the monks had broken their vows of obedience in actuality, and their other vows by desire. Dougal pleaded his powers as an exorcist in vain. Thereafter, for economy's sake, he gathered together the scrap-ends of his profligate experience – for he was a frugal man at heart – and turned them into a lot of cockeyed books, and went far in the world. He never married. (p. 142)

Is this, as it seems, indulgent amusement at Dougal's goings-on, or is something deeper at stake? The glancing reference to Catholicism – Dougal's becoming a Franciscan novice – suggests the latter. But then how serious is Muriel Spark's Catholicism? Barbara Vaughan in *The Mandelbaum Gate* is, after all, prepared to marry without the consent of the Church, though she would prefer not to have to do so. When that knot is finally cut her marriage still rests, unbeknown to her, on the bottomlessly insecure foundation of a forged birth certificate; and this state of affairs is apparently taken by the narrator, and by one of the priests whom Ricky consults to try to get at the reasons for the failure of Joe Ramdez's well-laid plot, almost as a sign, or a gratuitous grace.

The priests all said in effect, 'Well, if both parties remain in ignorance and the Church is satisfied, then it's a valid marriage.'

'According to the logic of the Catholics, that seems impossible.'

No, they mostly said, it was quite logical if one started from the right premise. Others said, well, logic or no logic, that was the case. One of them replied, 'With God, everything is possible.' (p. 245)

All this has a merry ring of Chestertonian paradox about it. But for Chesterton paradox was a device – paradoxically – for enforcing upon over-sophisticated minds the claims of an orthodoxy which he believed not merely to constitute the central tradition of Christianity but also to correspond to the ultimately sane, and naïvely realist, perceptions and sentiments of a child or a simple man.[2] In Muriel Spark paradox is not a means of leading us to an emphatic rediscovery of 'orthodoxy' or of the world as it 'really' and 'objectively' is. It seems rather to be sought for its own sake. But that raises the question of whether what underlies it is not the bottomless relativism Chesterton feared. Seen in this light the 'lightness of touch' for which Miss Spark has been praised may seem all too explicable: mere intellectual shiftiness; a paper screen concealing an abyss.

Once raised, the charge of shiftiness can be extended all too easily to plot and characters. Nothing is ever fully explained or given depth. When, at crucial points, the puzzled reader demands explicit enlightenment, he is invariably fobbed off with an authorial giggle or a significant silence. Or novels suddenly peter out into scraps and fragments of action and conversation, as at the end of *Jean Brodie* or *The Comforters*, and the reader is left to work out for himself why these particular fragments have been shored against the ruin of what had appeared until then, at least in long stretches, to be almost a conventional plot. If you see these things merely as failures of conception conveniently licensed by the canons of a fashionable 'modernism', then it is easy to see the most recent novels, *The Driver's Seat, Not to Disturb, The Hothouse by the East River* or *The Abbess of Crewe* for example, as representing the final decay of a small and over-praised talent. On this view, surface and fashionable enigma have finally won out: there is nothing to be seen but what is to be seen, and that is precious little, though terribly stylish.

II

There, bluntly and acidly stated, is a case against Muriel Spark which one often hears put in conversation but which I, at least, have seldom if ever come across in print. No doubt it rests on a superficial and unperceptive reading of her work; but still, I think, it expresses what many intelligent readers feel in their hearts; and hence there may be some practical utility in stating it clearly and meeting it head on. It must be answered, and not pushed aside, if we are to arrive at a more adequate reading.

One answer, of course, is that these are not 'traditional' novels. But that in itself gets us very little further. Even if '*the traditional novel*' is a real category, its principle of unity is clearly likely to turn out to be rather complex. Such a principle can be clearly formulated only by means of a good deal of discussion conducted upon a far more modest level of generality, and it is to this discussion that I wish, in part, to contribute at present. If we are to see where, and why, Muriel Spark's fiction departs from the canons of the traditional novel we need a concrete example of a 'traditional' technique of fiction, and some reasonably clear idea of what such a technique achieves, and how.

For this role I shall select Jane Austen. Her major novels are everything that Muriel Spark's seem not to be: both morally and psychologically they are impressively achieved and coherent structures[3] into which a vast amount of concrete detail is incorporated without arbitrariness or loose ends.

At the same time there are parallels. Like Jane Austen, Muriel Spark is a moral satirist. Like her she paints with fine strokes upon a small canvas, and yet achieves at her best a power and universality which transcend the littleness and provinciality of her characters and their world. Both are, in some sense which is at least partly the same sense, anti-Romantic writers. Both nourish a preference for the concrete over the general, for what is actually, materially given over idealising fancy.[4] Both mistrust antinomian individualism, and the rejection of familial or personal ties (and, in the logical extreme, of the whole fabric of what is concrete, given and intractable to the individual will about our existence) which springs from it. Neither has much time for sentimental moralising; that is, for moralising which is not under the control of a moral intelligence which is exact and discriminating precisely because it is exercised about some concrete and intimately known set of circumstances.

The most obvious disparity lies in the overt clarity and coherence of a Jane Austen novel. We feel in reading her indeed that 'our finest discrimination is being challenged'. And in fact it is. I think we can use this sonorous phrase of Leavis's with absolute literal appropriateness in her case. But what does the phrase mean? What is it to have one's finest powers of moral discrimination 'challenged' by a novel? It obviously cannot mean, I think, just that the characters are sufficiently well drawn to excite a moral response. For the response in question might be a facile and conventional one, like the boos that greet the appearance of the wicked stepmother at a pantomime. A more satisfying debunking interpretation, particularly tempting since the phrase is Leavis's, is that by 'finest powers of (moral) discrimination' we are to understand merely the conventional moral responses of a better class of person than the average pantomime-goer; the responses, let us say, of a clever, puritanical Cambridge don with a taste for acid wit. But, unhappily for the devoted literary polemicist, this won't do either. Anyone who embarks upon the reading of Jane Austen with an open mind is likely to encounter a phenomenon which is both familiar and yet, when one thinks about it, very odd, not to say startling; and which makes perfect and unexceptionable sense of Leavis's phrase. It is this: that in reading a Jane Austen novel one's accustomed habits of moral response may be altered by the book. It is not merely that one may be forced to revise one's estimate of a particular character; that one may pass from thinking Emma a good deal nicer and kinder than most people around her to thinking her a self-indulgent snob and manipulator, gravely in need of Mr Knightley's restraining hand; or from thinking Fanny Price a dreary, priggish mouse to seeing her undue seriousness and passivity as faults wholly separable from her kind-heartedness and her quick perception of other people's suffering, which is in the end inseparable from her perception of their moral flaws. Beyond that the novel may succeed in altering, for a time or even permanently, one's whole moral outlook. It may in short make one aware of the possibility of just moral distinctions which one had never noticed, or had been blind to, before: that is why talk of 'challenging our finest discrimination' is in order.

But now, this is very queer. It is obvious how one can find one's moral outlook shaken or changed by life. But how can it be changed or even shaken by a fiction? Emma and Fanny Price are – and it is a measure of the power and strangeness of what is happening that one needs to take a grip on oneself to remember it – not real; they never existed. They and all the characters and events of the novels in which they figure were made up by Jane Austen out of her head from beginning to end. Equally clearly the domain of moral discrimination is life: the real actions of real people. How can it possibly be challenged by the imaginary doings and sayings of creatures of fantasy; creatures after all, who are just not subject to the constraints of reality; who can be made to do and say anything their inventor chooses.

It is, I think, possible to give a fairly short and clear answer to this question if we look closely at the mechanisms by which Jane Austen constrains our moral assent. Put generally, the technique by which she achieves this consists of the arrangement of the fictional 'facts' of the novel, so that whenever we endeavour to put a different moral construction on events from the one Jane Austen intends, we are driven back from it – unless we wilfully refuse to see certain things which are 'there' in the text – by the remorseless pressure of 'reality': that is, of the fictional reality presented to us by the novel.

Take, for example, Knightley's insistence that Harriet Smith is fitted both by background and natural parts for the society of the Martins and nothing more. Suppose we try to see this, not as clear-sighted and realistic concern for Harriet's happiness but as snobbish and exclusive social pigeon-holing. We are obstructed at once by the contrast with Mrs Elton's eternal babble of Maple Grove (if *that* is what we take as our standard of snobbery then Knightley is very far from it) and by Knightley's own transparent kindliness as manifested in his rebuke to Emma on the excursion to Box Hill. Then again there is the manifest factual justice of Mr Knightley's estimate of Harriet. Her simplicity, docility and slowness of uptake are evident throughout the book. Contrariwise, indeed, these characteristics and the facts of Harriet's background cast doubt on the quality of Emma's concern for her friend. If Harriet were brighter, less biddable and of better family there would be more of true friendship and less of Lady Bountiful in Emma's relationship to her, and the way would not be prepared, as it is through most of the novel, for Emma's painful discovery of the nature of her own motives and desires.

What we must notice here is that the attempt to construe Knightley as a cold snob is being turned and defeated not by any single piece of countervailing evidence, but by the whole structure of the novel. If we see Knightley simply as a cold snob we have indeed no explanation for his rebuke to Emma on Box Hill (simple countervailing evidence); but in addition we have the ambiguities of Emma's relationship to Harriet, by contrast with which Knightley seems such a paragon of directness and plain justice of vision. Emma and Knightley, that is, are each known to us in the end by the relationship in which they stand to Harriet, and thus indirectly to one another. Each makes the character of the other intelligible as the opposite term of a moral polarity which can be grasped only if we attend to each not as he or she stands in isolation, but in relation to the other. Again, what sustains the polarity, and gives it a firm foundation, is the fact that we have independent knowledge (knowledge independent of what either Knightley or Emma say on the matter, that is) of Harriet Smith's simplicity and lack of sophistication or social *éclat*.

In short the reader who, following his own private moral predilections, classes Knightley as a cold snob (just as he might do if he ran into Knightley in real life at one of Mr Woodhouse's dinners) finds himself not merely up against a countervailing anecdote (Box Hill), but up against a moral structure in which Knightley's character, Emma's character, and Harriet Smith's independently known nature are held in a tension, a polarity, which defines not merely Emma's and Knightley's characters, but a general outlook on the world. You can look at other matters than Harriet Smith's prospects in terms of that contrast between a superficially benevolent and attractive romanticism and a dry pessimism which is the kinder just because it is the more honest and realistic. Indeed you can make out of it a vision, a philosophy and a way of life; and a long and important tradition of broadly liberal conservatism in English letters and English moral feeling has done so. In *A Passage to India*, for example, Fielding's sense that 'the British Empire really can't be abolished because it's rude'[5] seems to me a late and rather enfeebled expression of this tradition.

It is because they are concerned with the construction and exploration of a moral outlook of great potential generality that Jane Austen's novels, although profoundly concerned with morality, are not didactic fictions or moral fables. A moral fable simply illustrates a moral. It may illustrate, for example, how mere idleness, without any malicious intention, may cause great harm. It may show this as happening through a very plausible train of events and circumstances. But however plausible the fiction, and however strong the moral horror of idleness it produces in the reader's mind, the reader can always say, putting down the book and recollecting himself, 'But this is just a story; it never happened: and even though it *might* happen that does not show that idleness must have such consequences.' In short, moral fables suffer not only from being special pleading, but from being special pleading *founded upon a fiction*.

What we have in *Emma* is not at all this proving of a case, however plausibly, upon made-up evidence. We have the construction, through fictional exemplification, of a system of moral polarities and categories in terms of which we can, if we will, exhaustively partition and reduce to order the whole of our moral experience. The relationship of fictional 'fact'-making to the moral concerns of such a novel is quite different from its relationship to the moral concerns of a didactic fable. The 'facts' about Harriet's simplicity do not, any more than the 'facts' about who eventually married whom, support a 'moral'. They provide the foundation for a system of moral distinctions and oppositions which is not officiously pressed upon the reader, but which a candid and diligent reader learns and discovers as he reads the book, through learning by experience the ways in which the novel restricts his power to regard the characters otherwise than as Jane Austen intends. For this to happen, the fabric of the novel must be a seamless unity, so that no matter how the reader attempts to find footing for some 'private' view of his own, to the effect that Knightley is a cold snob or that Emma's wit and charm come to the same thing as moral intelligence, his foot will find no purchase. In addition novel-readers possess a great mass of miscellaneous knowledge drawn from everyday life about character and conduct. None of the 'facts' selected and assembled to form the 'reality' of the novel must be *ultimately* inconsistent with any of this: that is, inconsistent without an explanation internal to the novel which *is* consistent with it. That in turn means that the moral outlook which the reader learns from the novel must be one which the novelist can apply systematically throughout the fabric of the novel without either breaching the internal coherence of the outlook in question or, in pursuit of the coherence of his outlook, committing himself to events or characters which breach the canon of plausibility. Only a serious and powerful moral outlook can meet these demands; and indeed the capacity to organise a very complex and 'plausible' fictional structure can quite properly be taken for that reason as a species of empirical test of the seriousness and weight of the outlook in question, even though the material so organised is, strictly speaking, fictional.

We may, of course, if we are out of sympathy with Jane Austen's outlook, feel discomfort as we read her, and snipe in a limited and ineffectual way at her position. But to do more than snipe, to effect a real escape from the ordering polarities of her moral vision, requires an effort of creative imagination as serious and sustained as her own. And for that reason we are under a constant temptation to take her voice as the voice of morality *tout court*. The student who persists in seeing Harriet Smith as a working-class heroine provokes our impatience. He isn't *reading the novel*; he is letting 'external' moral considerations come between him and the text; in effect he is treating Emma and Mr Knightley as if they were real people whom he had just met, like the man who jumped on the stage during a performance of *Hamlet* to warn the Player King of the approach of the poisoner.

And we are right: this is not the way to read a novel. But there is another temptation; to take the moral polarities which the characters and events of the novel define as the form of morality itself, and the moral insights which it is possible to define within these polarities as the content of morality. Jane Austen does not tell us what to think about morality; we learn it; it proves itself upon the events of the novel, and these events are wholly plausible, and compose a naturalistically imagined world of great complexity, within which one can constantly stumble upon new insights which one missed on a previous reading. But learning the moral geography of this world is not learning the only moral geography there can be, or the moral geography of *the* world.

III

Because fiction and reality are held together in a Jane Austen novel by the tensions and constraints of simultaneously maintaining the plausibility of a complex fiction and the coherence of an organising moral viewpoint, readers feel that they 'know where they are' with Jane Austen, whereas with Muriel Spark they don't. Opening her novels one enters a world governed by ascertainable moral laws, by a viewpoint which proves itself exhaustively upon the events of the novel.

To every question there is an answer, because Jane Austen has made sure that there will be. The moral distinctions and polarities about which the novel turns govern its interior world as geometry and classical mechanics govern the world of Newtonian physics. To try to think oneself outside them and still read the novel *as a novel* is like trying to think of a material reality outside space, or to think of space itself as curved without recourse to the general theory of relativity. Similarly where the novel deals with moral growth, it is growth which proceeds against the background of, and is made intelligible by, this same Newtonian fabric of moral distinctions. When Emma discovers the ambiguity of her own motives, and by contrast the straightforwardness of Mr Knightley's, and knows at last to her chagrin that Knightley has always been right in their disagreements, she is discovering the inner logic of principles which her better self has held to all along, though blinded to their full implications by carelessness and self-indulgence. And this is no surprise: these principles are, within the novel, the only principles which can survive the scrutiny of an intelligent and clear-sighted critic: they *are* morality, and that is the end of it. Her self-discovery seems, indeed, less a confrontation with 'morality', conceived as a set of social norms of behaviour imposed upon life 'from outside', than a confrontation with reality itself. The greatness of the novel consists of its power to achieve this fusion of the form and the matter of morality; of values and the concrete realities of life which they nourish and organise.

But other novels offer other worlds, other air, which we can as easily learn to breathe as the air of Highbury or Mansfield. Opening *Le Rouge et le Noir* or *Pamela* we encounter moral outlooks as serious and as impressively fused with the fictional 'reality' of the novel, and through it, via the canons of plausibility, with real life, as Jane Austen's. We feel no strain in passing from one to another: we learn to do it as we acquire the habit of reading and the love of literature.

And this is strange, for we *should* feel a certain strain. What fills the space between these worlds? If one did not encounter them safely enclosed between the pages of books;

if one lived through the transition from one to the other, as people do live through experiences of conversion, or in a less conscious way and over long periods change their outlook on life through their particular experience of it, wouldn't one feel the very fabric of reality shifting beneath one's feet?

For obvious reasons the classical technique of novel-writing which we have been discussing will not easily permit you to deal with the experience of passing from one universe of values to another. It will not allow you to show the reader the gulf between a set of values taken together with the detail of the life, the *modus vivendi*, which they organise, and what gives life and content to all such partly conventional structures: the formless magma of human potentiality. But this, it seems to me, is Muriel Spark's peculiar subject-matter. In *The Mandelbaum Gate* Barbara Vaughan, a half-Jewish Catholic spinster on a pilgrimage in Israel, is questioned with flamboyant persistence about the ambiguities of her religious and racial identity by an Israeli tour guide:

Barbara thought, 'Who am I?' She felt she had known who she was till this moment. She said, 'I am who I am.' The guide spoke some short Hebrew phrase which, although she did not know the language, quite plainly signified that this didn't get them any further in the discussion. Barbara had already begun to reflect that 'I am who I am' was a bit large seeing it was the answer that Moses got from the burning bush on Mount Sinai when he asked God to describe himself. The Catechism, it was true, stated that man was made in God's image chiefly as to the soul. She decided, therefore, essentially 'I am who I am' was indeed the final definition for her. (p. 28)

But she cannot leave it there.

He was demanding a definition. By the long habit of her life, and by temperament, she held as a vital principle that the human mind was bound in duty to continuous acts of definition. Mystery was acceptable to her, but only under the aspect of a crown of thorns. She found no rest in mysterious truths like 'I am who I am'; they were all right for deathbed definitions, when one's mental obligations were at an end.   (pp. 28–9)

The last few sentences of this might serve as a general epigraph to the works of Muriel Spark. Her books are exercises for the reader in continuous redefinition. To see this it is easiest to begin with one of several books, *The Prime of Miss Jean Brodie*, *The Girls of Slender Means* or *The Mandelbaum Gate*, for example, which deal explicitly with conversion and the transcendence of a point of view. I shall concentrate for reasons of space on one of them, *The Prime of Miss Jean Brodie*. It is a curious feature of this book, which it shares with *The Girls of Slender Means*, that although it concerns a crisis in the beliefs and personality of one character, Sandy Stranger, as she emerges from childhood, the character in question is treated merely as one more character, and often a rather peripheral character, in the novel. We are not treated to a ringside view of Sandy's inner life, as we are to Emma's. At the same time we *know* in a rather external way all sorts of curious extrinsic facts about her. We know, for example, that when she slept with Teddy Lloyd 'she left the man and took his religion and became a nun in the course of time'. But we know nothing of Teddy Lloyd beyond his blond handsomeness and his capacity to turn every portrait into a portrait of Miss Jean Brodie. Of his *mind*, and thus of Sandy's mind from that source, we know nothing. Why does she become a nun in an enclosed order? What about her strange book of psychology, *The Transfiguration of the Commonplace* ('on the nature of moral perception')? Why put any of this in at all?

There are two answers, which are at first sight contradictory. The first is that the enigmatic and incomplete fragments of information which the novel drops casually concerning Sandy are meant to puzzle and irritate; to create in the reader a spirit of nervous dissatisfaction, of not knowing quite where he is going or what he is supposed to see when he gets there, which will make him work towards a reconstruction of Sandy's mind from the bits and pieces of information which the novel offers him.

The second and more important answer, which seems at first sight to contradict the first, but in fact complements it, is that the enigmas are there to obstruct the establishment of that systematic and unblemished unity of conception which it is of the essence of Jane Austen's genius to create and of her readers' pleasure to explore, and which makes possible the liberating, constantly surprising play of wit and moral perception which informs the interior of the novel precisely by the very rigour with which it restricts the range of what can enter the bounded, though not finite, world which it creates. The technique of a Muriel Spark novel is in fact exactly opposite to Jane Austen's: it works by continual *dislocation*, by setting up a fabric of faults and cleavages from one side of which the events of the novel can be construed in one way, while from the other they fall irrevocably (although we can recapture our first innocent vision by an effort of imagination) into another pattern. The pleasure of reading her lies in the unexpectedness and yet the justice of these discoveries. It is the pleasure of continually breaking out into a new-found world – a new level of sophistication – whereas the pleasure of Jane Austen is the pleasure of finding that each new vista, however surprising, is a vista of the same well-ordered park, and fits naturally and ineluctably with all the others. Muriel Spark's technique is inherently inimical to the setting-up of a single 'authorial' or 'ultimate' point of view from which alone everything in the novel can ultimately be seen as cohering with everything else (that point of view in a Jane Austen novel from which we stray only by dint of misreading or by ceasing to read the novel *as a novel*); although of course one can have a reading of a Muriel Spark novel which is *from a technical point of view* ultimate and 'complete' in the sense that it catches all the force (although perhaps not all the reverberations) of all the dislocations.

The Prime of Miss Jean Brodie is in this sense organised round Sandy's betrayal. Read straightforwardly from the first page on, the book can for some time be taken as a piece of amusing but rather lightweight social satire about the startling effect of a flamboyant and strong-minded spinster upon the girls of a drably conformist Edinburgh school. Of course even on that level there is an undercurrent of resistance and discomfort stemming from the urbane, deadpan irony of the style (one can trace the acknowledged influence of

Max Beerbohm here).[6] The book relies on one level on a stock response of liberal approval for the independent-minded, creatively subversive schoolteacher in order upon another level to subvert it, just as *The Girls of Slender Means* relies on and subverts a stock belief in the innocence and half-socialist community spirit of the war years and Golding's *Lord of the Flies* relies on and subverts a set of stock responses deriving from the boyhood reading of *Coral Island*.

However, even discounting style, the social-satire reading of the book runs steadily into choppier and choppier water. We pass from the idyll under the tree in the grounds of Marcia Blaine School for Girls, with Miss Brodie handing out to her enthralled little girls her coloured, delightful, half-sinful scraps of knowledge of the exciting adult world (so much more real and alive than the school subjects), to the isolation of her set in the whispering, private world of their precocity, to the strange fruits of political and sexual craziness that grow so naturally in this microclimate, untouched by the frosts of Edinburgh winters. Throughout this there is a constant swell, as of wind and tide in opposite directions, of uncertainty about what we are to think of Miss Brodie. Something obscure and darker struggles against the cosy, collusive intimacy of the 'Brodie set', which the reader at this point largely shares. After all, though, Miss Brodie *is* under attack from Miss Mackay and the governors.

'It has been suggested again that I should apply for a post at one of the progressive, that is to say, crank schools. I shall not apply for a post at a crank school. I shall remain at this education factory where my duty lies. There needs must be a leaven in the lump. Give me a girl at an impressionable age and she is mine for life. The gang who oppose me shall not succeed.' (p. 112)

And if she is a bit paranoid and has taken a leaf out of the Jesuits' book, well, she is under pressure. And she *is* a leaven in the lump. Doesn't she stand for independence of thought and for bold experiments in personal life?

'Interests you, forsooth,' said Miss Brodie. 'A girl with a mind, a girl with insight. He is a Roman Catholic and I don't see how you can have to do with a man who can't think for himself. Rose was suitable. Rose has instinct but no insight.' (p. 123)

Admittedly she is a fascist and she encourages her girls to sleep with the lover she will not, or dare not, commit herself to sleep with; and she encourages one, insanely, to go and fight for Franco. But after all, independence of mind and a boldly experimental attitude to personal relationships are bound sooner or later to lead one into deep water if one is serious about them . . .

The tolerant, easy-going voice in the reader's mind trails off. By the time we arrive at Miss Mackay's study, and Sandy's economical betrayal, we are mostly on Sandy's side, and the novel has turned retrospectively in our hands from a light social satire to a vision of metaphysical evil. Standing – like the half-adult Sandy – partly in and partly out of the Brodie set and its peculiar ambience, we are able to take Sandy's vengeful view of Miss Brodie as a secularised Calvinist.

> In this oblique way, she began to sense what went to the makings of Miss Brodie who had elected herself to grace in so particular a way and with more exotic suicidal enchantment than if she had simply taken to drink like other spinsters who couldn't stand it any more. (p. 109)

And later on: 'She thinks she is Providence, thought Sandy, she thinks she is the God of Calvin, she sees the beginning and the end' (p. 120). On this view Miss Brodie has sought a private election. She has sought to make the world intelligible on her terms by constructing a little world in which she can be, as none of us can in the real world, the source of all enlightenment. (It is no accident that this might also be a description of what a novelist does: on one level you can see Muriel Spark either as writing about her own craft and its predicament, or as using her own craft as a type of the human condition.) In this world love is a sentimental fiction. Jean Brodie's 'renunciation' of Teddy Lloyd is no more a real renunciation than her affair with Gordon Lowther is a real affair. Indeed it is hard to see what *reality* either man has for her: in the end they are both objects of her fantasies. To give body to this genteel, garish world of dream-sophistication she makes real children its accessories and servants, even to the extent of making them her sexual proxies: her 'set' is thus quite literally an extension of her person. And in other ways she deprives her protégees of innocence and of contact with reality (substituting for a knowledge of the real poor of Edinburgh her absurd visions of Mussolini's Italy, for example), and in one case of life itself. She has set herself in the place of God.[7]

Here at last is something which one might identify as the 'message' of the novel, and a very proper Catholic message too, which we can all greet with enthusiasm (especially if we are non-Catholics) and relief, since once one has discovered the message one can put the novel back, cheerfully unmoved like Miss Rickward in *The Mandelbaum Gate*, on the shelf with all the other books. But, thank God for Muriel Spark's intelligence, the novel's supply of concealed trap-doors is not yet exhausted, and the floor once again gives way beneath the reader's feet. The voice which delivers this impassioned judgement on Jean Brodie is Sandy's, charged with all the vengeful fires of adolescence, 'more fuming, now, with Christian morals, than John Knox'. This is the girl whose virtuous brutality in the demolition of Miss Brodie contrasts to such fine comic effect with Miss Mackay's genteel delicacy, no doubt rendered in a Morningside accent.

'I shall question her pupils on those lines and see what emerges, if that is what you advise, Sandy. I had no idea you felt so seriously about the state of world affairs, Sandy, and I'm more than delighted – '

'I'm not really interested in world affairs,' said Sandy, 'only in putting a stop to Miss Brodie.' (p. 125)

Here again, style is operating to disturb the reader's assurance that he is on the right track at last. Little stylistic land-mines of this sort pepper the concluding pages of the novel, and are the clue to their fragmentary, apparently offhand character. Thus Sandy herself, answering Jean Brodie's complaints about betrayal, sounds not, indeed, like the God of Calvin but like a cross between St Ignatius Loyola and the Christ of the Apocalypse casting out the lukewarm: 'Sandy replied like an enigmatic Pope: "If you did not betray us it is impossible that you could have been betrayed by us. The word betrayed does not apply . . ."' (p. 126).

But the real thrust of dislocation comes from Teddy Lloyd, who both loves Miss Brodie and sees through Sandy's new-found fanaticism.

Teddy Lloyd continued reproducing Jean Brodie in his paintings. 'You have instinct,' Sandy told him, 'but no insight, or you would see that the woman isn't to be taken seriously.'

'I know she isn't,' he said. 'You are too analytical and irritable for your age.' (p. 123)

The contrast between insight and instinct is, as we know, Miss Brodie's own. We are in no doubt that Miss Brodie prefers insight to instinct, which is indeed why she chooses Sandy as a natural confidante. Insight sets you above the mob; instinct plunges you into the ignorant darkness of passion and dangerous involvement. Sandy too, perched on her new-found rock of insight, finds love a dangerous enigma. It is for an answer to this that she rummages through Teddy Lloyd's mind.

To all this we have a footnote in the shape of Sandy's penultimate recorded judgement on Jean Brodie:

When Jenny came to see Sandy, who now bore the name Sister Helena of the Transfiguration, she told Sandy about her sudden falling in love with a man in Rome and there being nothing to be done about it. 'Miss Brodie would have liked to know about it,' she said, 'sinner as she was.'

'Oh, she was quite an innocent in her way,' said Sandy, clutching the bars of her grille. (p. 127)

In what way was Jean Brodie innocent? Well, there is a sense in which Jean Brodie is necessarily innocent: she has never *done* anything, has never *acted*. If you encounter the world as she does, only as shadows on the wall of your Platonic cave, then what you do to those shadows is in a sense not done to the people or things which cast them. The whole absurd charade of Jean Brodie's love-life is intelligible only as a series of devices to maintain an intangible barrier between the dream and the real world whose types and images figure in it: to ensure that no action passes this barrier. What happens to others as Miss Brodie tosses in her sleep is, poor innocent, not her fault. And it is significant that nothing much does happen to them. All the plain commonsensical girls like Eunice and Rose and Jenny pass through her hands unscathed. She harms only those who are like her: Joyce Emily Hammond, who shares her political romanticism, and Sandy, who loves daydreams, secret knowledge and the superiority which comes from 'insight'. What distinguishes Sandy from Jean Brodie is fear and desire. Edinburgh frightens her. To the man who comes to see her in middle age in her nunnery she says, 'I was once taken for a walk through the Canongate . . . but I was frightened by the squalor' (p. 34). As a child she does not go like the others to St Giles, 'with its tattered blood-stained banners of the past'.

Sandy had not been there, and did not want to go. The outsides of old Edinburgh churches frightened her, they were of such dark stone, like presences almost the colour of the Castle rock, and were built so warningly with their upraised fingers. (p. 35)

It is because she fears it that Calvinism is not a joke to her, as it is to Miss Brodie, but an alien presence which cannot be assimilated to the commonplace unity of her life but sticks out like a sore thumb.

Fully to savour her position, Sandy would go and stand outside St Giles Cathedral or the Tolbooth, and contemplate these emblems of a dark and terrible salvation which made the fires of the damned seem very merry to the imagination by contrast, and much preferable . . . All she was conscious of now was that some quality of life peculiar to Edinburgh and nowhere else had been going on unbeknown to her all the time, and however undesirable it might be, she felt deprived of it; however undesirable, she desired to know what it was, and to cease to be protected from it by enlightened people. (p. 108)

Desire leads her into the affair with Teddy Lloyd; jealously she wishes to know how he can love Jean Brodie, and she searches his mind to find out. Calvinism and Teddy Lloyd's mind: these two thrusting obstructions tear at the fabric of a life made from a nice Edinburgh suburb and the Brodie set. They let in light, give Sandy new ground to stand on, a vantage-point upon which to erect her critique of Brodieism and from which to act against it.

Sandy's betrayal is thus precisely *not* innocent; in one sense, obviously, because it destroys Miss Brodie for good – "'I'm afraid", Jenny wrote, "Miss Brodie is past her prime. She keeps wanting to know who betrayed her. It isn't at all like the old Miss Brodie; she was always so full of fight.'" (p. 127) – but more profoundly because Sandy knows and wills what she has done. It is the prime act of her liberation; it is the affirmation of her awakening from childhood and sleepwalking, from daydreams of Alan Breck among the heather and all that fatuity of *la crème de la crème* stage-managed by Miss Brodie. And therefore Sandy needs – must have – assurance that she *is* awake, that in her new and pristine state she sees straight, perceives reality at last: the commonplace transfigured. It is scarcely surprising that she should feel the need to write a book on the nature of moral perception; as we have seen, she is, like Jean Brodie, a great one for insight: she likes to feel on top of things as Miss Brodie, once Sandy has finished with her, plainly no longer does.

The loss of any assurance of reality, of the finality of any vision of what is or of what has worth, is the underlying theme of all Muriel Spark's fiction. In *The Mandelbaum Gate* two long passages occur, one an account of part of the Eichmann trial, the other a sermon by a young English priest in the Church of the Holy Sepulchre on fake shrines and commercialism in Jerusalem, which seem inconsequentially placed where they occur but which have, I think, a good claim to be the central pillars of the novel. Barbara Vaughan is a pilgrim in a land clotted with ambiguous history, with endless shrines among which it is impossible to distinguish the true from the false; in which a trial is going on which resembles 'one of the new irrational films which people can't understand the point of, but continue to see; one can neither cope with them nor leave them alone'.

The counsel for the defence consulted his document and drew his client's attention to specific names, Misters this and that and their sons, locked in reality. And his client, a character from the pages of a long *anti-roman*, went on repeating his lines which were punctuated only by the refrain, *Bureau IV-B-4*. Barbara felt she was caught in a conspiracy to prevent her brain from functioning.

. . . The man was plainly not testifying for himself, but for his pre-written destiny. He was not answering for himself or his own life at all, but for an imperative deity named Bureau IV-B-4, of whom he was the High Priest. (p. 179)

Later Barbara is arguing with Susi the impossibility of making religion something separate from life: a little block of sacred certainties of absolutely clear purpose and implications, against which we may measure and correct all the uncertainties of life.

'Well, either religious faith penetrates everything in life or it doesn't. There are some experiences that seem to make nonsense of all separations of sacred from profane – they seem childish. Either the whole of life is unified under God or everything falls apart. Sex is child's play in the argument.' She was thinking of the Eichmann trial, and was aware that there were other events too, which had rolled away the stone that revealed an empty hole in the earth, that led to a bottomless pit. So that people drew back quickly and looked elsewhere for reality, and found it, and made decisions, in the way that she had decided to get married, anyway. (p. 283)

Barbara's image of the empty grave catches the tone of familiar modern versions of the Victorian crisis of belief. God is dead, so everything is permitted; men's minds are transient sparks of consciousness adrift on the fathomless gulfs of time and space which confront us in the physical universe, a universe which is inanimate, springs from no ultimately assignable intelligible cause, is indifferent to human wishes and so on. We have an elusive sense that somehow Muriel Spark, through Barbara Vaughan, is making all this commonplace nihilism conned out of Nietzsche, or Bertrand Russell, look a bit vulgar and beside the point. But how?

Surely just turning one's back smartly upon the empty tomb of Christ as manifested in the Eichmann trial, and deciding to get married in defiance of one's church, is a grotesquely frivolous response to a genuine anguish?

Well, but it does not follow, because the Decalogue is not inscribed in the movements of the stars, that reality is an infinitely plastic substance which can be shaped to our dreams and desires in any way we please. That would be a real 'crisis of belief': to know that whatever we chose to believe or however we chose to live, the world would accommodate itself *without strain* to our wishes, so that anything we wanted could be made to cohere, without the need for any ingenuity, without the sacrifice of any other consideration, and without the need for any radical growth or maturing of our attitudes to things, with anything else whatsoever. Then we should really be in the padded cell. Philosophers sometimes manage to invent arguments which seem to show us to be in just such a position with respect to certain very special sorts of question. Do you see the things I see as green *as green*, or as blue? It can seem as if, provided the transposition were sufficiently systematic, no conceivable utterance or act of yours could reveal the difference, for whenever you see blue you will, after all, *call* it 'green'. But the cases which lend themselves to plausible scepticism of this sort are very special ones. Normally reality obstructs the free construction of private worlds of belief and feeling, as Edinburgh's churches, Teddy Lloyd, and the grating disparity between what Jean Brodie tells the girls about her love-life and what that love-life as witnessed and in part lived out by Sandy as confidante and proxy actually amounts to, obstruct and impede the influence of the Brodie set over Sandy's mind. We know reality, in short, by the inarticulate, mute resistance it offers to the human will. It is indeed true that reality offers us no final guaranteed description of itself, nor any real possibility of constructing one. But it is also true that its nature perpetually 'shows' itself, to use a term of Wittgenstein's, in the nature of the resistance it offers to our successive attempts to describe it, and that the nature it reveals in this dumb and in one sense passive way is not intrinsically vague and wavering but perfectly definitive and final, and, in short, real.

From this point of view Eichmann belongs in *The Mandelbaum Gate* as the polar opposite of Barbara Vaughan. He is fighting a long rearguard action against the evidence: the eroding drift of individually trivial, obstructive facts 'locked in reality'. In the process he is ceasing to be Adolf Eichmann, a man. He is not 'answering for his own life at all'. He is becoming the creature of the very construction which formerly gave him life, significance and importance – Bureau IV-B-4. He scuttles now over the disintegrating surface of Bureau IV-B-4 and the world to which it belonged, patching it together against the terrible, unremitting inroads of small facts. His condition is analogous to Pincher Martin's at the end of Golding's novel, and he stands here as a type of all those, including Miss Brodie and perhaps in the end Sandy herself, who, having built a world, occupy it until it breaks apart rather than admit its intrinsic separateness from reality. This is a process by which the self – the self as potential, the self whose life is creation – buries itself in the debris of its own constructions: 'The man was plainly not testifying for himself, but for his pre-written destiny.'

The Mandelbaum Gate is, in fact, about *letting go* of the world you have made for yourself. Barbara Vaughan, who is neither Gentile nor Jew, lets go of her comfortable condition of spinster schoolmistress with a sub-lesbian friendship when she meets Harry Clegg. In the same way she is not prepared to treat the doctrines of the Church on marriage as authoritatively deciding the question of whether she is to marry Clegg or not. But that does not mean that she treats the doctrines of the Church as of no importance. She treats them with perfect seriousness *as an impediment* to her marriage. It is indeed as an impediment, as something having the resistance and solidity of reality, that she values the Church, and that is why she hesitates to marry Clegg and have done with the charade – which for that very reason is not a charade – of the request for annulment, knowing that she will not find it easy to live without the Church to measure her life against. If she did not live in this curious tightrope fashion, between belief and apostasy, if she relapsed into being a Jew or a Catholic, a schoolmistress or a whore, someone bound by the chains of an ancient and authoritarian religion or a simple suburban pagan, she would become indistinguishable from many of Muriel Spark's nastier or more pathetic characters. You can measure her condition, for example, against the voice of Rudi Bitesch in *The Girls of Slender Means*, telling Jane Wright, from his fount of desiccating worldly knowledge of the limited possibilities of café ideology, of Nick Farringdon's general unsatisfactoriness as a sound party man.

Rudi said, 'You notice his words, that he says the world has fallen from grace? This is the reason that he is no anarchist, by the way. They chuck him out when he talks like a son of the Pope. This man is a mess that he calls himself an anarchist; the anarchists do not make all that talk of original sin, so forth; they permit only anti-social tendencies, unethical conduct, so forth. Nick Farringdon is a diversionist, by the way.' (p. 69)

Here, I think, we can find an answer to the charge of intellectual shiftiness with which we began. Curiously enough, it is not Barbara Vaughan's inventive Catholicism, nor the voice of the young English priest as he lists with muscular cheeriness one fraudulent shrine after another to the chagrin of the elderly priests who wait their turn to say mass, which gives us the sharpest vision of the empty tomb and the abyss which lies behind the screen of words. It is Rudi Bitesch's voice dividing life between dry and circumscribed doctrines which between them exhaust the very possibility of a new thought; or Eichmann's voice cataloguing the duties and responsibilities of an office in which official duty itself has become no longer a living expression of human community but a vapid and murderous fetish.

It is, indeed, precisely the refusal to admit that reality escapes all human formulas and established modes of response, and hence must continually be rethought, responded to freshly and incessantly each day, that lets in the void, that rolls away the stone to reveal an empty tomb. It is from this that Barbara turns away, to decide, to act. And it is because she can accept mystery 'only under the aspect of a crown of thorns' that she can accept mystery.

Teddy Lloyd, like Barbara Vaughan, understands the possibility of simultaneously accepting and relinquishing a vision of the world. Teddy Lloyd's mind 'invents Miss Brodie on canvas after canvas'. She is for him not something fixed in any single vision of his, but something outside all visions, which can thus serve as a perpetual and inexhaustible source of new creation, and is known through the resistance it offers to imagination in the work of creation. The real Miss Brodie is what each new-minted picture has in common with all those that went before it: but *that* cannot be expressed in a picture.[8] That is how he can know Jean Brodie to be just as ridiculous as Sandy makes her out to be, and yet still love her. Sandy's view of her is quite just, but it is not final: it has not the piercing security which 'insight' would have if it were not the epistemological chimera which it is.

Muriel Spark leaves open, I think, the question of whether Sandy cleaves to 'insight' to the bitter end. The fact that she tries to capture the nature of moral experience in a book suggests that she does, as does the final haunting image of her 'clutching the bars of her cell'. For if we cannot know the world from the standpoint of a single vision we cannot know it by detached contemplation at all. We can know it only through the experience of the resistance of the real, and to know that resistance we must commit ourselves, we must act, take chances. We find reality, as Barbara says, by making decisions.

The contrast between detached contemplation of the world, and exposure to the real in decision and action, runs as a connecting thread through all Muriel Spark's fiction.[9] But it is also, I think, the clue to her style and technique as a novelist. When Caroline in *The Comforters*, that curious novel about writing novels and being a character in a novel, leaves at the end of the book to write her novel, she leaves her notes behind her. This, I take it, is because the act of writing, if it is a real engagement with the world, must break from the husk of whatever preconceptions, hopes and expectations she may have entertained about it like a dragonfly from its larval skin. For a related reason Caroline *the character* leaves the novel when she begins to write, as Sandy does not. For again the process of writing, if it is a real engagement with the world, will change her. In creating we partly create ourselves, as Muriel Spark's Eichmann has ceased to do.

Writing is here a metaphor for living, in all those who have not so far chosen to die, and for reading. The purpose of Muriel Spark's technique, I think, is to construct novels that have to be read with the same sense of engagement with a perpetually obstructing reality. Certainly in reading *The Prime of Miss Jean Brodie* one passes, as I have tried to show, through a series of dislocations, each of which disturbs one's former conception of the novel and transforms it into something new. In the process the reader finds himself living through the stages of Sandy Stranger's childhood and conversion, and is finally led to see, *through* the texture of the novel, as it were, something about the nature of our relationship to reality which mutely shows itself in the ambiguities of Sandy's final state and of her relationship to Teddy Lloyd. This is not something the novel could achieve if it possessed the luminous integrity of surface and depths which Jane Austen's novels have. For then it would possess and generate a moral climate, on which the reader could repose his judgement, and the kind of reading which Muriel Spark needs for her purposes would be excluded.

In short whereas Jane Austen's art occupies the interior of a very serious and powerful moral point of view, Muriel Spark's is busy precisely at the still point at which worlds of consciousness, each organised and dominated by such a moral vision, cleave from the still and speechless surface of reality. I hope I have said enough earlier on to make it clear that in saying this I have no intention of denigrating Jane Austen, or of opening a polemic, which I consider wholly misplaced, as to which kind of novel is 'better'.

Quotations from Muriel Spark are from the Penguin editions: *The Ballad of Peckham Rye* (1960); *The Girls of Slender Means* (1965); *The Prime of Miss Jean Brodie* (1961); *The Mandelbaum Gate* (1962)

1   F.R. Leavis, *The Great Tradition* (Harmondsworth, 1972), 20

2   This aspect of Chesterton's work is discussed by Stephen Medcalf in his admirable essay, 'The Achievement of G.K. Chesterton', in John Sullivan (ed.), *G.K. Chesterton, A Centenary Appraisal* (London, 1974)

3   Doubts are most often expressed about the coherence of *Mansfield Park*, but I am inclined to discount them as resting on too ready an assimilation of Jane Austen's authorial moral outlook to the moral outlooks of Edmund and 'My Fanny'. The book is not a celebration of humourless and priggish passivity but a study of vanity, ambition and parental feebleness. That Jane Austen is aware of Fanny's deficiencies as a heroine is evident from, *inter alia*, the contrast with Susan, but Fanny is needed as she is to serve as a foil to the Crawfords; to show that wit and gaiety are neither necessary accompaniments nor sufficient conditions of goodness and moral intelligence

4   'One of the things which interested me particularly about the Church was its acceptance of matter. So much of our world rejects it. We're not happy with things.' Muriel Spark, 'My Conversion', *Twentieth Century* 170 No 1011 (Autumn 1961)

5   E.M. Forster, *A Passage to India* (Harmondsworth, 1961), 316

6   'What I like about Max Beerbohm is his attitude of not caring a damn about any of it, but under this he had a real style, a real humility. He didn't worry too much about what's not worth it' (Spark, 'My Conversion', p. 63)

7   A reader remarked here: 'It could easily turn into a sort of attack on God, couldn't it?' From seeing this it is a very short step to seeing why it doesn't, and to seeing why Miss Spark, despite her opaque laughter and her regular scourging of the orthodox, really is, after all, a Catholic novelist

8   Those familiar with Wittgenstein's *Tractatus Logico-Philosophicus* may perhaps recognise here the influence of his thought, particularly as it concerns pictures and propositions, and the distinction between 'saying' and 'showing'

9   Indeed it would not be all that far from the mark if one were to say that her books are about what Marxists call the Unity of Theory and Practice

12 'But time will not relent': modern literature and the experience of time

Gabriel Josipovici

I

I want to start with something so obvious that it hardly seems worth saying. But the obvious is sometimes overlooked and it is frequently important. Let me begin with the obvious then.

I open a book and begin to read. When the book is finished I pick up another – or write a letter, go to the cinema, to an art gallery, to a concert, talk to my friends. When the day is done I go to sleep and the next day carry on where I left off: I go out to work, carry on reading my book, play tennis perhaps. In other words I fill my days with various kinds of activities, and reading, writing, looking at pictures or listening to music happen to be among them. These activities follow one another in time, but they also help us to pass the time – help us, that is, to ignore the passing of time.

There are moments, however, when something in us rebels against this linear yet timeless existence. It is as if there were unexpected knots in the smooth rope of our lives. Wallace Stevens, in a poem called 'The Man Whose Pharynx Was Bad', has accurately described this state:

> The time of year has grown indifferent.
> Mildew of summer and the deepening snow
> Are both alike in the routine I know.
> I am too dumbly in my being pent.

The mind attendant on the solstices
Blows on the shutters of the metropoles,
Stirring no poet in his sleep, and tolls
The grand ideas of the villages.

The malady of the quotidian . . .
Perhaps, if winter once could penetrate
Through all its purples to the final state,
Persisting bleakly in an icy haze,

One might in turn become less diffident,
Out of such mildew plucking neater mould
And spouting new orations of the cold.
One might. One might. But time will not relent.[1]

We are creatures of time, and yet something in us longs for that impossible, that unique moment when winter will penetrate through all its purples to the final state. But nothing, not love, not religion, not even art, will set us free. Awake! a voice seems to cry. You are asleep! Awake to a new life, free of the eternal, meaningless ticking of the clock. But the frenzy engendered by the voice only thrusts us back more deeply into the arms of unrelenting time.

From one point of view all of Freud's work can be seen as the attempt to describe such knots in our smooth existence and to account for them. At the simplest level, Freud noted, there are slips of the tongue in everyday conversation, which literally force us to start again if we want to get what we want said. Then there are dreams, which pull us back to the events of the previous day or of our childhood, and sudden stabs of memory, which bring us into touch with areas of ourselves which had lain dormant for years. Finally there are neuroses of various kinds, from simple anxiety to fully developed hysterical paralysis, all of which assert the fact that some part of ourselves simply wants to stop, to put a brake on this meaningless forward movement. And one does not have to be a slavish follower of Freud to see the value of his insights. For the curious fact about the state I am trying to describe is that though we are completely subject to time, we are completely unaware of time. We are completely subject to time precisely because we are unaware of it. Thus Freud could argue that in all three cases – slips of the tongue, dreams, neuroses[2] – the smooth functioning of the organism is halted by pressure in two opposed directions. On the one hand part of us wants to keep at bay the recognition of time passing, since that would entail a recognition of our own eventual death; on the other hand part of us desperately wants to wake up from a situation in which time is not even acknowledged. In pursuing his linear existence, Freud would say, man is in flight from death, but also from his own body: the body calls out for recognition, but recognition of the body would entail the acceptance of the world in which that body has a place and thus of the fact that it will one day cease to occupy that place. And none of us, Freud came to see, is willing to give up the myth of his own immortality without a struggle.

To accommodate this insight Freud was forced to give up his dual schema of Conscious and Unconscious, or Reality and Pleasure Principles, and to replace it by a tripartite division. In this new schema he distinguished between the id and the superego on the one hand, and the ego on the other. The id is the unconscious, which knows neither time nor negation, but only immediacy; the superego, on the other hand, is man's consciousness and will as he uses them in the service of the id. That is, Freud came to see that man may and indeed does use all the wiles of his consciousness to protect himself from a real recognition of time and of the claims of the world.

Several years before Freud, Nietzsche had already begun to explore the curious paradoxes of man's subjection to time. Nietzsche was more interested in the superego as it manifests itself in history and culture than as it impinges on the individual. Early in his career he was struck by the odd fact that man is the only animal with a history. What, he wondered, are the implications of this? What is it that drives man forward into the future even as he builds monuments all round him in an effort to give permanence to the present? The enlightened men of his age had dismissed the belief in God as an ignorant superstition. But, Nietzsche noted, is not the belief in Progress held by these same enlightened men just as much in need of justification as the belief in God? For even the most seemingly disinterested scholarship is based on the implicit assumption that such work is valuable and that, when all the pieces are added together, they will form a meaningful whole. But why should they? The men of the eighteenth and nineteenth centuries had thought they could get rid of God, but all they had done, Nietzsche noted, was to substitute the God of Teleology for the God of Christianity.

For Nietzsche as for Freud, civilisation itself is Janus-faced: it reveals and it conceals. It reveals *as* it conceals. Like the dream or the neurotic symptom, it is a mute plea for help as well as a way of coping with an intolerable situation. When he asks, Why all this industry? Why this frenzied desire for Progress, for accumulation, for culture? he does this not in a spirit of mere nihilism, but in order to make men recognise the compulsive and irrational drives that inform even their most normal-seeming activities. And he does not of course exempt himself from his critique. He sees quite plainly that his own polemics against culture are themselves a part of culture and subject to the same criticism. Hence the growing despair of his thought and the growing fragmentation of his discourse.

Nietzsche sometimes talks about the entire history of the human race and sometimes only about the nineteenth century. Often it is difficult to decide what his target really is. But as with Freud, this does not lessen the suggestiveness of his insights. Indeed not only have the events of the last sixty years made it possible for us to be better readers of Nietzsche than his contemporaries could ever be, but developments in history and the social sciences, by drawing attention to various aspects of western society since his day, have made it possible to see more clearly the implications of many of his remarks. It is for instance possible to say that in Western Europe before the seventeenth century (and in much of the rest of the world to the present day) man did not live in so completely linear a fashion as he does today. Annual festivals, sacred and secular, once ensured a return to the

255

sources, a renewal through repetition. Time was accepted in the public celebration of mythical or historical events; rites of passage marked the key stages of a man's life, so that at each stage he was united both with other members of the community and with the history of his people. To some extent the liturgy still functions in this way for Christians (and Jews) today, but the numbers for whom this is meaningful have dwindled to such an extent that it retains little public or general significance. Sunday, far from being a day of renewal or remembrance, is a curiously empty, isolating day, an unreal hiatus in a life of continuous bustle. And it seems likely that the notion of a work of art as an aesthetic object, existing outside space and time, and asking of the viewer a contemplative rapture equally free of space and time, emerged only as other, more public, modes of escaping linearity were disappearing.

But linearity impinges on our history and culture in other, less immediately obvious, though more material ways. John Steane, in his book *The Northamptonshire Landscape*, writes, for example, about the changes that came over the village of Helpston during the lifetime of the poet John Clare:

Clare's vision was limited by the village which was the centre of a road system designed as an internal network to connect different places within the parish. This microcosmic universe was shattered by the work of the rural professional class and the new topography of enclosure was imposed on Clare's world. The ancient internal lanes vanished. Helpston was connected to the outside world with straight roads. The parish now simply became a place on the way to somewhere else. The linear landscape replaced a circular one.[3]

Gombrich has remarked how slow men are to grasp the implications of advances in their own technology and how conservative the design of technology remains. Thus the first trains had carriages that were still built merely as movable rooms. Reading Steane's remarks with hindsight one cannot but be struck by the thought that only a few years later railways would utterly transform not only the landscape of Europe and America, but also men's inner sense of what it meant to travel.[4]

Even more striking is the ease with which Steane's remarks can be applied to changes in the arts. In Fielding and Sterne the chapter is still the basic unit, just as in Hogarth even the rake's *progress* is presented by separate panels. The plot of *Tom Jones* may be hugely complex, but the book is really like a vast object suspended in eternity, in and out of which the author, with his guest, the reader, is free to wander, pausing to examine now this character or incident, now that, and then moving on. In the nineteenth century, however, even in so unromantic a writer as Jane Austen, the author has moved into the background (or rather has suffused himself into the very language of the book), and the chapter has become, like the paragraph, merely the indication of a pause in the swelling continuity of the narrative. In similar fashion the symphony of a Beethoven or a Berlioz has become a single unity, a wide arch stretching from first to last chord, and meant to be experienced as such, instead of as a group of discrete movements such as we find in Mozart or Hayden.

There are two important factors to note here. The first is that the work *leaves no gaps*. A Fielding or a Mozart remind us constantly that they are presenting us with a made world, something created by them for our pleasure and enlightenment. A George Eliot or a Verdi, by contrast, do their best to make us forget this, to make us enter right *into* the world they have created, to make us suffer with their heroes or heroines, until the novel or the opera is over. The second factor, closely connected with this, is what one might call *the tyranny of plot*. An opera by Verdi, a novel by Hardy is good in spite of its plot. And yet it would of course never have come into being without the extraordinary convolutions and unlikely coincidences which make up the plot. Even so restrained a novelist as George Eliot, in a novel like *Daniel Deronda*, which is in many ways closer to a twentieth- than to a nineteenth-century mode, is the victim of a convention of plot formation which she is forced to use without quite seeing its implications. Is it likely, for example, that Daniel should discover Mirah's brother with all London to search in? Is it likely that Mirah's father should chance upon *her*? And is it the slightest bit probable that

257

Daniel should find himself in Genoa and at just the right spot in that city at precisely the moment when Gwendolen is fished out of the water after Grandcourt has drowned? Such absurd coincidences would not bother us in Shakespeare or Fielding, but they do here, precisely because of the novelist's effort to create the impression that the novel is writing itself, that it is 'life', wholly unmediated by language.

Reading an intricately plotted nineteenth-century novel is very much like travelling by train. Once one has paid for one's ticket and found one's seat one can settle down in comfort and forget all everyday worries until one reaches one's destination, secure that one is in good hands. There are few pleasures in life greater than this, and it is Stevens again who catches the mood most perfectly:

> The house was quiet and the world was calm.
> The reader became the book; and summer night
>
> Was like the conscious being of the book.
> The house was quiet and the world was calm.
>
> The words were spoken as if there was no book,
> Except that the reader leaned above the page,
>
> Wanted to lean, wanted much most to be
> The scholar to whom his book is true, to whom
>
> The summer night is like a perfection of thought.
> The house was quiet because it had to be.
>
> The quiet was part of the meaning, part of the mind:
> The access of perfection to the page.
>
> And the world was calm. The truth in a calm world,
> In which there is no other meaning, itself
>
> Is calm, itself is summer and night, itself
> Is the reader leaning late and reading there.[5]

And yet, though few novel-readers can fail to respond to the accuracy of this, it is worth noting that the mood is captured precisely because the poet is both immersed and not immersed, both reader and watcher. One feels that at any moment for the reader the mood will be broken, and then the time of year will grow indifferent, the horror of meaningless routine will overwhelm the poet, he will suddenly feel that he is too dumbly in his being pent and experience sharply the malady of the quotidian: 'One might. One might. But time will not relent.'

II

Kierkegaard. Dostoevsky. Kafka. Three major writers who grew up in the great century of the bourgeois family, 1815–1914. Three writers who, whatever their differences, all share the same ambiguous relation to their own fathers. For in all three cases the father *is* the world into which the son has been born, and his acts and pronouncements have the weight of absolute authority. Yet in all three cases the acts and the pronouncements of the father can strike the son only as irrational and incomprehensible. Thus in all three cases the son is torn in two by conflicting needs: the need to obey something in which he cannot believe; and the need to rebel against something which is already planted so deeply inside him that rebellion is tantamount to suicide.

Kafka's is perhaps the most interesting case, because it is the most fully documented and because he was the most fully conscious of the vertiginous implications of the relationship. In his eyes the father stands for the world of progress, solidity, continuity, a world in which events and actions seem naturally meaningful. Yet his father, he soon discovers, is irrational, arbitrary, and tyrannical. Is his father then a petty autocrat who has no justification for his acts and pronouncements except for his own will? Or is there a sanction for these which Kafka for some reason cannot see? The issue soon takes the form (as it does for Kierkegaard): should he marry and become a father in his turn, or should he not?

Marrying, founding a family, accepting all the children that come [he writes in the letter to his father], supporting them in this insecure world, and even guiding them a little as well, is, I am convinced, the utmost a human being can succeed in doing at all. That seemingly so many succeed in this is no evidence to the contrary, for, first, there are not many who do in fact succeed, and secondly these not many usually don't 'do' it, it merely 'happens' to them; although this is not that Utmost, yet it is still very great and very honourable (particularly since 'doing' and 'happening' cannot be kept clearly distinct). And finally it is not a matter of Utmost at all, anyway, but only of some distant but decent approximation . . .[6]

The convolutions of this are typical of Kafka and they reveal clearly his central dilemma: is the ease with which other people lead their lives, marry, beget children, even die, the result of their lack of concern over the distinction between 'doing' and 'happening', or does it seem so only to one who is on the outside, and would the decision to get married, for example, automatically confer meaning upon the event? For it is meaning that is at stake here. Kafka's horror of committing himself stems from his profound sense of the sacrilege involved in lending oneself to a mere 'happening', especially if that involves the bringing of other human beings into the world. Yet the doubt always remains that this may be his own fault, that he may be personally excluded from a meaningful world precisely because of his doubts.

Kafka's art, to begin with, is the result of rebellion against his father and the lie of a life lived as though it had meaning. But almost at once he finds the father installed in the very heart of writing itself. The need for shape, for plot, for a forward movement of some kind, seems to be inseparable from the act of writing. And the act itself, the time spent alone in a room, filling blank pages with words, is surely a prime example of the assertion of will. But it is in order to escape such assertion, such wilfulness, that he has turned to writing in the first place. The rejection of the father thus turns into a rejection of himself, not just as businessman or father, but as artist. Hence the profound and quite incurable masochism that pervades every letter, every diary entry, every story that he ever wrote. The infernal circle has no outlet except for death, and one can perhaps see why Kafka welcomed the sudden flow of blood from his lungs which heralded his impending death. One can also understand why he genuinely wished his own work to be destroyed.

Until the moment of death, however, writing went on holding out for him the only hope of escape. In the first story with which he was fully satisfied (perhaps the only one ever), a father condemns his son to death by drowning and the son carries out his father's orders. The story ends as the son drops off the bridge into the river. By making his art out of the impossible conflict Kafka was able at least to carry on living. But the preponderance of unfinished stories in his *oeuvre* shows that this was no triumph: the conflict ran too deep for words like 'triumph' and 'human spirit' to acquire more than a hollow ring. It was a way of holding out, and the wonder is not just that so much did get written, but that even the tiniest fragments contain the seeds of the greatest tales.

Other twentieth-century artists have faced the same issues without finding that it cut quite so deeply into the fabric of their lives. I am thinking of Picasso, of Webern, of T.S. Eliot.[7] Let us look for a moment at one of Eliot's earliest poems, 'Rhapsody on a Windy Night'. Of its six stanzas only one does not begin with a statement of time: 'Twelve o'clock'; 'Half-past one'; 'Half-past two'; 'Half-past three'; 'The lamp said/"Four o'clock . . ."' And just as time here is only the ticking of the clock, so space is merely the eternal division of the long street by the regularly spaced street lamps:

> Every street lamp that I pass
> Beats like a fantastic drum,
> And through the spaces of the dark
> Midnight shakes the memory . . .

What both the clock and the lamp throw up are fragments of a world: 'Regard that woman/Who hesitates towards you in the light of the door/Which opens on her like a grin . . .';

'Remark the cat which flattens itself in the gutter/Slips out its tongue/And devours a morsel of rancid butter.' This seems to be the world of Imagism, but is it? The conclusion shows us why Eliot, for all his surface resemblance to the Imagists, was never one of them. There is no pleasure for the poet in this fragmentation of the world; on the contrary, this is a vision of meaninglessness which is forced upon him against his will, which he would dismiss if only a meaning could be found that would integrate the bits, but where every impulse towards integration is recognised as a dangerous temptation:

> The lamp said
> 'Four o'clock,
> Here is the number on the door:
> Memory!
> You have the key,
> The little lamp spreads a ring on the stair.
> Mount.
> The bed is open; the tooth-brush hangs on the wall,
> Put your shoes at the door, sleep, prepare for life.'

> The last twist of the knife.

Why the last line, separated as it is by all that space from the previous stanza? Because to enter the room, to leave the fragmented vision of the city at night, the awareness of the inconsequential ticking of the clock, the horror of events and moments which do not add up, is indeed to sleep. To sleep as Jonah slept at the bottom of the boat he thought would carry him away from God's insistent summons, the heavy drugged sleep of a man trying to escape awareness of himself. To enter the room is to take part in a falsehood; it is to assert as meaningful a world without meaning; to pause, to recognise its lack of meaning is at least to make possible the recovery of meaning. As Kierkegaard said, the deepest despair is not to know that you are in despair.

This is the theme of all Eliot's works up to and including *The Waste Land*. Every reader of Eliot has sensed this. And yet as soon as we try to articulate our feelings about his poetry, we fall prey to precisely the temptations he himself is trying to resist. We fill in the gaps, we assert continuity, we impute a meaning to the world he describes by searching for a meaning to the poem. Commentary, after all, grew up in response to sacred texts. It twined about the holy words like ivy on the walls of an old house. But Eliot and Kafka write out of a sense of the disappearance of that house. Their art is an effort to make us glimpse a world before sleep catches up with us again. Unfortunately even the best-intentioned commentator takes signs for wonders and turns art, like history, into a golden calf.

The power of Eliot's early poetry stems from its embodiment of a sense of awakening, and that awakening is always frightening, since humankind cannot bear very much reality. But there are other, less anguished responses to the same insight. One of Wallace Stevens's collections of poems is called *Parts of a World*, and many of the poems included in it repeat the emphasis of the title: 'You said/There are many truths,/But they are not parts of a truth' ('On the Road Home'); 'The squirming facts exceed the squamous mind' ('Connoisseurs of Chaos'); 'Yet having just/Escaped from the truth, the morning is colour and mist,/Which is enough . . .' ('The Latest Freed Man'). Truth, in Stevens's terms, is unity, and truth stops us seeing the world as it is. The free man is freed of the burden of truth, the imposition of unity, and so he can see again. 'The pears are not seen/As the observer wills,' he writes in the best evocation of the Cubist vision I know, 'Study of Two Pears'. But the most profound poem on this theme is perhaps the one called 'Add This to Rhetoric' – profound because it tackles the subtlest ally of 'truth', language. 'He has not got rid of God who still retains faith in grammar,' Nietzsche had written, and Stevens expresses it like this:

> It is posed and it is posed.
> But in nature it merely grows.
> Stones pose in the falling night;
> And beggers dropping to sleep,
> They pose themselves and their rags.
> Shucks . . . lavender moonlight falls.

> The buildings pose in the sky
> And, as you paint, the clouds,
> Grisaille, impearled, profound,
> Pftt . . . In the way you speak
> You arrange, the thing is posed,
> What in nature merely grows.[8]

To see, to report on what we see, is to perform a mysterious sleight-of-hand: it is to naturalise culture and therefore to culturalise nature. To recognise this is suddenly to be made aware of what we normally miss. The poem helps us to this awareness by laying out for us the purely human, man-made nature of our speaking and writing: adding this word to this word to this word.

The imagination of Robbe-Grillet, particularly in his finest novel, *Dans le labyrinthe*, is, it seems to me, closer to that of Stevens than to that of any French writer. In his novels he deploys his art to confound our instinct for linear progression and to deny us the luxury of 'the truth'. Thus *Dans le labyrinthe* begins:

I am alone here now, safe and sheltered. Outside it is raining, outside in the rain one has to walk with head bent . . .; outside it is cold, the wind blows between the bare black branches; . . . Outside the sun is shining, there is not a tree, not a bush to give shade. . .[9]

In *Les Gommes* the action appears to move forward only for us finally to discover that the book has ended where it began; in *Le Voyeur* there is a hiatus in the centre, where action and meaning ought to be. As with a Cubist painting, the reader is forced to move again and again over the material that is presented, trying to force it into a single vision, a final truth, but is always foiled by the resistant artefact: 'It is posed and it is posed. /But in nature it merely grows.'

III

Let us turn for a moment from books written within the last hundred years to one composed in the first decades of the fourteenth century. At the start of Dante's *Commedia* the poet, awakening in a dark wood, seeks to escape by climbing up a hill towards the sun which has just appeared over the summit, but is pushed back by three beasts who bar his way. Instead, with the guidance of Virgil, he turns and begins to move in a slow spiralling motion, first down to the centre of the cone of hell and then up the cone of the purgatorial mount, which is clearly none other than the hill he had first seen. At the top Beatrice appears to him, from the east, radiant like the sun, to name him for the first time in the poem and to carry him off to the manifold circles of the heavens.

Now the crucial difference between Dante the pilgrim and the inmates of hell is that they cannot move from level to level, but he can. As he descends lower and lower he discovers a greater and greater rigidity in the damned, a physical state which corresponds to their spiritual rigidity. The final, most moving image of the sequence is to be found at the very bottom of the universe, as Dante puts it, where those in the icy circle closest to Satan himself find that even their tears, the physical and spiritual token of life, change and compassion, are frozen on their cheeks and in their eyes, causing them intolerable torment. In purgatory, on the other hand, the pilgrims are, like the poet, on the move. As in life they exhibited enough suppleness to repent, so now they are given enough suppleness to wind round and round the mountain, rising, slowly at first but with gathering speed as they near the top, until at last, like Dante himself, they leave the cone and enter the circle of the heavens.[10]

The word 'turn' (*tornare*) plays a key role in the *Purgatorio*, reflecting the spiritual and physical suppleness of the souls encountered. Interestingly enough that word was to play a key role in Eliot's development as a poet. After the fragmentation of 'Rhapsody on a Windy Night', 'Gerontion', and *The Waste Land*, it seemed that no way forward was possible. How to write a long poem out of fragments? It had been done once and for all in *The Waste Land*. To write a narrative poem in the old Tennysonian or Browningesque modes was clearly impossible – the last twist of the knife. But it

is just here that the miracle occurred. Eliot, taking Cavalcanti's lines about his exile, about the impossibility of any
return to his homeland, and brooding on them, now found,
with Dante's help, a way out of the impasse:

> Because I do not hope to turn again
> Because I do not hope
> Because I do not hope to turn
> Desiring this man's gift and that man's scope. . .

The rhythm, like the sense, spirals slowly, returning to the
point of departure as if for reassurance, gradually gathering
momentum, until a whole long poem is generated by the
movement. And in the end it is that movement which allows
the semantic transformation to occur, as the poem moves
towards its conclusion:

> Although I do not hope to turn again
> Although I do not hope
> Although I do not hope to turn. . .

It must be clear by now that linearity, fragmentation, the
slow motion of the spiral are not ways of describing the
merely formal properties of a work, that we are talking about
aspects of art and of personality where questions of form
and content, of will and choice, are curiously irrelevant. Was
Eliot able to write *Ash Wednesday* because he had found
a faith, or was his conversion the result of a discovery in
himself of unexpected resources of suppleness made manifest
in the process of his engagement with his craft? Did Dante
the pilgrim find his way to heaven because Beatrice took
pity on him and sent Virgil to guide him out of the wood
of error, or did she take pity on him because she discerned
in him the desire for salvation? Dante wisely leaves that
question unanswered, and we would be well advised to do
the same.

As we might perhaps expect, Wallace Stevens has provided
us with his own version of the Dantean experience, and,
what is more, he has placed it at the gateway to both his
Collected Poems and his *Selected Poems*, thus underlining

its importance in his eyes. It is a short and simple poem called 'Earthy Anecdote':

> Every time the bucks went clattering
> Over Oklahoma
> A firecat bristled in the way.
>
> Wherever they went,
> They went clattering,
> Until they swerved
> In a swift circular line
> To the right,
> Because of the firecat.
>
> Or until they swerved
> In a swift circular line
> To the left,
> Because of the firecat.
>
> The bucks clattered,
> The firecat went leaping,
> To the right, to the left,
> And
> Bristled in the way.
>
> Later, the firecat closed his bright eyes
> And slept.

Just as Dante started by trying to move straight up the mountain, so the bucks try to run straight forward. But there is always an impediment in the way, barring the route. The only way to advance is to go on a long circular trek. Finally the firecat goes to sleep. Nothing now stops the bucks moving forward. But it is as though the bucks – *and the poem* – could keep moving at all only *against* pressure: with the shutting of the firecat's bright eyes the poem itself comes to an end.

We can see the spiralling mode at work in other master-pieces of the present century, most notably in *A la recherche du temps perdu*. The opening pages of that novel are just such a hesitant backward and forward movement as we find at the start of *Ash Wednesday*. It is as if we were watching a diver bouncing again and again on the spring board, gradually gaining height, until he is finally ready to take off. Only the gradual, hesitant spiralling motion can allow the huge novel to unfold, and even when it does start to move forward it keeps turning and returning to its roots, closer in mode to *Four Quartets* than to *The Forsyte Saga*. And the same is true, despite my earlier remarks, about *Dans le labyrinthe*, which stands in roughly the same relation to Robbe-Grillet's earlier novels as *Ash Wednesday* does to Eliot's early poetry. Instead of the Cubist fragmentation of *Les Gommes* and *Le Voyeur*, a way forward is discovered, a groping, hesitant spiralling, which eventually allows the 'I' of the first word to transform itself into the 'me' of the last:

I am alone here now, safe and sheltered. Outside it is raining, outside in the rain one has to walk with head bent, hand shielding eyes that peer ahead nevertheless, a few yards ahead, a few yards of wet asphalt; outside it is cold, the wind blows between the bare black branches; the wind blows among the leaves, sweeping whole boughs into a swaying motion, swaying, swaying, that throws its shadow on the white roughcast of the walls. Outside the sun is shining, there is not a tree, not a bush to give shade, one has to walk in the full sunlight, hand shielding eyes that look ahead, a few yards ahead only, a few yards of dusty asphalt where the wind traces parallels, curves and spirals.

I am not suggesting that the way of the spiral, the way of turn and return, is necessarily an advance on the way of fragmentation. Both modes (is mode the right word?) are responses to the deep dissatisfaction felt with purely linear modes by all the major artists of this century. In Eliot and Robbe-Grillet we have seen a movement from fragmentation to spiralling, but in other writers the reverse movement is discernible. After the spirals of *The Waves* came the fragmentation of *Between the Acts*; after the loops and hesitations of Beckett's trilogy have come works which seem to take a perverse pleasure in the refusal of even that consolation: *Krapp's Last Tape* and *Imagination Dead Imagine*.

IV

One more aspect of our theme deserves attention. In discussing the response of Kafka and Eliot to linearity I have tried to bring out the sense of betrayal that any 'talking about' engenders. But criticism is precisely the art of 'talking about'. How can criticism countenance the Nietzschian question: Why culture? Is criticism not itself the product of culture and committed to it? This helps to explain the ever-widening rift between modern art and the discourse about art which is criticism. The classic exploration of the nature and consequences of this rift are to be found in Thomas Mann's *Doktor Faustus*.

There is obviously more than a little of Mann himself in the figure of Serenus Zeitblom, the cultured academic to whose lot it falls to write *about* his friend, the composer Adrien Leverkuhn. Mann had a profound belief in Culture, in the value of art to society and in the ability of society to use art to enrich itself. Brought up as he was to revere the art of the nineteenth century, with its profound sense of organic growth and development, the new music must have come as a severe shock to him. For him it must have looked like a denial of the human in art, a denial of that happy marriage of thought and feeling which is the goal of civilisation. The art of Schoenberg and Webern, of the Cubists, of Joyce and Eliot, with its twin principles of fragmentation and discontinuity – was not such an art an affront to the humanist, since it founds its principles of form in the dislocation of linear time, the time, precisely, of talking about?

But the humanist is himself a product of the Renaissance. As we have seen, what we have here is not a clash between culture, represented by the art of the nineteenth century, and barbarism, represented by some aspects of the art of this century. Nor is such art a reflection or mirror of the barbarism of our time. The silence of an Eliot, a Beckett, a Webern has nothing to do with the events of Nazi Germany or with the bankruptcy of language, as apocalyptically minded critics have claimed. It is connected rather with the desire to release us, through art, from an adherence to false idols.

The principles of fragmentation and discontinuity, of repetition and spiralling, which we found underlying the works of Kafka, Eliot, Stevens, Proust and Robbe-Grillet do not reveal anything so banal as the final disintegration of the western imagination. What they reveal is the potential in each moment, each word, each gesture and each event, a potential denied by the linear way we live our lives and read our books.

But for this very reason there is something deeply worrying to the critic about such art. It seems to him to be anarchic, inhuman. It will not allow itself to be talked about, to be assimilated into the stream of culture and consciousness, yet the critic has chosen a profession which is devoted to doing just that. What is he to make of a novel like *The Unnamable*, which vanishes with a gurgle of icy laughter as soon as he tries to grasp it? What is he to make, even now, half a century after its publication, of a poem like *The Waste Land*, with its phrases petering off into the void and its unexplained juxtapositions of fragments of older literatures? That he must make something of them is not in doubt. And so he does one of two things: either he ignores the radical nature of such art and assimilates it to the mainstream of Western European art since the Renaissance; or, recognising the strangeness of much modern, non-linear art, he takes refuge from its implications *for him* by seeing it as a mirror or symptom of apocalypse, thus proving the continuing validity of Nietzsche's dictum that man would rather take the void for his purpose than be devoid of purpose.

Am I suggesting, then, that we do without any 'talk about', any book reviews, literary criticism, the academic study of literature? No, and for the simple reason that 'talking about' is not the prerogative of the critic or reviewer. It is there as a perpetual temptation for all of us, as we live, as we read, as we write. I would only suggest that what is important is to learn to wait, to listen, to see. And to remember the words of Wallace Steven's poem, 'The Latest Freed Man':

> Tired of the old descriptions of the world,
> The latest freed man rose at six and sat
> On the edge of his bed. He said

'I suppose there is
A doctrine to this landscape. Yet, having just
Escaped from the truth, the morning is color and mist,
Which is enough . . .'

1   Wallace Stevens, *Collected Poems* (London, 1955), 96

2   The reader familiar with Freud will know that I am referring to the tripartite division of the *Introductory Lectures*, which in turn refer to the three pillars of psychoanalysis: *The Interpretation of Dreams* (1900); *The Psychopathology of Everyday Life* (1904); and the *Three Essays on Sexuality* (1905)

3   John Steane, *The Northamptonshire Landscape* (London, 1973), 86

4   Daniel Boorstin, in his 1975 Reith Lectures, sees the same change but from a different angle: 'The great awakening of modern man was his finding out that life was not really as repetitious as it had always seemed . . . America was to play a crucial role in that awakening . . . A pilgrim is a religious devotee who journeys to a shrine or to a sacred place. Pilgrimage – the characteristic popular travel-institution of the age of Again-and-Again – is of course one of mankind's most ancient and familiar rituals . . . When the first Puritans and Separatists came to New England, they, too, saw themselves as going on a pilgrimage . . . |However| the shapers of American civilisation and the makers of America's influence on the world experience would not long continue to view their American mission in this way. New World experience and New World opportunities would effect a modern transformation. This was the transformation of a world of typology into a world of history' (*Listener* [20 November 1975], 667 and 668). The emptiness of the American continent thus played a crucial role, Boorstin argues, in the development of a linear view of time and history

5   Stevens, op. cit., 358

6   In *Wedding Preparations in the Country* (London, 1954), 204

7   Is it fanciful to suggest that this was so because in each case there was a 'good father' to hand, someone who admired and encouraged but did not overshadow, or someone who had already borne the burden of being the first? Kafka had no Cézanne, no Schoenberg, no Pound . . .

8   Stevens, op. cit., 198

9   Alain Robbe-Grillet, *In the Labyrinth*, transl. Christine Brooke-Rose (London, 1967)

10   My thoughts on Dante are heavily influenced by T.M. Greene's fine
     article, 'Dramas of Selfhood in the Comedy', in T.C. Bergin (ed.),
     From Time to Eternity: Essays on Dante's Divine Comedy (New Haven
     and London, 1967)

Notes on contributors

George Craig Lectures in the School of European Studies at the University of Sussex. His two main and overlapping areas of interest are modernism, particularly as it has affected writing in France since Mallarmé and Proust; and the relation between the psychoanalytic 'speaking subject' and the literary 'I'.

Bernard Harrison Reader in Philosophy at the University of Sussex. His books include *Meaning and Structure, Form and Content* and a study of *Tom Jones*.

Tony Inglis Lectures in the School of English and American Studies at the University of Sussex. His main areas of interest are nineteenth-century Scottish culture and modernist writing in English.

Gabriel Josipovici Has published three novels and a book of stories and short plays. His plays have been produced in London and Edinburgh and on Radio Three. Lectures in the School of European Studies at the University of Sussex, and is the author of a study of modern fiction, *The World and the Book* (1971).

Jeremy Lane Lectures in the School of European Studies at the University of Sussex. Has recently completed a doctoral thesis on the poetics of Joyce and Mallarmé, and has translated poetry from French, Spanish and Italian.

Robin Lee Published two volumes of poetry in his lifetime and, when he died, was completing a doctoral thesis on Virginia Woolf and English Romantic poetry.

273

Stephen Medcalf   Lectures in the School of European Studies at the University of Sussex. Has published essays on Virgil, Chaucer, Chesterton and William Golding. At present writing a book on biblical narrative.

John Mepham   Lecturer in Philosophy at the University of Sussex. His main interest is in the forms and development of human knowledge, and therefore in the theory of symbolism and the theory of science.

Roger Moss   Graduated in English in 1973 from the University of Sussex. Is writing a thesis there on 'burlesque' rhetoric in Chaucer, Nashe and Sterne, which, with the present paper, springs from his preoccupation with fiction as a mediation of private vision and public language.

Gabriel Pearson   Professor of English at the University of Essex. His main interest is in nineteenth- and twentieth-century English and American literature.

Gāmini Salgādo   Reader in English at the University of Sussex. His main interests are Shakespeare and Elizabethan drama, and D.H. Lawrence.

Rachel Trickett   Novelist and Principal of St Hugh's College, Oxford. Has written a study of Augustan poetry, *The Honest Muse* (1964), as well as numerous articles on English literature since Milton.

Index

Adams, Mrs Henry, 77
Alexander, C.F., 186
Auden, W.H.
  on Wodehouse, 189, 197
  on Falstaff, 201
Austen, Jane
  narrative style of, 146
  Harrison on, 225–50
  nature of her work, 257
  Emma, 230–4
  Mansfield Park, 251n
Austin, J.L., 191
author, *see* writer
authorial intent
  and shaping of stories, 3–5
  and autonomy, 56–7, 62–3
authority and authorship, 113–28

Ballantyne, R.M., *Coral Island*, 239
Balzac, Honoré de, 13, 72
Barth, John, *Lost in the Funhouse*, 122
Barthes, Roland, 6, 114
Bataille, Georges, 116
Bayley, John, 198
Beckett, Samuel Barclay
  effect of his work, 5
  and comic mode, 13
  Lee on, 14, 206–23
  and language, 139
  nature of his work, 269

How It Is, 210
Imagination Dead Imagine, 268
Krapp's Last Tape, 268
'Lessness', 222–3
Malone Dies, 211, 218–19
Molloy, 215–19
More Pricks Than Kicks, 208–9
Murphy, 206, 209–11
The Unnamable, 11, 206, 208, 218–23, 270
Watt, 208, 210–15, 218
  with Georges Duthuit, *Three Dialogues*, 211, 215
Beerbohm, Max, 251n
Beethoven, Ludwig van, 257
Belloc, Hilaire, 201
Benjamin, Walter, 6
Berkeley, Bishop George, 115
Berlioz, Hector, 257
Betjeman, John, 188–9
Biggles, *see* Johns, Capt. W.E.
Bildungsroman, 3
Blanchot, Maurice, 119
Boorstin, Daniel, quoted, 271n
Boothroyd, Basil, *Homage to P.G. Wodehouse*, 197
Borges, Jorge Luis, 12, 34
  'Funes the Memorious', 5
Boz, *see* Dickens, Charles
Bradley, F.H., 93
Brooke-Rose, Christine, 122

Browne, Hablôt K., 75n
Buchan, John, 7
Burroughs, William, 122
Burrow, Trigan, *The Social Basis of Consciousness*, 110–11
Butt, J., and K. Tillotson, *Dickens at Work*, 54–5
Byron, George Gordon, Lord, *Destruction of Sennacherib*, 192

Carroll, Lewis, 13, 35–6
Cavalcanti, Guido, 266
Cézanne, Paul, 271n
Chatman, Seymour, *The Later Style of Henry James*, 77–8
Chaucer, Geoffrey, 56, 190–2
Chesterton, Gilbert Keith
  on Dickens, 54, 59, 64, 73n, 194
  nature of his work, 188–9
  on theology, 193
  and paradox, 227
  Medcalf on, 251n
Churchill, Winston S., 188, 203
Clare, John, 256
Clarke, Colin, 96, 108–9
Confucius, quoted, 198
Conrad, Joseph, 12–13, 52
Craig, George, on language, 6
  on reading, 12, 15–36
Craye, Florence, *Spindrift*, 201
criticism
  language of, 10, 18
  French, 13
  see also critics, language
critics
  and structuralism, 4
  and theory of the novel, 9, 37
  on James, 77
  on *Hamlet*, 95

and *Ulysses*, 130, 147
and implications of modern discontinuity, 269–70

Dante Alighieri
  quoted, 190, 192
  La Divina Commedia, 65, 74n, 265–7
  La Vita Nuova, 65
Davidson, Lionel, 13
Descartes, René, 115
Dickens, Charles (Boz)
  style of, 4, 40, 46, 48, 133, 146
  as story-teller, 7
  examination of, 12
  and literary tradition, 13
  James and, 52–3
  Pearson on, 54–72
  Bleak House, 40–5
  Dombey and Son, 5, 54–72, 133
  Great Expectations, 72
  Hard Times, 59
  Martin Chuzzlewit, 59–60
  Nicholas Nickleby, 56, 74n
  The Old Curiosity Shop, 58
  Oliver Twist, 64, 74n
  Our Mutual Friend, 72, 92
  The Pickwick Papers, 64
  A Tale of Two Cities, 64
  The Uncommercial Traveller, 62
Dostoevsky, Fyodor
  Dickens and, 72
  James and, 93
  Wodehouse and, 202
  and his father, 259
Doyle, Sir Arthur Conan, *The Lost World*, 35
drama and narrative art, 38
Ducasse, Isidore, *see* Lautréamont, Comte de

Index

Duthuit, Georges, *see* Becket, Samuel Barclay

Eco, Umberto, quoted, 128
Eichmann, Adolf, 244–8
El Greco, 113
Eliot, George
  nature of her work, 37, 257
  narrative style of, 42
  James and, 52
  Adam Bede, 92
  Daniel Deronda, 92, 257–8
  Middlemarch, 45–9
Eliot, Thomas Stearns
  and existentialism, 93
  C.S. Lewis and, 186
  and modernism, 188
  and Wodehouse, 192
  and vision of discontinuity, 261–3, 269–70
  Ash Wednesday, 266, 268
  Four Quartets, 268
  'Gerontion', 265
  'Rhapsody on a Windy Night', 261–2, 265
  Tradition and the Individual Talent, 198
  The Waste Land, 262, 265, 270
Engels, Friedrich, *The Condition of the Working Class in England in 1844*, 60

Fielding, Henry, 257
  Tom Jones, 257
Flaubert, Gustave, *Madame Bovary*, 92
Ford, George, 96
Forster, John, 55
  Life of Dickens, 55
Forster, E.M., 93
  Aspects of the Novel, 206
  A Passage to India, 232

Freud, Sigmund
  and dreams, 4
  C.S. Lewis and, 186
  and time, 253–5
Frye, Northrop, 200

Galsworthy, John, *The Forsyte Saga*, 268
Garis, Robert, 54
Golding, William, 12, 188
  Lord of the Flies, 239
  Pincher Martin, 247
Gombrich, E.H., 256
Greene, Graham, 13

Hancock, Tony, 194
Handley, Tommy, 203
Hardy, Thomas, 12, 257
Harrison, Bernard, 225–50
Hayden, Joseph, 257
Hegel, G.W.F., 93
Homer, 113
Hopkins, Gerard Manley, 140
Hugo, Victor, 72

Inglis, Tony, on James, 77–93
intentional fallacy, 56

James, Henry
  nature of his work, 11
  on George Eliot, 52
  Inglis on, 77–93
  development of, 200
  Leavis on, 225
  The Ambassadors, 80, 86
  The Awkward Age, 86, 92
  The Golden Bowl, 79, 86–92
  In the Cage, 82–5
  Madame de Mauves, 78–81
  'The Middle Years', 13
  The Other House, 92
  Portrait of a Lady, 77
  'The Real Thing', 82
  What Maisie Knew, 86

The Wings of the Dove, 86–7, 91

Janouch, Gustav, 123

Johns, Capt. W.E., 12–13, 34

Josipovici, Gabriel, on time and the novel, 252–71

Joyce, James
  and comic mode, 13
  on truth, 118
  on his writing, 119
  and language, 124–5, 196, 198
  protagonists of, 126
  C.S. Lewis and, 186–7
  nature of his work, 269
  Dubliners, 133, 135
  Finnegans Wake, 119, 121
  A Portrait of the Artist as a Young Man, 116–17, 120–1, 123, 135–7, 140, 144
  'The Sisters', 130–2
  Stephen Hero, 136
  Ulysses, 9–10, 118, 122–3, 125, 128, 130–48, 209

Kafka, Franz
  James and, 86, 93
  and 'K' figures, 117, 126
  on truth, 123
  and space and time, 125
  nature of his work, 128, 263, 270
  and his father, 259–61, 271n
  and linearity, 269
  quoted, 12
  'The Metamorphosis', 125

Kermode, Frank, 96

Kierkegaard, Søren
  James and, 92–3
  C.S. Lewis and, 186
  on wit and humour, 203–4
  on the self, 217

and his father, 259
on despair, 262

Lane, Jeremy
  on critical language, 10
  and the effect of reading, 12
  on authority, 113–28

language
  and modern criticism, 6–7
  and meaning, 8–9
  and critical response, 15–16
  and the writer, 124

Lautréamont, Comte de (Isidore Ducasse), 13

Lawrence, David Herbert
  nature of his work, 11
  examination of, 12
  and creative writing, 86
  as mediator, 93
  Salgado on, 95–111
  language of, 146
  C.S. Lewis and, 186
  quoted, 54
  The Crown, 109
  Lady Chatterley's Lover, 74n
  Psychoanalysis and the Unconscious, 109
  The Rainbow, 96, 101, 103, 105
  The Reality of Peace, 109
  Sons and Lovers, 102
  Women in Love, 95–111

Lear, Edward, 13

Leavis, F.R.
  on Lawrence, 95–8, 100, 104
  on James, 225, 229
  For Continuity, 98
  The Great Tradition, 54
  and Q.D. Leavis, *Dickens the Novelist*, 54–5

Leavis, Q.D., *see* Leavis, F.R.

Lee, Robin
  on Beckett, 6, 206–23

on critical language, 10
death of, 14
Levin, Harry, 135–6
Lewis, C.S.
　on *Hamlet*, 95
　and language, 187–8, 190–2,
　　196, 203
　and tradition, 189
　The Abolition of Man, 198
　A Grief Observed, 188
　Surprised by Joy, 186
　Till We Have Faces, 188
　The Weight of Glory, 188
Locke, John, 78, 114–15
Luria, A.R., 6
　The Mind of a Mnemonist, 5

Mallarmé, Stéphane, 6
　quoted, 18
Mann, Thomas, *Doktor
　Faustus*, 269
Mao Tse-tung, 6
Marvell, Andrew, quoted, 193
Medcalf, Stephen
　on Wodehouse, 186–204
　on Chesterton, 251n
Mepham, John, on Woolf, 5, 10,
　149–185
Milton, John, 187
mimesis, 113–14
Mosley, Sir Oswald, 203
Moss, Roger, 10, 130–47
Moynihan, Julian, 66
Mozart, Wolfgang Amadeus,
　257
Murry, Middleton, 96–7, 100

narrative, as process in time,
　38–40
Nicolson, Harold
　language of, 188, 196, 198
　The Desire to Please, 188
　Diaries and Letters 1930–39,
　　203

Helen's Tower, 188
In Search of the Past, 188
Some People, 188
Nicolson, Nigel, quoted, 203
Nietzsche, Friedrich
　on purpose, 211, 270
　and nihilism, 245
　and time, 254–5
　on God, 263
　and culture, 269

oral fiction
　nature of, 7–8
　and dimension of time, 38–9

Pascal, Blaise, 193
Paz, Octavio, quoted, 128
Pearson, Gabriel
　on Dickens, 5, 54–72
　on critical language, 11
Picasso, Pablo, 261
Pollack, Oskar, 12
Pont (cartoonist), 203
Pound, Ezra, 271n
Proust, Marcel
　and experience, 93
　and the self, 117
　and nature of writing, 119
　and fictive persona, 126
　nature of his work, 128, 270
　and memory, 178
　language of, 188
　*A la recherche du temps
　　perdu*, 35, 119, 188,
　　267–8
Punch (magazine), 58

Quirk, Randolph, *Charles
　Dickens and Appropriate
　Language*, 40

Racine, Jean, 13
　Andromaque, 86
　Phèdre, 86

Ravel, Maurice, 143
reading
   and surrender of self, 17–21
   and the book as object, 22
   as exchange, 24–7, 33–6
   and the writer, 27–33, 122
   and speech, 37–8
   and reader as consumer, 116
revolution, 6
Ricardou, Jean, 6
Richards, Frank, 199
Richardson, Samuel, 86
Pamela, 235
Robbe-Grillet, Alain
   effect of his work, 5
   and discontinuity, 270
   Dans le labyrinthe, 264, 268
   Les Gommes, 264, 268
   Le Voyeur, 264, 268
Romantic literature
   and artist as prophet, 6
   and modern novel, 116
   and authority, 120
   Russell, Bertrand, 245
Ryle, Gilbert, 191

Sacks, Oliver, 6
   Awakenings, 5
Sade, Marquis de, 13
Salgādo, Gāmini, on Lawrence, 95–111
Sartre, Jean-Paul
   James and, 86, 93
   and 'Bad Faith', 161
   C.S. Lewis and, 186
   on imagination, 222
Saturday Evening Post, The (newspaper), 200
Schoenberg, Arnold, 269, 271n
Scott, Sir Walter, 46
   Waverley, 207, 222
Seuss, Dr, 34
Shakespeare, William

and literary tradition, 13
and intentional fallacy, 56
authorial identity of, 113
in Woolf, 179
and language, 198
nature of his work, 258
Hamlet, 95, 234
King Lear, 197
Smollett, Tobias, *Roderick Random*, 64–5
Sontag, Susan, *Death Kit*, 122
Spark, Muriel
   examination of, 12
   and comic mode, 13
   Harrison on, 225–50
   The Abbess of Crewe, 228
   The Ballad of Peckham Rye, 226
   The Comforters, 227, 249
   The Driver's Seat, 228
   The Girls of Slender Means, 237, 248
   The Hothouse by the East River, 228
   The Mandelbaum Gate, 225–7, 236, 241, 244–7
   Not to Disturb, 228
   The Prime of Miss Jean Brodie, 227, 237–44, 250
Sperber, Dan, *Rethinking Symbolism*, 9
Steane, John, *The Northamptonshire Landscape*, 256–7
Stendhal (Henri Beyle), *Le Rouge et le Noir*, 235
Sterne, Laurence, 257–8
   Tristram Shandy, 49–50, 214
Stevens, Wallace, 270
   'Add This to Rhetoric', 263–4
   Collected Poems, 266
   'Connoisseurs of Chaos', 263

'Earthy Anecdote', 267
'The House was Quiet and
  the World was Calm',
  258
'The Latest Freed Man', 263,
  270–1
'The Man Whose Pharynx
  Was Bad', 252–3
'On the Road Home', 263
Parts of a World, 263
Selected Poems, 266
'Study of Two Pears', 263
story-teller, *see* writer
structuralism, 4

Tel Quel (magazine), 6
Thackeray, William Makepeace
  style of, 49, 53
  quoted, 58
  The Newcomes, 50–2
  Vanity Fair, 58
Thody, Philip, 202
Tillotson, K., *see* Butt, J.
time
  and the shaping of narrative,
    37–40
  and art as escape, 252–3
  Nietzsche and, 254–5
Trickett, Rachel
  on Victorian novel, 7, 37–53
  on critical language, 10
Trollope, Anthony, 199

Valéry, Paul, 6–7
Verdi, Giuseppe, 72, 257
Virgil, *Eclogues*, 201

Wagner, Richard, 72
Walpole, Hugh, 201
Watts, Cedric, quoted, 97
Waugh, Evelyn
  exclusion of, 12

nature of his work, 188, 190
  on Wodehouse, 200
Webern, Anton, 261, 269
Williams, Charles, 187–8, 196
Winters, Yvor, 78
Wittgenstein, Ludwig, 9
  Philosophical Investigations,
    6–7
  *Tractatus Logico-
    Philosophicus*, 251n
Wodehouse, P.G.
  as story-teller, 7
  examination of, 12
  and comic mode, 13
  Medcalf on, 186–204
  and Walpole, 201
  Aunts Aren't Gentlemen,
    201–2
  The Code of the Woosters,
    193–4
  Leave it to Psmith, 200
  Mike, 200
  Money in the Bank, 201
  Psmith Journalist, 200
  Something Fresh, 200
  Summer at Blandings, 34
  What ho, Jeeves!, 11
Woolf, Virginia
  technique of, 10
  language of, 146
  Mepham on, 149–85
  Between the Acts, 268
  To the Lighthouse, 5, 149–
    85
  The Waves, 268
writer
  as story-teller, 7–8
  isolation from reader, 31–6
  see also authorial intent
    and narrative

Yeats, William Butler, 188